THE NATIONAL HOME MORTGAGE QUALIFICATION KIT

How To Qualify For And Obtain Your Mortgage Money 99% of The Time

By Benji O. Anosike, B.B.A., M.A., Ph.D.

Copyright © 2001 by Benji O. Anosike

Library of Congress Cataloging-in-Publication Data

Anosike, Benji O.
    The national home mortgage qualification kit : how to qualify for and obtain your
mortgage money 99% of the time / by Benji O. Anosike.
        p. cm.
    Includes bibliographical references and index.
    ISBN 0-932704-41-7 (alk.paper)
    1. Mortgage loans--United States. I. Title.

HG2040.5.U5 A758 2001
332.7'22--dc21

2001017464

Printed in the United States of America
ISBN: 0-932704-41-7

Library of Congress Catalog Number:

Published by:

Do-It-Yourself Legal Publishers
60 Park Place
Newark, NJ 07102

The Publisher's Disclaimer

We have, of course, diligently researched, checked and counter-checked every bit of the information contained in the manual to make sure that it is accurate and up-to-date. Nevertheless, we humans have never been known for our infallibility, no matter how hard the effort! Furthermore, details of a law do change from time to time. Nor is this relatively short manual conceivably intended to be an encyclopedia on the subject, containing the answer or solution to every issue on the subject. ***THE READER IS THEREFORE WARNED THAT THIS MANUAL IS SOLD AND DISTRIBUTED WITH THIS DISCLAIMER:*** The publisher (the same for the author) does NOT make any guarantees of any kind whatsoever, or purport to engage in the practice of law, or to substitute for a lawyer, an accountant, a tax expert, or rendering any professional or legal service; where such professional help is legitimately necessary in your specific case, it should be sought accordingly.

—*Do-It-Yourself Legal Publishers*

Table of Contents

INTRODUCTION: WHY YOU CAN, INDEED, GET YOUR MORTGAGE LOAN 99 PERCENT OF THE TIME

A. Beginning with the Beginning: Mortgage Fundamentals 1
B. Getting a Loan Is Not Mysterious; It is Easy to Get, If Only you Know How to Meet the Bank's Rules and Criteria for Getting One 1
C. How the Book is Organized 2
D. How to Read and Use This Book In securing Your Mortgage Goal 3

Chapter 1
THE BASIC PRINCIPLES THAT APPLY IN ALL MORTGAGES: HOW MORTAGES WORK

A. What is a Mortgage? 4
B. The Three Major Attributes of a Mortgage – The Mortgage "Big Three" 5
C. How the Mortgage "Big Three" Determine Your Home's Ultimate Cost 5
D. Loan Amortization: How it Works and The Basic Lessons To learn From It 7
E. Using the "Big Three" Factors in Planning The Terms of the Mortgage to Obtain 9
F. Conclusion: You'll Have To Decide on a Mortgage Based on the Mortgage "Big Three" Factors 10

Chapter 2
SOURCES FOR MORTGAGE MONEY AND HOW TO APPROACH EACH SOURCE

A. The Home Sellers 13
B. Savings and Loan Associations (S&Ls 13
C. Commercial Banks 14
D. Mutual Savings Banks 14
E. Mortgage Companies/Mortgage Bankers 14
F. Mortgage Brokers 15
G. Credit Unions 16
H. Insurance Companies and Pension Funds 16
I. Real Estate Brokers and Agents 17
J. State Assistance 17
K. Tips on How to Select the Best Mortgage Source 17

Chapter 3
THE VARIOUS TYPES OF MORTGAGES AND "CREATIVE FINANCING" PACKAGES AVAILABLE

A. Reasons for the Proliferation of "Creative Financing" 19
Creative Financing Methods will Generally Involve More Costs to You, the Borrower 19
The BIG FIVE of Mortgages: The Five Basic Types of Mortgages 20
B. Some Major Financing Plans in Today's Market 20
   1. Fixed-Rate Mortgages (FRMs 20
   2. Adjustable-Rate Mortgages (ARMS) 21
   3. FHA-backed Mortgage 22
   4. VA-backed Mortgage 22

5. Balloon Mortgage...22
6. Graduated payment Mortgage..23
7. Growing Equity Mortgage (Rapid Payoff Mortgage)..............................23
8. Shared Appreciation Mortgage..23
9. Assumable Mortgage..24
10. Seller Take-back or Owner-Financed Mortgage....................................24
11. Wraparound...25
12. Land Contract...25
13. Buy-down...25
14. Rent with Option..26
15. Zero Rate and Low Rate Mortgage...26
16. Reverse Annuity Mortgage (RAM)...26

Chapter 4
CONTRASTING THE TWO BROAD TYPES OF MORTGAGES in the MARKET: THE FIXED RATE MORTGAGE AND THE ADJUSTABLE RATE

A. **The Fixed Rate Mortgages (FRMS)**...28
  1. Advantages of the Fixed-rate Mortgages...29
  2. Disadvantages of the Fixed-rate Mortgages.......................................29
  3. Summary...30
B. **The Adjustable-Rate Mortgages (ARMS)**...31
  1. Advantages of the Adjustable-rate Mortgages...................................31
    Availability...32
    Better Rate...32
    Affordability..32
    Assumability..33
  2. Disadvantages of the Adjustable-Rate Mortgages.............................33
    Costs can rise...33
    High degree of uncertainty..33
C. **Summary and Conclusions** on ARMs and FRMs.......................................34

Chapter 5
THE TWO MAJOR TYPES OF GOVERNMENT-BACKED FINANCING: THE FHA AND VA MORTGAGES

A. An Overview...35
B. Procedures of the FHA Loan Program..36
C. FHA Closing Costs...36
D. FHA Loans Distinguished from Conventional Loans............................37
E. Interest Rates and Discount Points on FHA Loans...............................38
F. The Advantages of FHA Financing...38
G. The Procedure of the VA – Guaranteed Loan Program.........................40
H. Loan Characteristics of VA Loan..40
I. VA Closing Costs...43
J. Summary & Conclusions..43
   List of HUD Regional Offices in the U.S...44

Chapter 6
SELLER-ASSISTED HOME FINANCING

The "Second Mortgage" or Seller Take – Back..45

Chapter 7
HOW CAN YOU ASSESS THE BETTER DEAL USING "POINTS" OR INTEREST RATE TO COMPARE?

A. What is A "Point"?...47
B. Value of a Point 47
C. Interest Rate Versus Points 48
D. A Few Methods For Comparing Points Versus Interest Rates 48
    1. Two Quick Formulas 49
    2. Using The Points Equivalency Table..49
    3. Using The Annual Percentage Rate (APR) To Gauge 51
    4. Using the 10-year Analysis Calculation to Gauge 52

Chapter 8
MAKE AN HONEST ASSESSMENT OF YOUR CURRENT FINANCIAL CONDITION: YOUR INCOME, EXPENSES & NET WORTH

A. Figuring Out Your Present Finances..55
B. Analyzing Your Finances 57
C. Figuring Out Your Net Worth..57

Chapter 9
ARE YOU INTENDING TO SEEK A MORTGAGE? THEN, FIRST DETERMINE THE HOME PRICE RANGE YOU CAN ACTUALLY AFFORD & PRE-QUALIFY YOURSELF

A. First Thing First: Forget About Looking For a House; First Estimate the Home Price Range That You Can Afford..60
B. Getting Yourself Pre-qualified With A Lender Before You Even Locate A House To Buy 61
C. Some Quick Rule-of-Thumb Formulas 62

Chapter 10
KNOW THE TOTALITY OF ALL THE FINANCING COSTS THAT'S INVOLVED IN MAKING A HOME PURCHASE: THE CLOSING & OTHER COSTS

A. Summary of the Closing Costs You May Need to pay...67
B. Summary and Conclusion 70

Chapter 11
HOW A BORROWER TYPICALLY APPLIES FOR A MORTGAGE AND GETS PROCESSED: THE APPLICATION, PROCESSING, AND QUALIFYING PROCEDURES FOR A MORTGAGE LOAN

A. Borrower's Loan Application and Other Primary Documentation's.......................................71
B. Lender's Loan Application Analysis – Lender Makes Property Survey, Appraisal, Inspection, Etc. 72
C. The Truth-In-Lending Disclosure Statement & The Good Faith Estimate of Settlement Charges.................73
D. Credit Check, Employment Verification, Down Payment Verification, etc...........................74
E. Evaluating Your Ability to Pay..74
F. Loan Approval and Commitment 76

Chapter 12
THE SURE-FIRE SYSTEM TO SEEK OUT THE BEST AVAILABLE MORTGAGE LENDERS, AND FOR COMPARISON–SHOPPING FOR THE BEST MORTGAGE LOAN FOR YOU

A. Follow These Guidelines To seek Out The Best Possible Mortgage Source....................................84
B. You Must Then Do Some "Comparison Shopping Around" Before You Settle on Your Final Mortgage Pick..87

Chapter 13
YOU CAN SECURE YOUR MORTGAGE LOAN AT LEAST 99 PERCENT OF THE TIME! HERE ARE THE COMPLETE, SURE-FIRE FORMULA TO ACCOMPLISH THIS ALMOST ALWAYS

A. Yes, By Following A Few Simple Procedures, It's Possible to Secure A Loan Almost Always.................89
B. Step-by-Step Procedures for Getting Your Loan Approval Almost Every Time You Apply 90
 Step 1: Compile an Honest, Comprehensive, Objective Evaluation of Your Present Financial Condition. ..90
 Step 2: Study The Various Types of Mortgages Available and Determine Which Specific Type is Best to Choose.................90
 Step 3: Determine the Home Price Range You Can Afford 91
 Step 4: Seek Out the Best Lenders, and Then "Comparison Shop" to Select The One Best Loan For You ..91
  The Mortgage Shopping and Selection System.................91
 Step 5: Do Not Ever File a Loan Application Unless You First Have Certain Ideal Conditions And Don't Have Certain Problems.................93
 Step 6: Submit Your Loan Application to Your First Choice of Lenders and File For a Pre-Approval Before You Ever Pick a House to Buy.................96
  A. First and Last Rule: Make The Lender's Job Easier For Him/Her.................96
  B. Preparation For The Pre-Approval or Finance-Based Evaluation of Your Application......97
  Prepare the Following Documents in Advance To Take to Your Loan Appointment........99

Step 7: Lender's Decision-Making Process on Loan Pre-approval Application: What and What Would Make the Lender Decide in Your Favor.................99
  A Brief Summary: What Qualities Will Make You Get a Lender's Loan Approval............102

Chapter 14
SOME POINTERS ON WHAT TO DO IF DENIED APPLICATION FOR A LOAN

1. Check With The Lender.................106
2. Go Back to The No-fail Loan Approval Checklist and Check Everything Again.................106
3. Consider Making a New Application Altogether 106
4. Consider Applying for The FHA or VA Loan 106
5. Consider Filing Complaints For Discrimination, if Applicable.................106

Chapter 15
THE PROCESS OF BORROWER ANALYSIS FOR MORTGAGE LOAN FINANCING: HOW LENDERS FINANCIALLY QUALIFY THE BORROWER

A. Ratio Analysis.................109
Income Qualification, The Two Basic Debt-to-Income Ratios: The LT Debt Ratio; the P1T1 Debt Ratio.................109
B. The Total Long-Term Debt-to-Income Ration – LT Debt Ratio.................110
C. The Mortgage Debt-to-Income Ratio – P1T1 Debt Ratio 111
D. Which One to Use: The LT Debt Ratio vs. The P1T1 Debt Ratio?.................112
E. Cash-on-Hand Qualification 113
 The LTV Ratio 113
F. Financially Qualifying Yourself In A Conventional Loan Situation.................114
G. Analysis and Explanation of What Figure 15-1 Calculations Tell Us.................115
H. Financially Qualifying Yourself in an FHA Loan Situation.................118
 a. Primary Differences in Qualification Standards Between An FHA and Conventional Loan.................118
 b. Procedures for Financially Qualifying an FHA Backed Loan.................118
I. Another Method: The "Residuary Income" Formula For Qualifying An FHA Loan 119
 Let's Work Out a Specific Buyer's Loan Qualification Analysis for an FHA Loan.................120

J. Financially Qualifying Yourself in a VA Loan Situation..122
  (a) Primary Differences Between the FHA and VA Income Qualifying Standards 122
  (b) Procedures for Financially Qualifying a VA Loan 122
      Follow These Step-by-Step Procedure in Qualifying for A VA Loan....................................122
  (c) Let's work out a Specific Buyer's Loan Qualification Analysis for a VA Loan......................123
K. Another Alternative or Supplementary Qualifying Method Used by Some Lenders: The "Point Scoring System"...125

Chapter 16
LET'S SEARCH FOR THE PROPER HOUSE, NEIGHBORHOOD, AND/OR BROKER, FOR YOU

A. Consider What Kind of House and Neighborhood You Want and Can Afford 127
B. Now, Search for the Right House For You...127
  1. The Three Basic Channels for Searching For a House 127
  2. The Advantages of Using A good Real Estate Broker in Finding a House................................128
  3. General Pointers For Finding The Right House 129
  4. General Pointers For Finding The Right Broker...130

APPENDICES

A. Tables of Monthly Payments Necessary To Amortize a Loan at Stated Rates of Interest....................134

B. Loan Progress Chart: Table of Remaining Balances...143

C. Glossary of Real Estate and Mortgage Terms...152

D. Some Relevant Bibliography...164

E. List of Other Publications by Do-it-Yourself Legal Publishers..166

Index..167

INTRODUCTION

WHY YOU CAN, INDEED, OBTAIN YOUR MORTGAGE APPROVAL LOAN 99 PERCENT OF THE TIME

A. BEGINNING WITH THE BEGINNING: MORTGAGE FUNDAMENTALS

Forget all you might have thought, or been lead to think. Yes, you can – you really can – secure a mortgage loan approval some 99 percent of the time. *And yes, it's no slip of the tongue, you heard it right: 99 percent of the time!* The trick, not exactly sophisticated or mysterious, is simply to know the right way and the right procedures favored by lenders for loan-application making, the "short list" of lending rules and criteria favored by lenders for getting their mortgage money. And then just meet those requirements. This book will show you how.

Typically, here's how most people buy a home: first, they determine or simply imagine a neighborhood they'll love to live in, then they look through the 'home for sale' listings in the newspapers or find a real estate agent and begin searching for and looking at properties. Next, they find a house they think they can afford, and they make a purchase offer. And if the offer is accepted, then they go to a bank and start looking for a mortgage loan. *In other words, it is not until AFTER they have already decided on a home selection, that they begin to search out the financial possibilities or options.*

Unfortunately, though, there's one fundamental flaw about this 'typical' or 'popular' way: **It's plain DEAD WRONG!** This approach is exactly in the reverse order of what the proper sequence ought to be. The proper order should, actually, run this way: First, you consider your financial options; you apply for a mortgage loan to a lender and get pre-qualified for a loan; and then – and only then – you go for your house selection. Among many other important advantages, making sure, first that you meet the lender's qualifications for a loan, would mean that you already know beforehand exactly what kind of a house you can afford, and so, when you actually search for a house to buy, that knowledge narrows your search completely – you simply zero in precisely on the properties (and mortgage amounts) you can realistically afford, rather than on some dream houses you just can't possible afford.

The larger, central point that is intended to be made here, *is that a fundamental reason why prospective home buyers fail to obtain the lender's mortgage approval, is because they lack basic knowledge of, and fail to follow, certain basic rules and principles of mortgage lending that are required and favored by lenders and loan underwriters.*

B. GETTING A LOAN IS NOT MYSTERIOUS; IT IS EASY TO GET, IF ONLY YOU KNOW HOW TO MEET THE BANK'S RULES AND CRITERIA FOR GETTING ONE

THE FUNDAMENTAL PREMISE OF THIS BOOK IS SIMPLE. It is that, as a mortgage-seeker, *all you need to do is be armed and prepared with the right approach and procedures, the right facts and information that are commonly required by the bank to make its mortgage decisions – and you'll almost always get your loan approval.* To be sure, it will take a little background and preliminary work. Nor are there going to be any magic or easy gimmicks. But, by following several simple bank procedures and meeting certain simple criteria, *you can secure the mortgage of your choice 99 percent of the time, and you can do so in 24 hours* – an approval the day after your initial presentation to the bank.

Nor, in fact, are the procedures unusual. Nor mysterious. It's just that they may not be as widely known or used by most people. Knowledgeable real estate brokers, agents, and developers, especially the top-notch achievers among them who sell or build the most houses in their industry year-after-year, use these same methods and achieve fantastic results all the time.

This book aims at showing you some of these time-tested real estate industry "secrets" on how to accomplish this; how to prepare, assemble, and satisfy the magic "short list" of criteria and procedures that are critically required by the banks to get them literally excited and clamoring for your mortgage business: a fair picture of your overall financial profile as a prospective borrower, of your credit history and loan repayment potentials, of the value/quality of the property you plan to buy, and of the loan's profitability potentials for the lender, etc., etc.

C. HOW THE BOOK IS ORGANIZED

Mortgage financing involves basic finance and calculations. And while such skills may not be absolutely crucial in order for one to be a good mortgage shopper or negotiator, nevertheless those tasks are a lot simpler with an understanding of the basic principles. With that in mind, a significant portion of the book – Chapters 1, 7, 8, 9, 10, 11 and 15, among others – deals with aspects of loan making and loan qualifications analyses which could be said to be the analytical or computational dimensions of basic mortgage finance. This aspect has been assigned such significance in the book because knowledge of such issues is primary as an essential background, for understanding mortgage financing and mortgage loan granting.

Briefly summed up, the book literally 'walks' you, step-by-step, through the essential but proper processes of mortgage loan selection, evaluation, qualification, and shopping, for the loan applicant and the lender alike, and through the mortgage bank decision-making process.

For simplicity of analysis and comprehension, a reader could view the book as being divided or separable into two basic 'Parts.'
Part 1 would consist of those chapters which deal with the mortgage basics and background information:

- **Chapter 1** – describes the basic principles that apply to every mortgage, explaining what mortgage is and how a mortgage loan is structured.

- **Chapter 2** – gives a rundown of different types of mortgage lenders and various sources of mortgage money you'd need to contact in order to get a mortgage.

- **Chapter 3** – deals with various types of mortgages and financing arrangements available; and shows how each one works and the advantages and disadvantages of each.

- **Chapter 4** – deals with the two broad types of mortgages in the mortgage industry with the broadest appeal among homebuyers, the fixed-rate mortgage and the adjustable-rate mortgage, and explains the advantages and disadvantages of each type.

- **Chapter 5** – provides you the two major types of government-backed home financing, the FHA and the VA loans.

- **Chapter 6** – provides the seller-assisted home financing methods for a homebuyer.

- **Chapters 7 and 10** – could also be classifiable within this category, as they provide the tools or information to properly analyze or assess the total cost of mortgage.

And **Part 2** sections of the book. This would be those aspects of the book which deal with the mortgage choice and source selection methods and mortgage shopping process; the lender's qualifying criteria and procedures for a loan applicant, and the lending underwriter's decision-making process and considerations in deciding on whether to approve a given applicant's loan request or not to, and the like. For example, as a loan-seeker, one of the major, indeed decisive, questions for you will likely be whether you financially qualify for a mortgage, and if so, what size of loan you are qualified for. While ultimately only a lender can answer those questions for a loan applicant in a specific situation, a mastery of these relevant chapters will help give you a fairly good idea.

- **Chapter 8** – let's you assess your current financial condition.

- **Chapter 9** – let's you assess the house price range you can realistically afford, and let's you pre-qualify yourself for the type of house and price range you ought to have your sight on.

- **Chapter 11** – literally 'walks' you through a typical mortgage application processing and qualifying procedures.

- **Chapter 15** – does the same thing for you as Chapter 9, but in a manner more analytical, computational and detailed (use of formulas, financial ratios, and points scoring system), and is more geared to specific loan programs, such as conventional loans, FHA, and VA backed loans. This chapter (and Chapter 9, as well) provides you a rundown of the general formulas used by lenders to qualify loan applicants.

In **Chapter 13**, you have the most important and pivotal chapter of the whole book. This chapter, which lays out a systematic road map and method of seeking out and evaluating the best mortgage sources and mortgage loans available, and of winning the lender's favorable assessment and approval for a loan request, is the centerpiece – "the glue" – which ultimately ties the whole book together for you into a programmatic "system" for successfully filing and processing a mortgage loan application, from start to finish. ***By diligently following, step-by-step and systematically, the procedures and steps outlined in Chapter 13, you are almost 100 percent assured of meeting a bank's requirements and criteria for getting a mortgage money – at least 99 percent of the time.***

D. HOW TO READ AND USE THIS BOOK IN SECURING YOUR MORTGAGE GOAL

So, **the advice is this: First** of all, to begin with, read and master all essential "background material" chapters – Chapters 1 to 7, then 15. Next, read and master Chapters 8 to 11; work out on yourself a mortgage profile of the house price range you can afford, then pre-qualify yourself for a suitable loan (Chapter 9). These preceding chapters (and others, including the appendices, if you like) would give you the background materials and preparations you'd need in the making of an actual loan application. And, finally, go to the two chapters that tie it all together for you, Chapters 12 and 13, and SYSTEMATICALLY and SEQUENTIALLY follow, step-by-step, the loan application and processing program outlined therein to make your loan application.

One thing is certain, without contention: Armed with the knowledge and information and the guidelines outlined in this book, you'll find venturing out into the mortgage marketplace a far, far, less formidable, intimidating or uncharted task than it would otherwise have been. ***The overriding guiding principle here is:*** *Learn those same time-tested but little-known "short list" of principles and criteria desired by lenders for winning their ears and getting their mortgage money. Then, simply meet those requirements. And your chances of getting the right mortgage at the right price are greatly enhanced— indeed, even to the height of 99 percent of the time!*

CHAPTER 1

THE BASIC PRINCIPLES THAT APPLY IN ALL MORTGAGES: HOW MORTGAGES WORK

A. WHAT IS A MORTGAGE?

A mortgage is a loan contract, a borrowing of money, secured by property – the property you purchase - for the repayment of this loan. It's a special loan given especially for the purpose of buying real property. The loan lasts until the original "principal" amount of money (the amount borrowed) plus the interest, is paid off. Then the mortgage is dissolved and the property is owned free and clear by the borrower. The term is also used to mean a lien on real property given by a homeowner or buyer (the borrower) to his lender as security for the borrowed money.

Here's how it works. A lender agrees to provide you the money you need to buy a specific home or piece of real property. You, in turn, promise to repay the money based on the terms set forth in the mortgage (loan) contract. Under the *Federal Truth in Lending Law*, the contract should state the amount of the loan, the annual percentage rate (which, when computed, includes the mortgage interest rate, the premium paid for insurance, the mortgage, and "discount points"), the size of the repayment, and the frequency of payments.

As a borrower, you pledge your home as security. It remains pledged until the loan is paid off. If you fail to meet the terms of the contract, the lender has the right to "foreclose", that is, obtain possession of the property, but he must follow the prescribed formalities of law to exercise the right of foreclosure.

Under the laws of most states in the East, the mortgagor (the borrower) retains title to the property, and the mortgage document does not give the mortgagee (the lender) title to the property, but merely gives him a lien (a claim) against the property. For most states west of the Mississippi, however, the mortgage arrangement is slightly different. Here, instead of the buyer receiving the actual title of ownership directly from the seller at the time of the purchase deal, a document is created, known as a *TRUST DEED* (also called *"Deed of Trust"* *"Mortgage Deed"*, or *"Deed to Secure Debt"*, depending on which state) for "holding the title during the mortgage period." This way, the power to carry out a foreclosure, if there should be need, is, in effect, vested in a third party and thereby makes it even easier for the lender to force a sale of the property in the event that the borrower defaults on his mortgage payments since the lender would not now have to go through many of the legal formalities and complications involved in formal foreclosures. In such western and other states (Alabama, Arkansas, Connecticut, Illinois, Maine, Maryland, Massachusetts, Missouri, New Hampshire, New Jersey, North Carolina, Ohio, Pennsylvania, Rhode Island, Tennessee, Vermont, and W. Virginia), the mortgage is, in fact, the deed; and the lender is legally regarded as the virtual owner of the property – until the mortgage loan has been repaid.

In a word, if you really want to be technically correct about it, the "mortgage" is actually not the very loan that you, as a home buyer, take out to buy the property; it is, actually, the document, the legal agreement, that you sign for the money's lender which gives the lender the right to the property (the right to "foreclose") in the event you "default" (i.e., fail) in repaying the loan. To put it another way, the MORTGAGE document is the instrument that creates a "lien" (a claim) on the borrower's property, which then makes it possible for it to serve as a *collateral* to secure the promise of payment.

Throughout most of this book, however, when we use the term "mortgage", we will commonly think it to mean, as most people do, simply the MORTGAGE LOAN — the mortgage money with which the home purchase is generally made.

B. THE THREE MAJOR ATTRIBUTES OF A MORTGAGE – THE MORTGAGE 'BIG THREE'
For our purposes in this manual, there are THREE basic attributes essential to a mortgage, each of which affects your home's ultimate cost to you.

They are: •the principal (amount)

                    •the interest (rate)

                    •the payment term (time).

The PRINCIPAL is the loan amount taken, the amount of money borrowed. The INTEREST is what you pay the lender for the use of its money. (Interest plus principal, equals the total payment). And the payment TERM is the length (amount) of time it will take you to repay the mortgage.

C. HOW THE MAJOR MORTGAGE 'BIG THREE'
DETERMINE YOUR HOME'S ULTIMATE COST
Question: Generally speaking, when you think about a house in terms of its price and what it will cost for you to own it, what question immediately comes to your mind? Probably the purchase price issues about the house: 'What is its list price; will I be able to come up with the down payment? And will I be able to keep up the monthly payments on the mortgage?' Indeed, these, exactly, are what the average person who contemplates being a house owner basically thinks of as being the TOTAL cost of a house, as being all it will basically cost him (her) to own that dream house of his that he contemplates buying.

But, is that really the case? Is that really ALL it costs, or even most of what it costs, to own a house? NOT AT ALL! Not by any means. In truth, the hard reality concerning the buying and owning of a home is that the officially "contracted" costs of a house, such as the above mentioned costs, represent only a lesser fraction, a small portion, of the actual TOTAL COST of a house. The above mentioned costs do not even represent the larger part of a home's total cost. To put it simply, *what will cost you far, far, more in the end in purchasing your home, are not the more immediate or near-term cost factors, like the home's list price, or the down payment amount for its purchase, and the like, but the "long-term" cost factors of buying the home*. If you are like the average American homebuyer, the overwhelming odds are that you probably will, of necessity, finance your home purchase with a lender's mortgage. And that'll mean that you will, in the end, have to pay not merely the house purchase price figure you were quoted by the house seller at the time of purchase, but probably *two or three times more* than that amount. You'll pay that primarily in the form of INTEREST! (See the "ILLUSTRATION" below).

In other words, what you will wind up paying for your home will be determined by a combination of what we'll call the home mortgage 'Big Three' — the size of the loan amount of your mortgage (the principal); the interest rate of the loan (the interest); and the payment term (the period of payment). *The higher any one (or more) of these attributes is, the greater the amount of the TOTAL home cost you'll wind up paying in the end*. The total interest payment you'll pay on a $100,000 mortgage loan, will, for example, be much greater than what you'll pay on a $50,000 mortgage loan; the longer the term of the loan (say, 30 years instead of 15), the greater the total interest cost (though the lower the monthly payment you'll need to pay); and the higher the interest rate, the greater the total loan amount you pay in the end.

ILLUSTRATION. To give you an idea of this reality about the impact of the mortgage 'Big Three,' let's use just one element of the Big Three factors, the 'interest factor,' to illustrate how much you are actually going to wind up paying on a given home purchase. We'll use something called an INTEREST FACTOR TABLE —Figure 1-1 below. Designed for a standard 30-year, fixed rate mortgage, this table allows you to compute the total interest charges you are to pay out over the term of your mortgage loan. You simple multiply the loan amount with the "interest factor" applicable to your mortgage interest rate. Thus, let's say you're buying a home worth $200,000, and that you put 10% of that as down payment and borrowed the remainder (i.e., $180,000) at 9.75 percent fixed rate of interest for a 30-year term. Now, using the interest factor from Table 1-1 for 9.75%, you can determine that you'll pay $180,000 x 2.093 or $376,740 in total interest cost (the interest alone) over the 30-year life of the mortgage. Now, this represents the INTEREST COST only. To determine the total cost of the mortgage, you now add this interest cost to the amount borrowed ($376,740 + $180,000),

Figure 1-1. Selected Interest Factors Table For Loans

7% = 1.395	10.5 = 2.293	14 = 3.266
7.25 = 1.456	10.75 = 2.361	14.25 = 3.337
7.5 = 1.517	11 = 2.428	14.5 = 3.408
7.75 = 1.579	11.25 = 2.497	14.75 = 3.480
8 = 1.642	11.5 = 2.565	15 = 3.552
8.25 = 1.705	11.75 = 2.634	15.25 = 3.624
8.5 = 1.768	12 = 2.703	15.5 = 3.696
8.75 = 1.832	12.25 = 2.772	15.75 = 3.769
9 = 1.897	12.5 = 2.842	16 = 3.841
9.25 = 1.962	12.75 = 2.912	16.25 = 3.914
9.5 = 2.027	13 = 2.982	16.5 = 3.987
9.75 = 2.093	13.25 = 3.053	16.75 = 4.059
10 = 2.159	13.5 = 3.124	17 = 4.132
10.25 = 2.226	13.75 = 3.194	17.25 = 4.286

Here's the simple formula for this:

$\underline{\$\quad\quad}$ X $\underline{\quad\quad}$ = $\underline{\$\quad\quad}$
amount   interest   total interest
financed   factor   paid

$\underline{\$\quad\quad}$ + $\underline{\quad\quad}$ = $\underline{\$\quad\quad}$
total interest   amount   total cost of
paid   financed   your mortgage

($ amount financed) × (interest factor) = $ total interest paid

($ total interest paid) + ($ amount borrowed) = $ total of
your loan

$ total of your loan + your down payment = total direct cost of
the house

and to determine the TOTAL COST[1] of the home to you, you further have to add the amount of the down payment you had put down on the home, making it $376,740 + $180,000 + $20,000, or $576,740!

D. LOAN AMORTIZATION: HOW IT WORKS AND THE BASIC LESSON TO LEARN FROM IT.

The term "amortization" refers to the gradual, systematic liquidation or repayment of a debt through normal, regular payments. Indeed, interestingly, the term is directly derived from a Latin word meaning "deadening" – denoting the gradual killing off of a debt for the benefit of the lender! The usual way of financing a mortgage loan is through the loan "amortization" method over the term (duration) of the loan.

Suppose that, as an 'average Joe' with no special expertise or knowledge in these matters, you merely are interested in getting a rough idea of how the amortization of a mortgage will work out, say on a $100,000 loan at an interest rate of 10 percent for the standard 30-year term? Just off hand, what you might probably think is that you'll probably pay $10,000 in interest for the loan (10 percent of the $100,000 principal), plus 1/30th of the principal, or $3,333. That's seemingly logical, isn't it? So it might seem. But it's also all wrong. Loans simply aren't structured that way!

Rather, loans are structured in a drastically different way. For example, your repayment plan ("amortization") would likely call for a series of regular, equal monthly payments. Each monthly payment is applied, first to pay the INTEREST which has accrued, and the remainder then to pay the outstanding PRINCIPAL. Thus, in the typical long-term loan (15 to 30 years), the payments will be divided into either 180 or 360 monthly payments. By simply tracking closely the loan amortization process and analyzing it, we are able to see quite clearly just how much of the payment go for INTEREST and how much towards reducing the loan debt itself, and at what speed and to whose benefit, the homeowner's or the lender's.

BUT HERE'S THE IMPORTANT POINT FOR YOU TO NOTE: because of the special way loans are structured, *in the EARLIER years of the mortgage term most of the mortgage payments (those equal monthly payments) you make consist almost entirely of INTEREST, with the loan PRINCIPAL left virtually untouched. Only many, many years down the road, after you shall have already made a large amount of payments to the lender with virtually all of it being credited to INTEREST (his profit), will a slowly increasing share of each payment that you make begin to go toward paying the PRINCIPAL.* Then, month by month, gradually, you pay more of the principal and less of the interest, until, toward the end, your payments become mostly principal.

To put it another way, mortgage loan amortizations are structured in a unique way; they are structured in such a way that when your loan balance (the actual amount you still owe) is high, more of each monthly payment you make goes to INTEREST (the lender's profit) and only a small amount goes toward the loan itself (the principal). The interest (the lender's profit) on the loan is said to be "front-end loaded"— that is, paid first upfront to the lender *before* the principal begins to be paid. Consequently, because of the nature of the mortgage loan structure — because the amount of interest chargeable on a loan is figured based on the remaining loan balance, meaning the amount of the loan still unpaid — the loan balances (the amount still owed or unpaid) decline only very, very slowly, indeed painfully so.

To illustrate, let us track a typical 30-year mortgage; as we do, just notice closely how excruciatingly *slow* the loan is paid down, how slowly the balances (what is still owed or unpaid) actually decrease over long stretches of time.

Look at the monthly payment schedule, known as "Amortization Schedule," shown below in Figure 1-2 — for a mortgage of $100,000 amortized (i.e., paid off) over a 30-year term, at 10 percent interest.[2] The payment

---

[1] This figure does not include all and every conceivable costs, obviously, costs such as the closing costs for the home purchase, the insurance or real property taxes, home improvement or repair and maintenance costs, and the like.

over the 30-year period is $877.57 per month, each divided between what goes towards paying the "principal" (the specific amount you actually borrowed), and what goes towards paying the "interest" (the lender's profit for lending you the money). As you can see from Figure 1-2 below, each month's payment ($877.57) always breaks down to two parts: between the INTEREST and the PRINCIPAL. For example, the very first month's payment of $877.57 breaks down as follows: Principal $44.24, and Interest $833.33, for the combined total of the $877.57 per month. Thus, Figure 1-2's Amortization Schedule shows how payments on a $100,000, 30-year term, 10 percent loan, breaks down each month — in interest, principal, and the balance — for the 30-year duration of the loan period.

Figure 1-2. Sample Amortization Table

30-year, $100,000 Mortgage at 10 Percent

Month	Starting Balance	Payment Principal	Interest	Ending Balance
1	$100,000.00	$44.24	$833.33	$99,955.76
2	99,955.76	44.61	832.96	99,911.16
3	99,911.16	44.98	832.59	99,866.18
4	99,866.18	45.35	832.22	99,820.84
5	99,820.84	45.73	831.84	99,775.12
6	99,775.12	46.11	831.46	99,729.02
7	99,729.02	46.49	831.08	99,682.52
8	99,682.52	46.88	830.69	99,635.64
9	99,635.64	47.27	830.30	99,588.38
10	99,588.38	47.67	829.90	99,540.72
↓	↓	↓	↓	↓
351	8,394.96	807.61	69.96	7,587.35
352	7,587.35	814.34	63.23	6,773.01
353	6,773.01	821.13	56.44	5,951.88
354	5,951.88	827.97	46.90	5,123.91
355	5,123.91	834.87	42.70	4,289.04
356	4,289.04	841.83	35.74	3,447.21
357	3,447.21	848.84	28.73	2,598.37
358	2,598.37	855.92	21.65	1,742.45
359	1,742.45	863.05	14.52	870.24
360	870.24	870.24	7.33	-0-

As you can clearly see for yourself, the following facts can immediately be gleaned from this scrutiny:

FIRSTLY: That the EARLIER YEARS of the loan, when the borrower's loan balance is high, is when MORE of the borrower's payments go to INTEREST, while a SMALL AMOUNT goes toward the PRINCIPAL (the loan itself). For example, in the first month's payment in the table, while the interest (the lender's profit) is a whopping $833.33, only a pitiful $44.24 is for the principal, the actual amount that's applied towards reducing the debt.

SECOND: That in the LATER years of the loan, when the borrower's loan balance is low (or lower), there is a complete switch: gradually, MORE of the borrower's payments now go to the PRINCIPAL, and smaller and

---

[2] When your mortgage loan is issued, your lender will often give you an Amortization Schedule or Table, which will show you, month-to-month, the principal and interest payments and the declining balance. You also can get such a table from your real estate agent or from a prospective lender.

SMALLER AMOUNTS go to INTEREST. For example, while the interest part in the first month of payment in Table 1-2 is a whopping $833.33, in the 351st month the interest part is way down to only $69.96, and by the 359th month, it's a meager $14.52. But, on the other hand, by the 351st month a staggering $807.61 of the borrower's payment now goes to liquidating the principal (the actual debt), and in the 359th month, it's up to $863.05 — up from a measly 444.24 in the first month!

THIRDLY: That in the EARLIER years of the mortgage, the borrower's loan balances (the amount still owed) decline very, very slowly, if barely, while in the LATER years there is a switch: the balances decline in that period in ever GREATER amounts each month, and do so more rapidly.[3] For example, as can be seen from Table 1-2, upon making the lst month's payment of $877.47 (interest plus principal), the loan balance only declines to $99,955,76, and by the 10th month's payment, with a total of $8,775.70 already paid in by then, the loan balance has barely moved, declining to only $99,540.72 – a decline of just $459.28. But now, in contrast, take a look at the comparable LAST 10 payments of the mortgage, and you'll find, on the other hand, a dramatic and rapid decline in the loan balance: the drop in the balance in the one month period from the 351st to 352nd month, for example, is a steep $807.61, and in the very last one month period, the 360th month, it is a gigantic drop of $870.24.

Indeed, on this loan, as in the average 30-year mortgage, at the end of the 10th year, just when you are at the one-third mark of the loan term, only 9 percent of the total loan shall have been paid off. Out of the $100,000 loaned you, you will still owe about $90,000 to your lender at that point, after 10 years. In fact, by the middle of the 24th year, all you shall have paid off is only one-half of the loan, and only in the last 6 years of the 30-year term will you pay off the second one-half![4]

THE MAJOR IMPLICATION: Since the clear reality of the amortization process is that in the EARLY years each payment you make consists almost entirely of INTEREST that accrues solely to your lender's benefit, and that it is only towards the ENDING part of the loan term that the payments largely begin to go to the PRINCIPAL for the actual paying down of your loan, this thus strongly suggests two things: (1) that there's a critical need, in the greater financial benefit of the borrower, for some acceleration (speeding up) of the payment process by the borrower to pay off the mortgage within a shorter period; and (2) that the earlier the borrower can begin such a program of additional or increased payment on his mortgage, the greater the financial benefit it will yield for him.

E. USING THE 'BIG THREE' FACTORS IN PLANNING THE TERM OF THE MORTGAGE TO GET

Let us look at the above-described implications for the moment. Let us look at it in terms of doing some strategic planning with regard to certain important considerations about the loan you are to take – how long a loan should it be, for example, what the interest rate should be, and so on. For, put in the simplest term, what the above-described realities say concerning the way the process of loan amortization works, is simply this: that if you would be able to find a way by which you can effect a change, downwards, in just one (or more than one) of the BIG THREE factors of your mortgage, you would have correspondingly effected a change, also downwards, in the ultimate cost of your home to you. *To put it another way, whenever you have to choose a*

[3] Indeed, the reason why this is so simple. In the earlier years, since it is on the still outstanding balance of a loan that the interest chargeable is figured, much of the payment that is made will necessarily have to go towards interest, and not to the loan itself!

[4] As a rule, the two major parts of the mortgage payment, the principal and interest, do not even get to equal each other in amount until halfway through the term of the loan. Before the halfway point (15 years on a 30-year loan), more money goes to paying the interest than does to paying the principal. After the halfway point, the greater amount now goes towards the principal and lesser amount goes toward interest. In sum, the central point is this: that the far larger share of the amount of money you pay monthly on the first half of your mortgage is INTEREST – i.e., PROFIT TO YOUR BANK OR LENDER!

mortgage, if you can choose one that has a comparatively shorter term of payment, or one with a comparatively lower interest rate (or amount), you would directly, indeed even quite dramatically, reduce the overall total cost of the home to you.

HOW LONG A LOAN TO GET, FOR EXAMPLE?

One of the primary decisions you'll need to make, for example, at the time you decide on which loan package to pick over the others (Chapter 12), is whether the loan you're to take would be for a 15, 20, 25, or 30-year term. Indeed, the duration of one's mortgage (called the "term" of the mortgage), is the most significant of the three main factors, the BIG THREE factors, of a mortgage. Stretching out your mortgage for an extended period of years lowers your monthly payments, but it would also mean that you pay far more in total interest cost on the longer-term loan. Indeed, because the long-term mortgage loan lasts for 30 years, the difference in total interest costs is enormous since the interest has to be "compounded" for up to three decades.

For example, let's say you're buying a $140,000 home with a $40,000 down payment, and you borrow $100,000 from the bank. To make matters simpler, let's assume that your option is choosing between a 15-year and 30-year loan at a 10% interest rate. (Actually, in practice, the shorter term loan – the 15-year term loan in this example – will usually carry a slightly lower interest rate since the shorter term commitment is deemed somewhat less risky for the lender). Here's how the figures, in terms of the monthly payment amounts and the total overall costs to you (the borrower), will come out:

Figure 1-3

PAY MORE NOW, SAVE A LOT MORE LATER

Even if you have to pay more money each month, the key to saving on your mortgage in the long run is to pay for as few months as possible. Here's a comparison of your total costs on a typical $100,000 loan at 10 percent interest rate

Figure 1-3. The Impact of The Length of Time Taken In Paying Off a Loan

TABLE 1.2 *Impact of the Loan Term*

Monthly payments and total interest payments for a basic $100,000 fixed-rate mortgage loan at 10 percent interest

Length of Loan	Monthly Payment	Total Interest Paid
15 years	$1,074.61	$ 93,430
20 years	965.02	131,605
25 years	908.70	172,610
30 years	877.57	215,925

As can be readily gleaned from the above table, you pay a "mountain" of EXTRA costs more in interest expense by taking the longer-term 30-year loan, than by taking the shorter-term, 15 year loan. How much of a mountain of difference between the two loan terms? A whopping $122,495 ($315,925 - $193,430) in comparative total interest costs between the two mortgages! Put another way, if you took the 30-year loan, you would have paid back <u>more</u> <u>than</u> <u>twice</u> as much in interest costs as the home itself costs; and if you took the 15-year loan, you would have incurred a total interest cost that's only 43% of the total interest cost for the 30-year loan.

F. CONCLUSION: DECIDING ON WHAT MORTGAGE TO TAKE SHOULD BE MADE ON THE BASIS OF THE MORTGAGE 'BIG THREE' FACTORS.

As can be readily seen from the same Table 1-3, one other reality that stirs you in the face in analyzing the numbers, is that there is a "mountain" of difference also between the monthly amounts that will need to be paid under each of the two types of loan: $1,074.61 per month, if you take the 15-year loan, and $877.57, if you take the 30-year loan. *In short, the big, old, "affordability factor" – the question of whether or not you'll be able to afford a home if you were to pay a higher mortgage amount (say, $1,074.61) per month, as opposed to something lower (say, $877.57) per month – is a hugely major consideration in deciding on the term of the loan you are to go for. Briefly summed up, as a rational consumer out shopping for a mortgage loan, given the apparent, big extra interest burden involved in taking the longer term loan, you should almost always shoot for the shorter term loan – if you can handle the monthly payments involved.* **Here's the rule,** simply: *after you* **shall have fully shopped around and taken a careful, hard look at the various mortgage terms available (Chapter 12), if you find that you can afford the monthly payments on a shorter-term loan without squeezing too severely the other parts of your** budget, **then generally the shorter-term loan would be preferable to the longer-term one.** Meanwhile, another option, also, might be to consider a middle ground. You don't necessarily have to go for the standard 15-year mortgage. You can go for a 20-year, or even a 25-year mortgage.

Figure 1-4   **Comparison of a 30-year mortgage with a 15-year mortgage at varying interest rates.**

MONTHLY PAYMENTS: 30-YEAR MORTGAGE

RATE OF INTEREST	AMOUNT OF MORTGAGE ($)						
	70,000	75,000	80,000	85,000	90,000	95,000	100,000
6%	419.69	449.66	479.64	509.62	539.60	569.57	599.55
6.5%	442.45	474.05	505.65	537.26	568.86	600.46	632.07
7%	465.71	498.98	532.24	565.51	598.77	632.04	665.30
7.5%	489.45	524.41	559.37	594.33	629.29	664.25	699.21
8%	513.64	550.32	587.01	623.70	660.39	697.08	733.76
8.5%	538.24	576.69	615.13	653.58	692.02	730.47	768.91
9%	563.24	603.47	643.70	683.93	724.16	764.39	804.66
9.5%	588.60	630.64	672.68	714.73	756.77	798.81	840.85
10%	614.30	658.18	702.06	745.94	789.81	833.69	877.57
10.5%	640.32	686.05	731.79	777.53	823.27	869.00	914.74
11%	666.63	714.24	761.86	809.47	857.09	904.71	952.32
11.5%	693.20	742.72	792.23	841.75	891.26	940.78	990.29
12%	720.03	771.46	822.89	874.32	925.75	977.18	1,028.61

MONTHLY PAYMENTS: 15-YEAR MORTGAGE

RATE OF INTEREST	AMOUNT OF MORTGAGE ($)						
	70,000	75,000	80,000	85,000	90,000	95,000	100,000
6%	590.70	632.89	675.09	717.28	759.47	801.66	843.86
6.5%	609.78	653.30	696.89	740.44	784.08	827.55	871.11
7%	629.18	674.12	719.06	764.00	808.95	853.89	898.83
7.5%	648.91	695.26	741.61	787.98	834.31	880.66	927.01
8%	668.96	716.74	764.52	812.30	860.09	907.87	955.65
8.5%	689.32	738.55	787.79	837.03	886.27	935.50	984.74
9%	709.99	760.70	811.42	862.13	912.84	963.55	1,014.27

9.5%	730.96	783.17	835.38	887.59	939.80	992.01	1,044.22
10%	752.22	805.95	859.68	913.41	967.14	1,020.87	1,074.61
10.5%	773.78	829.05	884.32	939.59	994.86	1,050.13	1,105.40
11%	795.62	852.45	909.28	966.11	1,022.94	1,079.77	1,136.60
11.5%	817.73	876.14	934.55	992.96	1,051.37	1,109.78	1,168.19
12%	840.12	900.13	960.13	1,020.14	1,080.15	1,140.16	1,200.17

To figure out the total interest payable by you, find your monthly payment in the table. Then multiply by 360 (the number of months), for a 30-year mortgage, and by 180, for a 15-year mortgage. And subtract the principal, in either of the two cases. The difference is how much you'll save if you take a 15-year instead of a 30-year mortgage.

CHAPTER 2

SOURCES FOR MORTGAGE MONEY, THEIR CHARACTERISTICS, AND HOW TO APPROACH EACH SOURCE

Where do you go to get your mortgage money? Most American consumers think a bank is the only source of mortgage financing. What's more accurate, however, is that banks make most of the mortgages given out in the United States. However, there are other options, some of them often less expensive and more flexible. Indeed, mortgage money is so available from so many different sources that at times it can make the selection of the proper source down-right confusing.

Given below in this chapter, is a review of the many different major sources of mortgage financing that are available, the kinds of financing they offer, and the ideal conditions under which you are most likely to get their financing.

A. THE HOME SELLERS

Sellers of real estate often finance a part or all of the purchase of their property. Often overlooked, the best source of financing, when you can get it, is the person from whom you buy the property since he/she is especially motivated to make a deal. More often than is generally realized, the seller will help you finance. And it's not as hard as one might think to negotiate: all you'll need to do is simply make your offer contingent upon the seller's readiness to provide a specific amount of financing. You might ask, for example, that the seller provide the full first mortgage at a fixed rate, or that he is to assume his loan with a secondary mortgage to help you with the down payment.

Seller financing is more common in periods of high interest rates. Seller financing is usually for short terms and carry what is known as a "balloon" payment. (In a balloon loan, the entire principal becomes due at maturity). The seller's greatest motivation may be to make the sale happen, and if he has to help you finance in order to realize that goal, he will. (See Chapter 6 for fuller discussion of the procedures for seller-assisted mortgage loan financing).

B. SAVINGS AND LOAN ASSOCIATIONS (S & Ls)

Despite all the changes in the real estate lending industry in the past few decades, the Saving and Loans (S & Ls) industry still make the majority of residential loans in the United States. Historically, these specialized financial institutions have always been active lenders in the residential real estate market; they are accessible in each community and generally have mortgage officers on staff who are eager and willing to place their funds with residents in the community.

Savings banks are one of the easiest institutions to approach. Go and chat with them BEFORE you start looking for property. Ask them about availability of money, the current rates of interest, and the types of properties for which they currently offer mortgages. If you can establish some rapport with a mortgage officer *before* you buy, it will make the actual commitment of the bank much easier and quicker to get the moment you find the property to buy.

C. COMMERCIAL BANKS

Many of the mortgages not issued by Savings and Loan Associations are often issued by commercial banks. In some cases, their rates may be slightly higher than those of S&Ls, or their application process more complex. That may be so because mortgage lending is only one of many activities of a commercial bank, whereas it's the main bread and butter of an S&L. But it's hard to generalize; some commercial banks offer reasonable mortgage rates and efficient loan processing.

Commercial banks usually attract the kind of bank deposits called "demand deposits" (checking accounts), and make short-term loans primarily to businesses. They tend to be more conservative than savings banks; they are often excellent sources for larger amounts of money, particularly those requiring larger investments. Perhaps due to their history of loaning money to businesses, commercial banks are often more likely than savings banks to give confirmation loans for medium to large-scale income properties because these loans will have shorter maturities. (Frequently, when such banks offer loan-term real estate loans, they will usually turn around and sell them to other financial institutions, rather than keep them in their own investment portfolio). Commercial banks are also often more likely than savings banks to loan money beyond the initial mortgage (a second mortgage) to finance residential expansion projects. If you need an extra $20,000 or $40,000 to fix up a house, for example, or extra money to finance a two-car garage or an additional bedroom, they are the place to go.

You should approach a commercial bank as you would other banks, with questions as well as information about the property and about your financial circumstances, questions about availability of money, their current interest rates, the types of properties they currently offer mortgages for, etc. In negotiating interest rates and terms, be aware, however, that such banks have more of a need for profitability than other banks. Commercial banks are stock-holder owned corporations that seek a return on invested capital, thus often making the interest rates they charge slightly higher than those charged by mutual or cooperatively owned banks.

D. MUTUAL SAVINGS BANKS

A major source of mortgage money is the mutual savings banks. Probably less known than the S&Ls and commercial banks, mutual savings banks go by a variety of names in different areas of the country – mutuals, savings banks, cooperative banks, and the like. Said to be "cousins" of the S&Ls, mutual savings banks are a hybrid of a commercial bank and an S&L and invest a very high percentage of their available funds in mortgages. They compete aggressively for savings deposits and offer accounts similar to those offered by S&Ls. However, there's one distinction that separates them from some of their more commercial competitors: they are owned by depositors. They are not corporations with stockholding owners; rather, they are large joint ventures or partnerships which operate similar to cooperatives, in which depositors have a major say about the bank's policies and encourage good public relations in the community with the bank. Mutual savings banks number less than 1,000 in the whole nation and are concentrated on the Northeast coast; they tend to be small although in recent times many have become large by merging with other banks. Like pure savings and loan banks, mutual savings banks have easily accessible offices in each community and are equipped with a team of mortgage specialists actively engaged and eager to place their money in the community in which they're located. They, too, are easy to approach. However, they often require that you open a savings account with the bank for a nominal amount in order to be eligible for a loan.

E. MORTGAGE COMPANIES/MORTGAGE BANKERS

Mortgage companies, also known as mortgage bankers, are specialized financial companies which represent funding sources, such as insurance companies and pension investors. Unlike banks and savings institutions, they don't make a wide variety of loans: they make mortgage loans only. Again, unlike banks and savings institutions, they don't take deposits from the public. Rather, they obtain the money they lend from their own partners and from outside investors, such as insurance companies and pension funds, and from money they themselves have borrowed from others (often by issuing bonds).

For locating a borrower who meets the qualifications of their loan investors and for closing the loan, mortgage bankers generally receive 1% to 3% of the loan at the time of the loan origination, and ¼ percent to ½ percent of the outstanding balance each year to service the loan. As a rule, after originating the loans, mortgage bankers generally sell the mortgage to financial institutions and large investors all across the country. Because of such activities, mortgage bankers play an important role in VA and FHA lending as a large part of the mortgage banker's business involves FHA and VA loans on owner-occupied single-family houses. Mortgage bankers also specialize in fixed-rate mortgages.

In recent years, mortgage bankers have become increasingly important, picking up much of the lending business lost by savings and loans. *It's estimated that they now issue as many new mortgages as banks or S&Ls do.*

Their drawback? It is said that because mortgage bankers don't provide other banking services but would often collect their origination fee and sell the mortgages to other financial institutions, they may have less incentive to treat you well as would a company intent on keeping you as a long-term customer. Also, it is said, because mortgage bankers typically sell off mortgage loans after they make them, you stand a great chance of having your mortgage transferred. Nevertheless, if you can get a good rate from a mortgage banker, it is a loan source very much worth considering. The fact that mortgage lending is the only business of the mortgage banker can be considered an advantage for the borrower; it must serve the mortgage borrower effectively, or it won't be around in business! Finally, for borrowers whose preference is a fixed-rate type of mortgage, mortgage bankers may offer a special appeal since fixed rate mortgages are their specialty.

F. MORTGAGE BROKERS

In a strict sense, mortgage brokers are not true sources of mortgage financing. Rather, they're middlemen who, for a fee, connect lenders (such as banks or mortgage bankers) with borrowers. In other words, mortgage brokers match borrowers with investors. They do not lend money themselves, and usually do not service the loan. Your real estate agent would, for example, often double as a mortgage broker.

What the mortgage broker does is to find the loan for you (the borrower), do all the loan origination (placement) work for you, and help you out with the application, for a fee. Don't expect to find a mortgage broker in a large, bank-like building; more often than not, he's located in a nondescript office storefront.

The advantage of using a mortgage broker is that he or she can comparison-shop for you among many, many lenders who may be located within and outside your own state. A good mortgage broker would typically have business connections with as many as ten or more lenders. The disadvantages of mortgage brokers are that they are not always a good source for residential or home loans as they usually prefer large deals, such as loans for investment property, apartments, condominiums, and commercial stores; their rates are not always competitive, they charge an extra percentage or two beyond the normal cost of money in order to accommodate their fees. Mortgage brokers are also fond of charging "points," and it has been said that, as a group, mortgage brokers are so difficult to work with that, after dealing with them, a loan-seeker may well feel that the mortgage broker is probably intent on making it, not easy, but as hard as possible for the borrower to be able to negotiate a loan. Finally, a usual disadvantage of mortgage brokers voiced by experts, is that they may be too cozy with a handful of their favorite lenders with whom they do business and from whom they receive a steady flow of fees, which may give rise to the temptation for the mortgage broker to select for the borrower, not a mortgage that's necessarily best for the borrower, but one that's best for the mortgage broker and his favorite lenders.

Nevertheless, a good mortgage broker can comparison shop effectively for you regarding the interest rates and other terms, and for certain types of loans they may be an efficient source since they cut red tape to a minimum, ensuring you a quick commitment. Indeed, in recent times, more and more Americans have been using mortgage brokers to find for them their mortgage loans. THEIR ROLE AS LOAN-FINDERS HAS

BECOME QUITE SIGNIFICANT: *The percentage of all home mortgage applications in the United states that are written by mortgage brokers has grown dramatically from about 20 percent in 1987, to the point where it is now about 50 percent today!*

More Buyers Turn to Mortgage Brokers

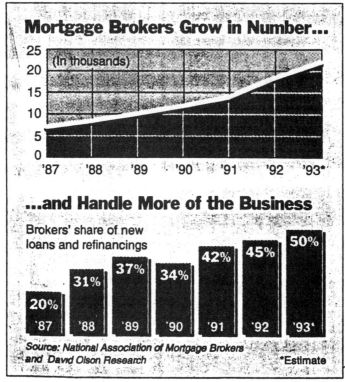

Mortgage Brokers Grow in Number...
(In thousands)

...and Handle More of the Business
Brokers' share of new loans and refinancings

'87	'88	'89	'90	'91	'92	'93*
20%	31%	37%	34%	42%	45%	50%

Source: National Association of Mortgage Brokers and David Olson Research *Estimate

The New York Times

G. CREDIT UNIONS

If you belong to an employee union at your place of employment, or have access to one through an association you belong to, your credit union can be your best source of mortgage. They are often an excellent source for a reasonably priced loan. Often established for employees of large businesses or universities and government entities, credit unions are like a miniature bank run for the benefit of their employee members. An important drawback may be that not all credit unions are in the mortgage business, and even those that are, may have lending limits that are too small for your financing needs.

However, assuming your credit union has sufficient mortgage money available to lend, seeking mortgage money from a credit union is well worth considering: rates of credit unions are often below those of local banks. Furthermore, because the credit unions aren't as experienced in placing mortgages full-fledged mortgage or savings banks, any information you can give them on the value of the property and your own economic resources, goes a longer way in gaining a favorable decision since credit unions do not usually have the capability to do extensive research themselves.

H. INSURANCE COMPANIES AND PENSION FUNDS

Because of their unique situation whereby premiums earned from their policyholders and payouts paid to beneficiaries can be calculated, insurance companies and pension funds usually loan money on long-term investment projects. They invest huge amounts of money each year in real estate financing, but their major area of interest is in commercial financing for large projects, such as large apartment complexes, shopping centers or office buildings. In fact, they are almost the exclusive source of money for hug projects that are valued at several millions of dollars.

Because of the magnitude of the amounts they loan and the long-term nature of the projects, insurance companies and pension funds often loan under complex arrangements and a complex loan process: the necessary paperwork and formal appraisal work involved in granting such commitment take time and it is rare to get a mortgage commitment in less than several weeks; numerous people in different levels of management are involved in approving the loan; a group of investors must have detailed architect's plans and a variety of computer workouts of financial projections, including detailed architect's plans and a variety of computer workouts of financial projections, including building and zoning approval from the local authorities, and so on. All of these documents and documentations cost money, of course, and are time-consuming. Furthermore, these companies often charge heavy fees up-front to negotiate fees with them. For example, fees are charged for preliminary investigation by the insurance company or trust fund, which alone may be in the thousands of dollars.

Nevertheless, the insurance companies and pension funds are in the business of lending money. Approach them, if you have to, preferably with the help of competent attorneys, architects, mortgage brokers, and builders.

I. REAL ESTATE BROKERS & AGENTS

Real estate brokers and agents do not make loans themselves, but they often are knowledgeable about local banks and lenders, or have a business relationship or tie-in with them. Above all, some real estate agents may be quite knowledgeable about the local mortgage market and can often provide you some very useful mortgage information that will steer you in the right direction and to the right mortgage sources. Indeed, one survey by the U.S. Department of Housing and Urban Development (HUD) found that about 40 percent of homebuyers choose their lenders based on the recommendation of a real estate broker.

Be fully aware, though, that real estate agents are not always an objective source of advice. Hence, by all means listen to the mortgage advice and suggestions from your agent. But stop there; just don't totally rely on him or her alone.

J. STATE ASSISTANCE

Your state government or some agencies within it may have programs (not every state does) designed to help first-time homebuyers or low-income homebuyers, or homebuyers who pledge to rehabilitate property in depressed neighborhoods. Mortgages obtained through such state-assisted programs often have attractive interest rates, often some that are well below the market interest rate. The state itself will rarely lend the money; rather, its sponsorship will be in the form of encouraging private lenders to do the actual lending by way of giving some guarantee or subsidy to the lender. You can find out about the availability of any such state programs in your area by simply asking your real estate agent. Or, you may call the housing development division of your state government offices.

K. TIPS ON HOW TO SELECT THE BEST MORTGAGE SOURCE

Not all mortgage money sources may be available or even advisable in every instance. *Here are a few tips on the best way to select a source for your mortgage:*

❖ Educate yourself about, and become familiar with, each and every one of the available sources even before you find the property you propose to buy. The idea is this: you should never narrow down your choice to a single institution until after you shall have investigated to assure who have the most favorable terms and interest rates. Establish contact with the mortgage officers of each institution.

❖ Develop an ongoing personal relationship with one, two, or more bankers. This is critical for negotiations. It is acceptable if you can take him (or her) to lunch, make him familiar with you and

- ❖ your finances. Loan officers like people who come to them already prepared and who think ahead as such attitude by a borrower makes the banker's job easier. With such attitude, loan officers can often help you, they can often take your side and support your mortgage plans, and influence the decision-makers in the bank.
- ❖ Get as much information as possible from the real estate sellers and agents, the mortgage brokers, and others, about what's happening in the area's mortgage market.
- ❖ *Do not ever rush the decision.* Shop around for both the property and the rates. Assemble all the necessary information to make a valid comparison; then make a comparative analysis of the loans in terms of the rates, points and terms.
- ❖ When you are considering a house to buy, find out where the existing loan is placed: other than the seller himself, the mortgage-holding bank that currently has the money invested in the property, is often the best possibility for financing a purchase and such banks are usually anxious to do business even if with a little extra monetary incentive. Such banks, for example, are often flexible enough to reduce or even eliminate points! (For a more complete discussion of mortgage lender selection procedures, see Chapter 12).

CHAPTER 3

THE VARIOUS TYPES OF MORTGAGES AND 'CREATIVE FINANCING' PACKAGES AVAILABLE

Until recently, the types of mortgages available in the real estate industry were a relatively simple, uncomplicated and predictable matter – they generally had an affixed interest rate and a full amortization (or transfer of equity) over a relatively fixed period of 20 to 30 years. Much of that has changed dramatically, however, in recent times! Today, beside the traditional mortgages with fixed interest rates and long terms, there has now emerged a whole new variety of mortgage plans – the so-called "creative financing" mortgages. Lenders and borrowers alike have discovered many ways to finance the purchase of a home.

A. REASONS FOR THE PROLIFERATION OF CREATIVE FINANCING

The most common reason often given for the existence — and then the proliferation — of creative financing, is that, without it, a number of homebuyers would simple not qualify for a mortgage loan. Lenders and the lending institutions point to the fact that the majority of home purchase deals that fail to materialize, do so largely because of buyer qualifying problems in terms of not being able to secure financing. Consequently, they say, buyers whose income may be too low to meet the lenders' normal standards, need to have other alternatives that are designed to meet a broad range of requirements for a different number of borrowers, namely, some "creative financing" methods.

(a) Creative Financing Methods will Generally Involve More Costs To You, However

As a lender (or potential lender), you should bear in mind, however, that while the challenge of qualifying for a loan might at times require that you finance your purchase in a more creative way, the fact, however, is that, as a rule, *the more "creative" the method used to get your financing, the higher the costs that will usually be involved for you.* ***Indeed, no form of financing is really even likely to reduce for you the interest costs or price of your home. Think of it this way: creative financing exists, really, to help prospective home buyers pay for a house when traditional methods are probably not available to them to do the job — that is, when they can't qualify through the more ordinary methods. That, quite likely, usually means having to pay more!*** The vast majority of creative financing methods are, for example, designed in the following manner with the following objectives: to reduce initial payments so that a borrower can then qualify; to leverage money; or to defer the payment of the loan. Other forms of creative financing are aimed at reducing the initial price of the house. All of these ideas are expensive, and consequently they add to the cost of the home purchase. For example, a 'creative financing' plan that entails interest-only payments might be much lower in monthly payments; you qualify for the loan alright, but the "higher cost" element for you is that the overall interest cost you pay on the loan is much greater. By its nature, virtually all forms of creative financing must involve some delay of interest expense or a higher level of interest payments in the long run, and, by this nature, the house you buy with a 'creative financing' method of financing will cost more than the one bought with traditional methods.

All these said, however, it should still be emphasized, that there are many situations when creative financing might be appropriate for a homebuyer, even though it would mean a higher cost for the home purchase. The reality is that, there are many instances and certain circumstances when you simply may not be able to buy a house without some arrangement away from traditional financing. For example, creative financing methods may be necessary for a borrower in a particular situation just to meet the lender's specific loan qualification requirements (say, for example, to reduce the monthly payments to an affordable level in terms of one's income); or such methods may at times be necessary in a particular situation because, although the borrower can qualify, the monthly payments called for are too high or, because a borrower can't afford a down payment requirement unless with a creative financing arrangement, and so on. *Consequently, if you are a prospective homebuyer who finds you cannot meet the conventional rules and requirements for obtaining a mortgage loan, some creative financing methods may well be a suitable necessity for you. For sure, the creative financing method you use would probably cost you more in the long run. But that's alright. Just be sure you get a convenient financing arrangement, as well as a financially sound one.*

Different borrowers seek special creative financing arrangements for different reasons, and the "creative" financing method one borrower wants, may not be appropriate or practicable for another, because of differences in borrowers' financial status, investment objectives, income, credit background, the home price, the lender, and any number of other considerations.

(b) The Big Five Of Mortgage Types: The Five Basic Types

The most commonly used types of mortgages are the traditional fixed-rate mortgages and the adjustable-rate mortgages or the ARMs. The other three basic types of mortgage loans are, respectively, the two principal government sponsored mortgage loans, namely, the FHA-insured and the VA-guaranteed loans, and the seller-assisted home financing.

Because these five types of mortgages or home financing methods, together, constitute the choice for the overwhelming majority of homebuyers in America, they have been more elaborately discussed in separate chapters in the book (see Chapters 4, 5 and 6, respectively). Fortunately, for most homebuyers, though there has been a proliferation of various types of mortgages in recent decades, a good deal of these "creative financing" types of mortgages – e.g., balloon mortgages, graduated-payment mortgages, equity mortgages, and reverse equity mortgages, to name just a few – are rarely used today. Nevertheless, they are covered below in this chapter for the general information of readers: by understanding what these types of mortgages are, you'll be in a better position to know whether you want to consider them or not, anyway. Not all of these mortgage alternatives are offered by every lender. In fact, most lenders actually offer only a limited number of choices, and frequently you might have to work with a mortgage broker or other mortgage sources (see Chapters 2 and 12) to shop for and find the specific arrangement you want, or to find the proper lender that carries a specific variety.

B. SOME MAJOR FINANCING PLANS IN TODAY'S MARKET[5]

Given below, are some 16 home financing plans and techniques, representing the basic variants of mortgage types on the market today, some of them falling under the "creative financing" category proper. It's not attempted to outline every new or currently existing financing technique on the market since new financing alternatives are frequently being introduced while many of the existing ones frequently grow obsolete or disappear from the scene just as fast.

1. Fixed-Rate Mortgages (FRAs)

Fixed-rate mortgage is one having an interest rate and monthly payments that remain *constant* over the life of the loan. For example, suppose you borrow $50,000 at 10% interest for 30-years. Your monthly payments on this loan would be $632.22 and will never exceed that fixed predetermined amount.

---

[5] Much of The rest of this appendix is excerpted from "*The Mortgage Money Guide,*" an excellent booklet prepared and published under the auspices of the Federal Trade Commission by its staff members as a public service to homebuyers. The present author is indebted to the FTC and its staff for this material

From the standpoint simply of simplicity and security, fixed-rate mortgages are simply the best mortgage for most buyers in most cases. With a fixed rate mortgage, since the interest rate is determined at the start and never varies, you know exactly what rate you'll be paying; no matter how interest rates fluctuate in the financial market, you know exactly what your monthly payments will be and what the amortization schedule for your loan is. Consequently, you can budget accordingly. (See Chapter 4 for a full discussion of this mortgage variety and how it contrasts with the traditional adjustable-rate mortgages).

2. Adjustable-Rate Mortgages (ARMs)

Adjustable-Rate Mortgages or ARMs (also called "rollover," "adjustable," "flexible," "variable" interest mortgages) are a mortgage with an interest rate which *increases or decreases* over the period of the loan according to pre-determined market conditions. The interest rate (the "price" of the loan) is not fixed, but is recomputed from time to time according to a certain financial index. For example, the mortgage rate could be tied to the so-called "prime rate", the rate banks charge their most creditworthy customers to lend them money, which is one of the most commonly used indices. Or, the mortgage rate could just as well be tied to any of the other financial indices less frequently used — e.g., the 3 to 5 year U.S. Treasure bill rate, or the Federal Home Loan Bank Board's interest rate, or some other price index.

The fundamental reason why lenders have a liking for adjustable-rate type of mortgages, is to protect themselves against inflation and higher interest rates for their money, as a fixed rate mortgage assures that they will be constantly able to keep their mortgage charges up as the market rates change (upwards) from time to time. There are many **variations** within the adjustable-rate mortgage category.

To build predictability into your flexible (adjustable) rate loan, some lenders would include provisions for "caps" that limit the amount your interest rate may change – a so-called "rate cap." Then, there is the "periodic cap'" which limits the amount the rate can increase at any one time [for example, a provision in the mortgage that even if the index increases by 2% in one year, the borrower's rate can only go up 1%]; and there's the "aggregate cap," which limits the amount the rate can increase over the life of the loan [e.g., a provision that even if the index increases by, say 2% every year, the borrower's rate cannot increase more than 5% over the life of the loan].

Another variation of the adjustable-rate mortgage is to fix the interest rate for a period of time – 3 to 5 years, for example – with the understanding that the interest rate will then be renegotiated. Loans with periodically renegotiated rates are also called *rollover mortgages*; and because the interest rate is fixed for at least a reasonable length of time, such loans make monthly payments more predictable. And, a final variation of the

Rollover Mortgages: An Example

Tables show mortgage rates and monthly payments on a $75,000, 30-year rollover mortgage with an initial rate of 12.5 percent that is renegotiated (or "rolled over") every three years. The rate may rise or fall by a maximum of 5 percentage points over the life of the mortgage, and that the rate can fluctuate by no more than 1.5 percentage points during each renegotiation. Assume the rate rises or falls by the maximum allowed at each renegotiation.

If Rates Go UP:	MORTGAGE RATE	MONTHLY PAYMENT	If Rates Go DOWN:	MORTGAGE RATE	MONTHLY PAYMENT
Year 1	12.5%	$ 800.44	Year 1	12.5%	$800.44
Year 4	14.0%	$ 885.95	Year 4	11.0%	$717.16
Year 7	15.5%	$ 970.21	Year 7	9.5%	$640.76
Year 10	17.0%	$1,052.57	Year 10	8.0%	$573.01
Year 13	17.5%	$1,078.92	Year 13	7.5%	$553.37

Source: Federal Home Loan Bank Board

The New York Times / May 31, 1980

flexible rate mortgage we shall take note of here, is the ***pledged account buy-down mortgage*** with a flexible rate. Under this plan, the buyer (or it could be the builder, or anyone else willing to subsidize the loan) makes a large initial payment to the lender at the time the loan is made. The payment is placed in an interest-earning account with the lender, thereby offsetting the mortgage rate you pay and helping lower your interest rate for at least the first few years.

To encourage you to take an ARM, the lender will often offer you a lower interest rate at the start of the loan payment. It's very important, however, for you to know just how long the lower, beginning rate lasts, how frequently the interest rate is adjusted, and how high it can go. [See Chapter 4 for a more comprehensive discussion of this mortgage variety and how it contrasts with the traditional fixed-rate mortgages].

3. FHA Mortgage

This is a mortgage insured (guaranteed) by the Federal Housing Administration (FHA). They are available only to owner-occupants of homes and for residential homes. The FHA does not make the loan itself, but grants the lender a guarantee for repayment of the loan. The one great advantage of the FHA type loan to a borrower, is that the down payment required from the borrower to qualify for such mortgage is minimal, usually an amount equal to between 3 and 5 percent of the home purchase price. The property is appraised and inspected by the FHA, and must meet certain minimum standards and conditions before the borrower's application may be approved. [See Chapter 5 for a fuller discussion of this mortgage variety and the eligibility requirements and application procedures].

4. VA Mortgage

This is a mortgage guaranteed by the Veterans Administration (VA). They are available to qualified U.S. war veterans. An owner-occupant can apply for such a loan if he/she is a veteran or the spouse of a veteran. Like the FHA loans, one great advantage of the VA-backed mortgage to a borrower, is that the loan is granted with little or no down payment but with minimal closing costs. [See Chapter 5 for a fuller discussion of this mortgage variety, and the eligibility requirements and application procedures].

5. Balloon Mortgage

A balloon mortgage is one in which only the interest due is paid during the term of the mortgage, with the entire loan principal due and payable at the end of the term (which is usually a short one, commonly 3 to 5 years). To put it another way, a balloon-payment mortgage features regular, usual level, monthly payments for a period of a few years, followed by an extra-large payment – the so-called ***"balloon"*** — at the end. The equal monthly payments to be paid in balloon mortgage plans are usually for the interest charge only. But that interest rate is a fixed rate throughout the life of the loan.

Here's how a typical balloon plan works. Suppose you borrow $30,000 for a 5-year term at a 15% interest rate. And suppose your payments per month are only $375. In this example, payments of $375 per month for a 5-year period only amounts to a sum just equal to the interest charge on the loan, which means that the $30,000 principal becomes due at maturity – at the end of the 5 year period. That means, in other words, that after you shall have made 59 monthly payments of $375 each, you will then have to make one final, big ("balloon") payment of $30,375. And what if you can't make that final payment? Then you'll have to refinance the property, if that is available, or sell the property.

Some (not all) lenders guarantee refinancing when the balloon payment is due, though no guarantee is usually made on the associated interest rate. When no such guarantee on refinancing exists, the borrower (homebuyer) could be forced to start the whole business of shopping for housing money, as well as of paying the closing costs and front-end charges, all over again.

Balloon mortgages are used most frequently in times when interest rates are so high that few people want, or can afford, to take out a conventional mortgage. Thus, the balloon arrangement option is made primarily because it allows the person who otherwise could not have afforded a house to manage buying one, and because it allows the developer to sell his house which would otherwise remain unsold in a period of high interest rates. Furthermore, it is expedient for the buyer who doesn't want to lock himself into a high-rate mortgage — he is, in effect, betting that by the time the big balloon payment is due, the rates shall have vastly come down from the existing rates and so he'll be able to refinance the balloon amount with a new mortgage at a lower rate. But, on the other side of the equation, the borrower's risk is also rather obvious: if, for whatever reason (continuing high interest rate, depressed housing market, etc.) he's unable to repay the balloon at its due date, or unable to obtain a new mortgage to refinance the balloon, he'll lose the house.

6. Graduated Payment Mortgage

Graduated Payment Mortgage (GPM) is designed for homebuyers who expect to be able to make larger monthly payments in the near future. During the early years of the loan, the borrower makes lower monthly payments. The payments are structured to rise at a set rate over a set period, say 5 or 10 years. Then they remain constant for the remaining duration of the loan.

Even though the payments change, the interest rate is usually fixed. So, during the early years, the borrower's payments are lower than the amount that would have been warranted by the interest rate. During the later years, the difference is made up by higher payments. At the end of the loan period, the borrower is to have paid off his entire debt. The idea is to allow you to *pay less in the early years,* when your earning power is modest, and *more in the later years,* when inflation and career progress shall have (hopefully!) made the higher payments easier to meet. The obvious danger: there's no guarantee that you will, in fact, have a higher earning power at the later time!

7. Growing Equity Mortgage (Rapid Payoff Mortgage)

The "Growing Equity Mortgage" (GEM) and the "Rapid Payoff Mortgage" are among the more recent of mortgage plans on the market. These mortgages combine a fixed interest rate with a changing monthly payment. The interest rate is usually a few percentage points below the market rate. Although the mortgage term may run for 30-years, the loan will frequently be paid off in less than 15 years because payment increases are applied entirely to the principal.

Monthly payment changes are based on agreed-upon schedule of increases or on an index. For example, the plan might use the U.S. Commerce Department index that measures after-tax per capita income, and your payments might increase at a specified portion of the change in this index, say 75%. Suppose you're paying $500 per month. In this example, if the index increases by 8%, you will have to pay 75% of the 8%, i.e., 6%, additional. Your payment increase, then, is to $530, and the additional $30 you pay will be used to reduce your principal.

To be able to use this mortgage plan, you have to have an income that is rising rapidly enough to keep pace with the increased payments. The chief advantage of this plan is that it can often permit the borrower to pay off his loan and acquire equity in the property rapidly.

8. Shared Appreciation Mortgage

In Shared Appreciation Mortgage (SAM), you make monthly payments at a relatively low interest rate. You also agree to share with the lender a sizable percentage (usually 30% to 50%) of whatever appreciation comes about in your house's value after a specified number of years, or when you sell or transfer the home.

The principal advantage of this plan to a borrower (which, it is to be recognized, comes about because of the *shared appreciation* feature), is that he gets to enjoy monthly payments which are lower than those available with many other regular plans. However, he's subject to some potential risks associated with the plan. For example, he may still be liable for the dollar amount of the property's appreciation even if he does not wish to sell the property at the agree-upon date. Also, if property values do not increase as anticipated, the borrower may still be liable for an additional amount of interest agreed upon.

Here is how one variation of this idea, called **shared equity mortgage plan,** works, for an example. Let's suppose you've found a home for $100,000 in a neighborhood where property values`are rising, and that the local bank is charging 18% on home mortgages. Assuming you paid $20,000 down and chose a 30-year mortgage term on the $80,000 balance, your monthly payments would have to be $1,205.67 — which, let's say, you'd find to be about twice what you can afford. But, along comes a friend who offers to help. He offers to pay half of each monthly payment, or roughly $600, for 5 years. At the end of that time, you both assume the house will be worth at least $125,000. You can sell it, and your friend can recover the share of the monthly payments he had made to date (i.e., $36,000), plus half of the home's appreciation, or $12,500, for a total of $48,500 to him. Or, you can at that time pay your friend the same sum of money out of your pocket and gain increased equity in the house.

Shared appreciation and shared equity mortgages were inspired partly by rising interest rates and partly by the notion that housing values would continue to grow and grow over the foreseeable future. It should always be realized, therefore, that if property values fall, or don't rise as high or rapidly as anticipated, these plans may not be as available or advisable.

9. Assumable Mortgage

An assumable mortgage is a mortgage that can be taken over or passed on to a new owner at the previous owner's interest rate. For example, suppose you're interested in a $75,000 home. You make a down payment of $25,000, and you still owe $50,000. The owner of the home has paid off $20,000 of a $30,000, 10% mortgage. You assume the present owner's old mortgage, which has $10,000 outstanding. You also make additional financing arrangements for the remaining $40,000, by, for example, borrowing that amount from a mortgage company at the prevailing market rate of 16%. Your advantage here: your overall interest rate is lower than the market rate because part of the money you owe is being repaid at 10%.

It should be noted that, as a practical matter, during periods of high rates, most lending institutions are reluctant to permit assumptions, preferring to write a new mortgage at the prevailing market rate. In such times this results in many lenders calling in the loans under **"due on sale"** clauses (see Appendix C). Because these clauses have increasingly been upheld in court, many mortgages are no longer legally assumable. Be especially careful, therefore, if you are considering a mortgage represented as "assumable." Read the contract carefully and consider having an expert or professional check to determine if the lender has the right to raise your rate in those mortgages.

10. Seller Take-back or Owner-Financed Mortgage

This type of financing goes by several names: owner financing, taking back a mortgage, seller-assisted financing, etc. Whatever the label used, however, the seller (owner) is issuing the buyer a mortgage. This mortgage, which is provided by the seller, is frequently a **"second trust"** and is combined with an assumed mortgage. The second trust (**or "second mortgage"**) provides financing in addition to the first assumed mortgage, using the same property as collateral. (In the event of default, the second mortgage is satisfied only after the first). Seller take-backs frequently involve payments for interest only, with the principal due at maturity.

For example, suppose you want to buy a $150,000 home, that the seller owes $70,000 on the house on a 10% mortgage, and that you assume this mortgage and make a $30,000 down payment. You still need $50,000. So the seller gives you a second mortgage, or take-back, for $50,000 for 5 years at 14% (well below the market rate) with monthly payments of $583.33. However, your payments are for interest only, and in 5 years you will have to pay the $50,000 principal. The seller take-back, in other words, may have enabled you to buy the home. But it may also have left you with a sizable "balloon" payment that must be paid off in the near future.

Some private sellers are also offering first trusts as take-backs. In this approach, the seller finances the major portion of the loan and takes back a mortgage on the property. [See Chapter 6 for a fuller discussion of the procedures of seller-assisted financing].

11. Wraparound

Another variation on the second mortgage is the *wraparound*. Suppose you'd like to buy a $75,000 condominium and can make a $25,000 down payment, but can't afford the payments at the current rate (let's say it's 18%) on the remaining $50,000. The present owners have a $30,000, 10% mortgage. They offer you a $50,000 "wraparound" mortgage at 14%. The new loan "wraps around" the existing $30,000 mortgage, adding $20,000 to it. You make all your payments to the second lender or the seller, who then forwards payments for the first mortgage. You'll, in effect, be paying the equivalent of 10% on the $30,000 to the first lender, plus an additional 4% on this amount to the second lender, plus 14% on the remaining $20,000. Your total loan costs using this approach will be lower than if you obtained a loan for the full amount at the current rate (for example, 18%).

Wraparounds may cause problems if the original lender or the holder of the original mortgage is not aware of the new mortgage. Upon discovering this arrangement, some lenders or holders may have the right to insist that the old mortgage be paid off immediately.

12. Land Contract

Borrowed from commercial real estate, this plan enables you to pay below-market interest rates. The installment land contract permits the seller to hold onto his or her original below-market rate mortgage while "selling" the home on an installment basis. The installment payments are for a short term and may be for interest only. At the end of the contract the unpaid balance, frequently the full purchase price, must still be paid. The seller continues to hold title to the property until all payments are made. Thus, you, the buyer, acquire no equity until the contract ends. If you fail to make a payment on time, you could lose a major investment.

These loans are popular because they offer lower payments than market rate loans. Land contracts are also being used to avoid the **due-on-sale clause** (see Appendix C). The buyer and seller may assert to the lender who provided the original mortgage that the due on sale clause does not apply because the property will not be sold until the end of the contract. Therefore, the low interest rate continues. However, the lender may assert that the contract in fact represents a sale of the property. Consequently, the lender may have the right to accelerate the loan, or call it due, and raise the interest rate to current market levels.

13. Buy-down

A buy-down is a subsidy of the mortgage interest rate that helps you meet the payments during the first few years of the loan. Suppose a new house sells for $150,000, that after a down payment of $75,000, you still need to finance $75,000, and that a 30-year first mortgage is available for 17%, which would make your monthly payments $1,069.26, or beyond your budget. However, a buy-down is available: for the first three years, the developer will subsidize your payments, bringing down the interest rate to 14%. This means your payments are only $888.65, which you can afford.

There are several things to think about in buy-downs. First, consider what your payments will be after the first few years. If this is a fixed rate loan, the payments in the above example will jump to the rate at which the loan was originally made — 17% — and total more than $1,000. If this is a flexible rate loan, and the index to which your rate is tied has risen since you took out the loan, your payments could go up even higher.

Second, check to see whether the subsidy is part of your contract with the lender or with the builder. If it's provided separately by the builder, the lender can still hold you liable for the full interest rate (17% in the above example), even if the builder backs out of the deal or goes out of business.

Finally, that $150,000 sales price may have been increased to cover the builder's interest subsidy. A comparable home may be selling around the corner for less. At the same time, on the other hand it may well be the case that competition encouraged the builder to offer you a genuine savings. So, it simply pays to check around.

There are also plans called ***consumer buy-downs***. In these loans, the buyer makes a sizable down payment, and the interest rate granted is below market. In other words, in exchange for a large payment at the beginning of the loan, you may qualify for a lower rate on the amount borrowed. Frequently, this type of mortgage has a shorter term than those written at current market rates.

14. Rent With Option to Buy

In a climate of changing interest rates, some buyers and sellers are attracted to a ***rent-with-option*** arrangement. In this plan, you rent property and pay a premium for the right to purchase the property within a limited time period at a specific price. In some arrangements, you may apply part of the rental payments to the purchase price.

This approach enables you to lock in the purchase price. You can also use this method to "buy time" in the hope that interest rates will decrease. From the seller's perspective, this plan may provide the buyer time to obtain sufficient cash or acceptable financing to proceed with a purchase that may not be possible otherwise.

15. Zero Rate and Low Rate Mortgage

These mortgages are unique in that they appear to be completely or almost totally interest free. The buyer makes a large down payment, usually one-third of the sales price, and pays the remainder in installments over a short term.

Suppose you want to buy a $90,000 home but you find the prevailing market interest rate unacceptable. You opt to use your savings to make the down payment, say $30,000, on a "zero rate" (or no-interest) mortgage. Then you pay a front-end finance charge — for example, 12% of the money you need to borrow, or about $8,400. You then agree to repay the principal ($60,000) in 84 monthly installments of $714.29. In 7 years, the loan will be paid off.

In these mortgages, the sales price may be increased to reflect the loan costs. Thus, you could be exchanging lower interest costs for a higher purchase price. Partly because of this, you may be able to deduct the prepaid finance charge and a percentage (for example, 10%) of your payments from your taxes as if it were interest.

16. Reverse Annuity Mortgage

If you already own your home and need to obtain cash, you might consider the reverse annuity mortgage (RAM) or ***"equity conversion."*** In this plan, you obtain a loan in the form of monthly payments over an extended period of time, using your property as collateral. When the loan comes due, you repay both the principal and interest.

A RAM is not a mortgage in the conventional sense. You can't obtain a RAM until you have paid off your original mortgage. Suppose you own your home and you need a source of money, you could draw up a contract with a lender that enable you to borrow a given amount each month until you've reached a maximum of, for example, $10,000. At the end of the term, you must repay the loan. But remember this, though: if you do not have the cash available to repay the loan plus interest, you will have to sell the property or take out a new loan.

HIGHLIGHTING THE ESSENTIALS OF CREATIVE FINANCING PLANS

Type	Description	Considerations
Fixed Rate Mortgage	Fixed interest rate, usually long-term; equal monthly payments of principal and interest until debt is paid in full.	Offers stability and long-term tax advantages; limited availability. Interest rates may be higher than other types of financing. New fixed rates are rarely assumable.
Flexible Rate Mortgage	Interest rate changes are based on a financial index, resulting in possible changes in your monthly payments, loan term, and/or principal. Some plans have rate or payment caps.	Readily available. Starting interest rate is slightly below market, but payments can increase sharply and frequently if index increases. Payment caps prevent wide fluctuations in payments but may cause negative amortization (see box, page 15). Rate caps, while rare, limit amount total debt can expand.
Renegotiable Rate Mortgage (Rollover)	Interest rate and monthly payments are constant for several years; changes possible thereafter. Long-term mortgage.	Less frequent changes in interest rate offer some stability.
Balloon Mortgage	Monthly payments based on fixed interest rate; usually short-term; payments may cover interest only with principal due in full at term end.	Offers low monthly payments but possibly no equity until loan is fully paid: When due, loan must be paid off or refinanced. Refinancing poses high risk if rates climb.
Graduated Payment Mortgage	Lower monthly payments rise gradually (usually over 5-10 years), then level off for duration of term. With flexible interest rate, additional payment changes possible if index changes.	Easier to qualify for. Buyer's income must be able to keep pace with scheduled payment increases. With a flexible rate, payment increases beyond the graduated payments can result in additional negative amortization (see box, page 15).
Shared Appreciation Mortgage	Below-market interest rate and lower monthly payments, in exchange for a share of profits when property is sold or on a specified date. Many variations.	If home appreciates greatly, total cost of loan jumps. If home fails to appreciate, projected increase in value may still be due, requiring refinancing at possibly higher rates.
Assumable Mortgage	Buyer takes over seller's original, below-market rate mortgage.	Lowers monthly payments. May be prohibited if "due on sale" clause is in original mortgage (see box, page 12). Not permitted on most new fixed rate mortgages.
Seller Take-back	Seller provides all or part of financing with a first or second mortgage.	May offer a below-market interest rate; may have a balloon payment requiring full payment in a few years or refinancing at market rates, which could sharply increase debt.
Wraparound	Seller keeps original low rate mortgage. Buyer makes payments to seller who forwards a portion to the lender holding original mortgage. Offers lower effective interest rate on total transaction.	Lender may call in old mortgage and require higher rate. If buyer defaults, seller must take legal action to collect debt.
Growing Equity Mortgage (Rapid Payoff Mortgage)	Fixed interest rate but monthly payments may vary according to agreed-upon schedule or index.	Permits rapid payoff of debt because payment increases reduce principal. Buyer's income must be able to keep up with payment increases.
Land Contract	Seller retains original mortgage. No transfer of title until loan is fully paid. Equal monthly payments based on below-market interest rate with unpaid principal due at loan end.	May offer no equity until loan is fully paid. Buyer has few protections if conflict arises during loan.
Buy-down	Developer (or third party) provides an interest subsidy which lowers monthly payments during the first few years of the loan. Can have fixed or flexible interest rate.	Offers a break from higher payments during early years. Enables buyer with lower income to qualify. With flexible rate mortgage, payments may jump substantially at end of subsidy. Developer may increase selling price.
Rent with Option	Renter pays "option fee" for right to purchase property at specified time and agreed-upon price. Rent may or may not be applied to sales price.	Enables renter to buy time to obtain down payment and decide whether to purchase. Locks in price during inflationary times. Failure to take option means loss of option fee and rental payments.
Reverse Annuity Mortgage (Equity Conversion)	Borrower owns mortgage-free property and needs income. Lender makes monthly payments to borrower, using property as collateral.	Can provide homeowners with needed cash. At end of term, borrower must have money available to avoid selling property or refinancing.
Zero Rate and Low Rate Mortgage	Appears to be completely or almost interest free. Large down payment and one-time finance charge, then loan is repaid in fixed monthly payments over short term.	Permits quick ownership. May not lower total cost (because of possibly increased sales price). Doesn't offer long-term tax deductions.

CHAPTER 4

Contrasting The Two Broad Types of Mortgages in The Market: The Fixed-Rate Mortgage and The Adjustable-Rate Mortgage

As elaborated elsewhere in this manual (see Chapter 3 at p. 19), until recently, mortgages and mortgage instruments were a fairly straightforward matter, relatively uncomplicated and simple – they generally had a fixed interest rate and a full amortization over a relatively fixed, long period of time. Today, however, with the advent of "creative financing" in mortgage financing largely due to higher home prices and volatile changes in housing values, there have developed many different methods in the way a home loan can be structured.

In this chapter, we deal in some greater detail with *the two broad and most commonly used types of mortgages in the home financing industry:* the Fixed-Rate Mortgages (FRMs), and the Adjustable-Rate Mortgages (ARMs). Previously in Chapter 3, we have listed some 16 mortgage varieties and "creative financing" devices that are available in the market today.

A. FIXED-RATE MORTGAGES (FRMs)

This is the basic, "plain vanilla" American mortgage: the old reliable kind of mortgage your grandparents, father, and mother, may have had on the family house! Indeed, just until a few decades ago (the 1970's and early 1980's), this was the primary and dominant type of mortgage in the American housing industry. It is also viewed in the eyes of many as the best mortgage for homebuyers in most cases, the kind that most consumers should prefer, primarily because of its simplicity and security for the borrower.

As the name implies, with a fixed-rate mortgage, the interest rate is set at the start and remains fixed and unvaried at the same rate throughout the life of the mortgage. For example, suppose you took a $100,000 fixed-rate type of mortgage at 10% (FIXED) interest rate for a 30-year term. Your monthly payment on this loan (see Amortization Table in Appendix A) would be $877.58, and will never vary or change for the whole 30-year loan term.

The attraction of the fixed-rate type of mortgages for, and the reason for its preference by, the average homeowner is rather simple and understandable: the great sense of security it provides the borrower; the certainty it provides him (or her) of knowing exactly what the rate he'll be paying is, exactly what his monthly payments will always be, and what the amortization schedule of his loan will always be. A fixed-rate mortgage gives the home buyer the assurance of knowing that no matter how the interest rates may fluctuate or how the general economic conditions change in the future, his mortgage payments will remain the same. As a homeowner, you can budget accordingly. As long as you are able to keep up with your monthly mortgage payments, you will not lose your house. If mortgage interest rates were ever to soar again to 20 percent or so, as they did in the 1970s and early 1980s, other homeowners who have adjustable or variable-rate types of loans will be the ones who'll need to worry, or perhaps even lose their homes. But not you!

One disadvantage of fixed-rate mortgages, however, is that somehow you have to pay for the "privilege" of having a fixed rate: generally, the rates on fixed mortgages are higher than the rates charged on adjustable rate mortgage (ARM), although the rates for ARM can sometimes rise too, often far above the level charged by the FRM. Furthermore, the FRM mortgages are generally not assumable by the new owner.

1. Advantages of the Fixed-Rate Mortgages

The FRM has the following major advantages:

(a) Your housing costs not only remain constant, but actually decline over time in terms of constant dollars. With the fixed-rate mortgage, given the reality of inflation over time, the consistency of payments for the mortgage means even more than just the fact of your housing costs merely remaining <u>constant</u> and not rising over time. Rather, even more important than that, it means for you a <u>decline</u> in your housing costs over time even as your payments remain the same. This is because as a consequence of inflation over time, the value of the dollar falls, hence the mortgage payments you make become literally lower in terms of constant dollars; and, secondly, personal income tends to rise over time, at the same time that the mortgage payments (under the fixed-rate mortgage plan) will not.

EXAMPLE #1: Assume that in 1999 the purchasing power of the dollar is 2 percent lower than it was 2 years earlier in 1997. Then the fixed-rate mortgage payment you make in 1999 is also 2 percent below the real spending level in 1997.

EXAMPLE #2: Assume the following: that your salary when you first took out your mortgage some 5 years ago, was $3,500, and that your monthly mortgage payments are $700, which is 20 percent of your gross; but that today, 5 years later, you have gained a promotion and now earn a higher salary of $4,900 per month.

You'll find that the mortgage payment you make is now ***lower in proportionate terms*** — now constitutes only 14.3 percent of your gross pay, which is <u>less</u> than the previous 20 percent figure. This means that you would have been paying less of your salary now – a *lower proportion* of your salary – in housing costs each month.

(b) It's easier to do long range financial planning with the fixed-rate mortgage. You can, for example, easily compute what is required to speed up your pay-off date on your mortgage with a fixed-rate mortgage. Since your monthly payment amount under the FRM is definite, and never varies, you will be better able to rearrange your budget to pay more for the move. On the other hand, if your mortgage were to be a variable-rate one, a long range plan to pay off your mortgage ahead of schedule could easily be disturbed when interest rates rise, which will then result, correspondingly, in rising monthly payments for you, making any long range mortgage acceleration plan you might wish to make impracticable.

(c) With a fixed-rate mortgage, your lender is more likely in the future to agree to refinance your loan, especially if interest rates rise. A general rise in interest rates will mean that the pre-existing payment you are making is relatively lower – an obvious motivation, from the lender's standpoint, to want to honor a refinancing plan from you to replace your pre-existing loan with another one.

2. Disadvantage of the Fixed-Rate Mortgage

The following are among the major disadvantages of the fixed-rate type of mortgages:

(a) ***Higher Interest Rates on Points***

The rates on fixed-rate mortgages are generally higher than the rates charged on adjustable-rate mortgages (or ARM), although it should be pointed out, however, that the ARM can rise too, often far above the level charged by the FRM. It is as though you have to pay, as though it has to cost you, something extra for the "privilege" of having a fixed rate! Generally, obtaining the loan itself as well as meeting the payments on a fixed-rate mortgage is more expensive for the borrower. This is so because, as a rule, in borrowing from a lender, you will start out with a higher interest rate than what the adjustable mortgage holders pay, and if the market interest rates remain the same, or fall, then your fixed-rate mortgage will be expensive to keep as you will have to live with paying more than you could elsewhere. Or, alternatively, you could decide to refinance the mortgage but then you'll need to pay all the closing and lender's refinancing charges all over again, not exactly a cost-free option!

(b) Higher Qualifications Standards

The second disadvantage associated with fixed-rate mortgages, is that generally speaking the average homebuyer may have a problem qualifying for a loan with a fixed-rate mortgage, than with an adjustable-rate mortgage. This is because generally fixed-rate mortgages start out with a higher rate, which, in turn, translates to higher monthly payments for the borrower to pay. A fixed-rate mortgage offered, for example, at 2 or 3 percentage "points" (see Chapter 7) above the adjustable-rate mortgage, will mean that the borrower will need to make a _higher_ monthly payment of $100 to $200. Such differentials could easily put the loan applicant over the limit of the typical income-to-payment ratio applied by lenders in deciding on a loan approval. Indeed, by common consensus, ***it is this differential which exists between the monthly payment required for the fixed-rate mortgage relative to that required for the adjustable-rate mortgage, that commonly force most borrowers to take out the adjustable-rate mortgage in the first place***. The scenario typically goes this way: at the time of the application for a long, the borrower, finding that he'll be unable to meet the lender's qualifying income level set for a fixed-rate loan, is compelled, out of necessity, to take out the adjustable-rate loan, instead, which generally start out with a _lower_ interest rate (and, therefore, lower monthly payment amounts) and then increases later based on some price indices. Thus, notwithstanding the borrower's insecurity about the inevitability that the monthly payments under an ARM arrangement would change and rise over time with increase in the price indices, the borrower still goes along with the adjustable-rate type of mortgage primarily for the sake of just being able to qualify for a loan.

(c) Higher Loan Fees and Charges

The third disadvantage associated with fixed-rate mortgages, is that generally the fees charged by lenders for contracting for fixed-rate mortgages, particularly for long terms, are substantially higher. Again, it's sort of like an expected premium you pay for the "privilege" of having a fixed-rate mortgage! Lenders, fully conscious of the reality that granting a long-term mortgage at a fixed rate of interest means taking the "extra" risk of committing themselves to earning the same rate of return for some 20, 25 or 30-year period of uncertainty, during which time the general rates – and their own cost of money for securing their funds – might very well rise far above the rate they're giving you today, seek to be compensated for that risk up front. That is, by charging more TODAY. Consequently, the average fixed-rate mortgage is often a few points higher, and involves higher lender's fees and charges at the beginning of the loan term.

(d) Non-Assumability

The fourth disadvantage associated with fixed-rate mortgages is that the FRMs are generally not assumable by the new owner. Thus, for most fixed-rate mortgages, if some emergencies were to hit which require you, unavoidably, to let someone else, a relative or customer, "assume" (take over) your loan payments, either temporarily or permanently, you won't be able to do so.

3. Summary

To summarize, the problem with fixed-rate mortgages — its central disadvantage – is that many prospective homebuyers simply can't qualify for the loan, as their incomes will often not be high enough to meet the standards under the lender's rules and requirements. As a rule, if you firmly believe you'll remain in the house for a long time, say for a full 25 or 30-year term of your mortgage, it will generally make a sound financial sense to take a fixed-rate mortgage. [See Chapter 7 for more on this]. In reality, however, the typical first-time home buyer stays an average of 5-years in the house, and, according to a recent U.S. census report, overall the average American home owner stays in a home for a period of 8.5 years. The security derived from knowing that your principal housing expense will never go up throughout the life of the loan, no matter how the interest rates fluctuate or how the general economic conditions change in the future, is a tremendous and invaluable economic advantage to a home owner.

B. ADJUSTABLE RATE MORTGAGE (ARMs)

An adjustable-rate mortgage (often called an ARM, for short), is a mortgage loan whose interest rate can change from time to time, usually every six months or annually. The rate moves up in tandem with some generally acceptable economic index, which is written into the loan contract. For example, some lenders may base their ARM rates on U.S. Treasury Securities rates, while others may base their ARM rates on the Federal Reserve Bank rate or Federal Home Loan Bank rate, which measures the cost of funds to lenders. And as that chosen index changes, so does the effective rate which you'll pay for your loan under an ARM deal. As a way of providing some degree of security to the borrower, a "cap" is usually placed in the contract limiting the degree beyond which the interest rate would not rise. In addition, there may also be restrictions on the rate and payment increases permissible from one period to the next.

The underlying rationale for the need to have variability of rates in the adjustable-rate mortgage, is for the lenders to protect themselves against rapid changes in the interest rates market, and thus to reduce their risks. The idea behind the "adjustable" or "flexible" rate mortgage, is simply to limit the lender's risk factor against possible future higher inflation and higher costs of funds. If, for example, a serious inflation were to set in, and the interest rates and the banks' cost of funds were to skyrocket (as they did, for example, in the late 1970s and easily 1980s when they reached 20 percent and drove many mortgage banks into insolvency), the bankers would be able to cope: their income would be able to rise just as well, as homeowners would pay them more on their mortgages.

In simple terms, here's how the adjustable-rate mortgage works: the initial interest rate charged is usually lower than the fixed-rate mortgage rates, perhaps as much as two to three percentage points lower. But the rate then increases over a period of years, based on the changes in the independent index rate that is agreed to be used. As that particular index changes, so does the effective rate that the borrower will have to pay.

A few safeguards and restrictions are also built into the ARM loan contracts as a way of giving protection to the borrower:

- A "cap" (limit) is placed on the permissible frequency of rate increases – to only once per year for most lenders, or to once every six months for others.
- A "cap" is placed on the degree of interest rate increase permissible annually – a contract might specify, for example, that the lender may not increase the loan rate more than 2 percent, or more than 2 ½ percent, per year.
- Most important of them all, a "lifetime cap" is included in the ARM loan contract, meaning a specification of a maximum, total number of percentage points beyond which the loan cannot be increased over the life of the loan. For example, a loan might provide for an initial rate of 10 percent, with a provision that at no point could the interest rate ever rise above, say, 15 percent.

1. Advantages of Adjustable-Rate Mortgages (ARMs)

Adjustable-rate mortgages have many shortcomings. (See below). Summed up in one sentence, what the adjustable-rate mortgage does, is shift much of the risk of rising interest rates from the lender, to you, the borrower. Nevertheless, despite the shortcomings of the ARM, it's not at all uncommon for homeowners and borrowers to find themselves seriously considering taking the adjustable-rate loan when buying a home. For a good number of reasons. Here are some of the major positive points and arguments in favor of the ARMs:

(a) Availability

Some lenders, concerned with the economic uncertainties of the future and fearful that inflation may set in and interest rates skyrocket at any unforeseeable times in the future, simply refuse to make fixed-rate mortgages at all. Consequently, adjustable rate mortgages are generally more available than FRMs. True, in today's mortgage market, adjustable-rate mortgage has come to be widely offered by lenders along with fixed-rate mortgages. But, while fixed-rate mortgages are widely offered, at certain times, particularly in times when the prevailing interest rates are quite high, most of the mortgages offered are of the adjustable variety. As a rule, the higher the prevailing interest rates go, the more common the adjustable mortgages tend to become, and the more the buyers and the lenders alike tend to prefer the adjustable mortgages: the buyers, because they would rather not lock themselves into fixed-rate mortgages at what have to be high rates, and the lenders, because the adjustable-rate mortgage gives them the protection they desire against the risk of large changes occurring in interest rates market.

(b) Better Rate

Because the adjustable-rate mortgage takes some of the risk out of lending for the lender, the lender, feeling freer, will usually give a better initial rate on the adjustable loan — often one to 2 percentage points below the rate of a fixed-rate loan.

The ARM is the best choice when you plan to stay in a home for only one to five years. Why? Because, since the adjustable-rate mortgage contract starts out at a much lower interest rate than the fixed-rate mortgage, you are likely to have left the home (and the loan) behind BEFORE the interest rate on the adjustable loan has a chance to grow to unacceptable levels. [See chapter 7 for more on this]. For example, let's say that the ARM contract starts out with an 8 percent rate when the FRM alternative is going for 10 percent, and that the adjustable-rate lender can raise the rate by no more than 2 percent per year. In such a case, at the very most, you can't come out behind on the adjustable loan until you've stayed in the home for 3 years – it would go from 8, to 10, to 12 percent, an average of 10 percent per year, which matches the fixed-rate mortgage. In this worse case scenario, the ARM still costs less. The principal balances to which the higher interest rates are applied, will be LOWERING balances since the loan shall have been slightly paid down during the first 2 years. By the start of the 4th year, you will come out ahead with the ARM. And you'd probably be looking for a new house by then!

(c) Affordability

The adjustable-rate mortgage might be necessary in order for you to be able to qualify for a mortgage, in the first place. For homebuyers with limited income now but with prospects of better income later, an adjustable-rate loan can mean the difference between being able to afford a house or not quite being able to. When lenders decide on whether to give you a loan, you may have the best job history and the most excellent credit and references, but they often decide based on one strict rule: DO YOU PASS THE INCOME-PAYMENT RATIO TEST AT THAT MOMENT? [See Chapters 9 and 15]

In brief, you can get the loan ONLY IF the lender can conclude that your income is sufficient to meet the proposed loan's payments in the *first* and *second* year of the loan. Since the first, and often the second, year's rate on an adjustable loan is typically below that of a fixed-rate loan, that often means that many homebuyers qualify for and sign up for an adjustable-rate mortgage, rather than a fixed-rate mortgage. This adjustment could make the critical difference in your being able to qualify when you would have no chance to get the higher, fixed-rate mortgage.

Furthermore, some lenders, in an attempt to improve the attractiveness of the adjustable-rate mortgage and to encourage borrowers to take out ARMs, will offer many attractive market incentives: relatively tight caps; low points or even no points; no appraisal fees; etc. Also, some ARM contracts include a conversion feature giving the right to convert the ARM to a fixed-rate mortgage at a given time (usually within 5 years or so). And finally, the closing costs, such as origination fees and other costs, might be substantially lower with adjustable-rate mortgages than with their fixed-rate counterpart.

Admittedly, being able to qualify for a larger loan under adjustable-rate standards in comparison to fixed-rate standards is obviously a significant advantage for a borrower. It's a powerful advantage alright. But up to a point: as long as life progresses as planned and the future prospects of better and rising income do actually materialize. If, however, the family income were to stagnate, contrary to expectation, or if it were to fall while the interest rates are rising, that could spell a catastrophic disadvantage for you as a homeowner.

(c) Assumability
Certainly, not all adjustable-rate loans are automatically assumable. However, adjustable-rate loans are more likely to be assumable than are fixed-rate loans. As a homeowner, assumability of your mortgage by a potential future buyer of the house is a great advantage for you to have because it makes your house easier to sell any time you might want to do so. The central reason why lenders of adjustable-rate loans are more predisposed to grant mortgage assumability, is because in an adjustable-rate situation the lender doesn't have to give up the right to increase the interest rate payable by a new buyer of the home if he were to let a future buyer take over ("assume") an existing mortgage. Thus, for the lender involved in an adjustable-rate contract situation, if the prevailing rates were to be on the increase, the new mortgage holder will simply be obliged to pay a higher rate, and the lender really loses nothing.

2. Disadvantages of Adjustable-Rate Mortgages
For the homeowner or the borrower, the main disadvantage of the ARM can be summed up in one sentence: it has a greater financial risk for him or her.

(a) Costs Can Rise
Whereas, in times of general rising interest rates the fixed-rate loan is the loan with the big advantage for the borrower, it is also true that the exact reverse is the case for borrowers with respect to adjustable-rate loan in such times of rising interest rates: they are at a disadvantage in such times in that they must pay a larger and larger amount of interest on their mortgage and suffer real financial hardship. Indeed, in times of rising interest rates, if the rise in interest rates gets appreciable high, borrowers with adjustable-rate mortgages might find themselves unable to make the higher payments called for, and could well end up losing their homes — a reality which, in fact, occurs in real life to many homeowners on a regular basis. In times of high inflation, or a rise in interest rates, or in periods of hard times when people lose their jobs or are unable to work for a long period of time due to ill health, or when they change employment at reduced incomes, homeowners who have adjustable-rate mortgages may be in great financial danger: they may be unable to keep up with the increasing higher mortgage payments at the same time that their income is either dropping or non-existent. And while borrowers with fixed-rate mortgages do face similar problems as well, the evidence available shows that a disproportionate number of homeowners who fall in the extreme category of actually losing their homes, are homeowners with adjustable-rate mortgages.

(b) High Degree of Uncertainty
With adjustable-rate mortgages, because you don't know in advance what your monthly mortgage expenditure will definitely be, budgeting for the immediate and long term is a lot more difficult, particularly because a mortgage is often the biggest expense item in most families' budgets. Any future substantial rise in the interest rate, or other economic difficulties, could well jeopardize your housing investment. Especially for homeowners on fixed incomes, the adjustable-rate mortgage could present a serious problem in the near future. If the lender does, in fact, raise your payments, the rate of increase in monthly payment could outpace the increase in your monthly family income; you must then pay an ever-growing portion of your income towards your housing costs, thus affecting your ability as a homeowner to continue to retain the house.

C. SUMMARY & CONCLUSIONS ON FRMs AND ARMs

Generally speaking, the fixed-rate mortgage is the best mortgage for a homeowner to have in most cases, primarily because of its simplicity and security for the borrower. Given the choice and its affordability, homeowners prefer a fixed-rate mortgage: it provides a great sense of security for the mortgage holder, a great sense of certainty in knowing exactly what rate he'll be paying, and what his monthly payments and the amortization schedule for his loan will be, and gives the borrower the assurance of knowing that whatever the fluctuations in interest rates or the changes in the general economic conditions in the future, his mortgage payments will remain the same and never change. Thus, you can budget and plan your finances better with an FRM. On the other hand, for the home buyer the fixed-rate mortgage is more costly and more difficult to obtain: the interest rates are generally higher relative to the rates charged for the adjustable-rate mortgages; as an aspiring borrower you may have a problem meeting the lender's higher income-to-payment ratio to qualify for a fixed-rate mortgage because since the fixed-rate mortgages generally start out at two or three percentage points above the adjustable-rate mortgage, the monthly payment amount required to amortize a given loan amount for the adjustable-rate loan is also usually higher.

As a practical matter, the reality is that most home buyers who take the adjustable-rate mortgage, do so primarily because they have no choice – because they simply can't qualify for the fixed-rate mortgage, their income just isn't high enough under the lender's rules, and they are therefore forced to take out an adjustable to at least get a mortgage.

SUGGESTION: By what criteria do you get to choose between an FRM and an ARM? In general, if you believe you will stay in the house you're buying for many years, say up to 5-years,[1] at least, the fixed-rate mortgage is probably the better choice for you; and if you are certain that you'll remain in the house for the full 30-years, it makes even perfect sense to get a fixed-rate mortgage. You should recognize, however, that in practical terms the reality is that the typical first-time homebuyer stays in the home for an average of 5-years, and that the tendency is for a long-term loan (the older rate) to be replaced rather quickly, either by sale of the home and repurchase, or by refinancing. With the adjustable-rate mortgage, because of the ever-present risk that interest rates can rise, thereby off-setting the protection against inflation which home ownership is supposed to provide you, adjustable-rate mortgage financing should be considered as a short-term alternative to the fixed-rate mortgage. *The adjustable-rate mortgage is appropriate until you can refinance and replace it with a fixed-rate mortgage, or if you can plan to sell the house within the next 5 years.*

With an ARM, if the lender does, in fact, raise your payments – a prospect, which you should, in fact, always assume is quite likely in planning ahead and evaluating an ARM – the difference could mean paying a lot more for your house. Hence, if you take an ARM loan, you'll need to plan ahead for a target date when you will replace the ARM with permanent, fixed-rate financing, or when you will move and find a house where you will want to stay longer than 5 years or so. In that event, you might also want to replace your ARM with a FRM.

Finally, note that the VA Mortgages (See Chapter 5) are exclusively fixed-rate mortgages, and the FHA loans (Chapter 5) are permitted to be either a fixed-rate or an adjustable-rate mortgage, but the overwhelming bulk of the FHA loans are of fixed-rate type.

---

[1] More precisely, the U.S. Census Report released in October 1998 states that nationally, the medium time Americans lived at one residence was 5.2 years (meaning that half moved sooner than that, and half remained in their nest longer). Homeowners, however, tend to stay put somewhat longer, averaging 8.2 years, while renters relocate every 2.1 years.

CHAPTER 5

The Two Major Types of Government-Backed Financing Available: The FHA & VA Mortgages

A. AN OVERVIEW

The Federal Housing Administration (the FHA), was created by Congress in 1934 under the National Housing Act and helps homebuyers secure financing by insuring the loan. Today, the FHA is part of the Department of Housing and Urban Development (HUD), and its primary function is to insure loans. The FHA does not build homes or make the loans. Rather, FHA insures FHA-approved lenders against losses caused by borrower defaults on FHA-insured loans. On its own part, the Veterans Administration (VA) has a loan guarantee program that was established in 1944 as part of the GI Bill of Rights. Originally established only for World War II veterans, the VA program has been expanded to include veterans of the Korean and Vietnam wars.

Both of these loan programs (FHA and VA), have one central thing in common: because they are insured or guaranteed by the government, by and large the loan can be obtained with smaller down payments and lower interest rate than conventional loans. *An important point for you to remember as a prospective homebuyer, is that often buyers who may be unqualified for a "conventional" (i.e., non-government-backed) loan, may be able to qualify for either an FHA or a VA loan as these loan programs have been set up by the federal government with the primary aim of encouraging people of more moderate means to become homeowners and to make home ownership more affordable for more Americans.*

Historically, for many families in America, the main obstacle standing in the way of home ownership has been the inability to come up with the down payment (usually 20 percent of the home purchase price) required for most conventional mortgages. Lenders, concerned about protecting themselves in the event that a borrower falls behind on his mortgage payments or defaults on the loan, often won't lend a borrower more than 80 percent of the home value. With respect to government-backed mortgages, however, such a problem largely doesn't exist for the borrower; lenders are therefore able to afford to be more liberal in their lending requirements, and will lend as much as 95, 97 or even 100 percent of the home purchase price.

Today, FHA and VA mortgages have become so significant that they now account for about one-fifth (20%) of all U.S. mortgage loans. Like the FHA, the VA does not issue mortgages directly. They merely give lenders assurance that loans made to people under the VA programs will be paid back. The FHA program provides lenders with *"insurance"*, the cost of which is partly paid for by the borrower, while the VA program gives lenders a direct (though partial) *"guarantee"* on the loan. In either case, the effect is the same: in the event the borrower fails to pay back the mortgage loan, the federal government (the FHA or VA) will pay off the balance due, either in full or up to an agreed limit. Because of this vital element of government assurance for lenders, FHA and VA-loan lenders feel more secure in offering mortgage money to those who might not otherwise have qualified, and to offer loans at a lower rate.

B. PROCEDURES OF THE FHA LOAN PROGRAM

Under the FHA loan program, lenders who have been approved by the FHA to make insured loans either submit applications from prospective borrowers to the local FHA office for approval, or, if authorized by the FHA to do so, perform the underwriting functions themselves (i.e., review of appraisal, mortgage credit examination, etc.). Lenders who are authorized by the FHA to fully underwrite their own FHA loan applications are called **direct endorsers**. As the insurer, the FHA incurs full liability for any losses that may result from borrowers' default and property foreclosure. In turn, the FHA regulates many of the conditions of the loan. *FHA regulations and the procedures and practices, have had such strong impact on the housing industry that over the years these regulations and practices have had the force and effect of law in the real estate industry.*

Unlike the VA mortgages, which are only for Veterans, FHA mortgages are not so restricted. Rather, while there are certain FHA mortgages that are reserved specifically for people of modest means, there are others open to anyone, rich or poor, who would want and can use the kinds of houses financed by an FHA mortgage. As a practical matter, however, because of the limited size of the loan amount available under the FHA program, a wealthy person would probably have little use for an FHA mortgage since such amount (a maximum sum of $124,875 in recent times) can only buy a very modest house in today's real estate market.

Again, unlike the VA mortgages which are always fixed-rate mortgages, an FHA mortgage is permitted to be either a fixed interest rate type or an adjustable rate type. If the rate is adjustable, it can't change more than 1 percentage point per year, or 5 percentage points over the life of the loan. The bulk of the FHA-issued mortgages, are fixed rate mortgages, however.

The nature of the guarantee to the lender is also different from that which applies in respect to FHA mortgages. With a VA mortgage, the government guarantees only a *portion* of the loan balance, usually 25 percent. With a FHA mortgage, 100 percent of the loan amount is covered by insurance. The FHA borrower, however, pays for part of the cost of this insurance premium, which is often sizable (as high as 3.8 percent to 4.3 percent of the loan amount).

FHA mortgages can be obtained on condos as well as cooperatives for loan amounts up to the prevailing FHA limit (about $124,875 in recent times).

C. FHA CLOSING COST

As with the VA loans, the closing costs in FHA loans tend to be on the high side. As explained in the VA Section (see p.43) , although on paper the VA regulations prohibit lenders from charging points to the buyer of a VA mortgage, lenders have often circumvented this rule; they'll have the home seller himself pay the points but then raise the price of the home to compensate for the cost. And, quess what! This same phenomenon prevails, as well, in the FHA lending program. In the case of the FHA, the FHA rule is that the buyer and seller may split the points in whatever proportion they are able to work out. But here, what happens in the real world of the market place, is that the home sellers will often raise the price of the home enough to cover their portion of the points. The buyer, on his part, may then be allowed simply to add his portion of the points cost to the loan amount, and to finance the whole amount over the 15, 20, 25, or 30-year life of the mortgage.

In addition to points, FHA borrowers would generally incur one substantial cost that would usually be avoidable on conventional loans:[1] the mortgage insurance premium or MIP, which is a default insurance designed to reimburse the lender in case you default on the mortgage, is required for FHA loans. The FHA will provide the insurance for the lender; but you have to reimburse it for at least part of the costs. (The fee for this service, a rather steep one, equals at least 3.8% of the loan amount, plus a surcharge of 0.5% in addition to that). Then, there are an assortment of other closing costs: a one percent loan "origination fee," charges for survey of

---

[1] In conventional loans situation,, mortgage default insurance generally becomes necessary only if the borrower's down payment is less than 20% of the home price, and upon one's equity reaching the 20% level such default insurance is cancelled and not required any further by the lender.

the home, title search, title insurance, recording fees, etc. FHA mortgages have one unique feature that is typically not available with conventional mortgages: they specifically allow some of the closing costs (about 57 percent of the total closing costs) to be added to the loan amount and financed over the life of the loan, instead of the whole thing having to be paid at once in one lump sum.

D. FHA LOANS DISTINGUISHED FROM CONVENTIONAL LOANS

FHA loans have a number of features, which distinguish them from conventional (i.e. non government-backed) loans. *The most significant differences are:*

1. No secondary financing for the downpayment

The FHA minimum downpayment for a particular loan may not be borrowed but must be paid by the borrower himself in cash. The buyer may not resort to secondary financing from the seller or another lender to borrow any portion of the minimum downpayment or other closing costs. FHA mortgages usually call for a down payment of between 3% and 5% of the loan amount (the formula is 3% of the first $25,000, and 5% on the rest); this is still well below the down payment required by lenders on conventional mortgages, which is usually 20% of the loan value.

2. Buyer must pay own impounds (reserves)

The borrower must prepay the reserves on FHA loans for property taxes, homeowners' insurance and mortgage insurance. (Tax and insurance reserves are referred to by several different terms, including "impounds," "prepaid items" and "prepayable expenses.")

3. Mortgage insurance (MIP) is required on all loans

Regardless of the size of the downpayment, mortgage insurance is required on all FHA loans. Conventional loans do not usually call for mortgage insurance (PMI) unless the loan-to-value ratio exceeds 80%.

4. Mortgage Assumability Issues

As with the VA mortgages, FHA mortgages used to be **assumable** — that is, the mortgages used to contain an **"alienation"** or **"due-on-sale"** clause, meaning a clause which gives the lender the right to demand full payment of the loan amount any time the property is transferred, or the right to approve the transfer and assumption of the loan by the new buyer. Modifications added in recent years, however, have made FHA mortgages less assumable than they were in the past. For example, under the new rules, mortgages issued before December 1, 1986, are assumable and the buyer need not be approved by the lender. However (unless the new buyer had first been approved by the lender and met the FHA standards), the original mortgage holder remains responsible indefinitely for making the mortgage payments if the person assuming the mortgage fails to pay. For mortgages issued from December 1, 1986 to December 14, 1989, another set of rules apply: these are assumable, but the original mortgage holder is liable for payments for a period of 5 years, unless the new mortgage holder has been FHA-approved. And for mortgages issued after December 14, 1989, they are subject to yet another set of rules which are the most restrictive of all: these are assumable only if the new home buyer is approved by the FHA, and only owner-occupants, as opposed to investors, are eligible for making assumptions.

In sum, by and large, only if you (i.e., the prospective home buyer) can expect to meet the FHA loan eligibility standards for earning a lender's approval, should you count on being able to assume a mortgage under the current FHA standards. Nevertheless, the privilege of mortgage assumption may still be worth it, however, especially on a mortgage that carries a below-market interest rate.

5. No prepayment charges

Many conventional loans contain prepayment provisions, which impose charges on the borrower if the borrower pays off the loan *earlier*, within the first few years of its term. These charges can be quite substantial.

FHA and VA loans, do not, however, contain prepayment clauses; they may be paid off by the borrower at any time without additional charges or penalty.

E. INTEREST RATES AND DISCOUNT POINTS ON FHA LOANS

Interest rates on FHA-insured loans are freely negotiable and are, therefore, determined by market trends in the financing industry. However, interest rates on FHA mortgages are generally about half a percentage point to one percentage point below the rates available on conventional mortgages. This is due to the government insurance factor.

THE MIP. The feature which distinguishes FHA mortgage payments from conventional and VA mortgage payments, is the fact that something called the *mutual mortgage insurance* premium, more popularly referred to as the *mortgage insurance premium (MIP)*, is included in the FHA mortgage.

For most FHA programs, the MIP is a one-time premium that may be either paid in cash at closing, or financed over the term of the loan. The amount of the premium varies, depending on both the term of the loan and whether the premium is to be paid in cash or financed. Premiums are smaller for shorter-term loans and for premiums paid at once in cash. If paid in cash at closing, the premium for a 30-year loan is equal to 3.66% of the loan amount; if financed, the premium would be 3.8% for a 30-year loan. In 1991, a surcharge was added. The surcharge, which was meant to shore up the FHA guarantee fund because it was felt to be in danger of running out of money, can add up to another 0.5 percent, sometimes making the total insurance fee as high as 4.3 percent of the loan amount. If the premium is paid in cash at closing, it may be paid by the borrower or by a third party, such as the seller; if financed, it must be paid by the borrower. If the MIP is financed, the amount of the premium is added to the loan to find the total amount financed. Monthly payments are then calculated to pay off the loan, including the MIP, according to the particular loan program.

PMI companies have many different insurance payment plans for borrowers. The most used plan, is a two-part pay plan: first, a cash premium paid at closing (referred to as the upfront premium); then, monthly premiums that are included in the mortgage payments. Mortgage companies usually require two months' premiums in advance, to be put aside in an escrow account.

At the present, the required mortgage insurance premium (MIP) for the FHA on a 30-year loan, is computed as follows: 22% cash at closing and 2% monthly premium for five years on loans with less than a 90% loan-to-value (LTV); 2% monthly premium for twelve years on loans with 90% to 95% LTV; 2% monthly premium for 30-years on loans over 95% LTV. An FHA 15-year loan term carries a different MIP at closing, namely, the cash MIP at closing, which is 2%, and all other LTV and monthly premiums remain the same.[2]

F. THE ADVANTAGES OF FHA FINANCING

It is fair to say that the FHA is consumer oriented; when administering its various programs, the FHA makes reasonable efforts to protect the interests of the borrower and to make home financing available on the most favorable terms. *Attractive features incidental to FHA-insured loans include*:

1. **Low downpayments.** FHA down payment requirements is usually much less than those set for conventional loans.

2. **No prepayment penalty**. FHA loans may be prepaid at any time without penalty. Lenders can require the prepayment to be made on a regular installment due date, however, and for loans made before August 1985, a 30-days' written notice of prepayment may be required.

---

[2] Note that these percentages and amounts are subject to change and do not apply to all FHA loan programs. The best and most current information should be obtained from the FHA office nearest you or from a mortgage company that participates in FHA programs.

3. **FHA loans may be assumed**. FHA loans may be assumed for a nominal handling fee under certain conditions. In contract, even when a conventional loan may be assumed, a hefty assumption fee is often charged.

4. **Long-term loans**. Most FHA loans are written for 30-years. The long term helps to minimize monthly payments.

5. **Less stringent qualifying standards**. It is generally easier for a borrower to qualify for an FHA loan than for a conventional loan. This is particularly true when FHA qualifying standards are compared to the recently stricter FHA conventional qualifying standards for lowdown payment loans.

DIFFERENT TYPES OF FHA LOAN PROGRAMS

The FHA has several programs which are of interest to homebuyers. These programs, named after the section of the statute that authorizes them, include:

Section 203b – For residential loans on single-family dwellings, duplexes, triplexes and fourplexes. It is the standard FHA loan and accounts for almost 75% of all FHA-insured loans. This loan program is discussed in more detail below, and in this chapter generally.

Section 222 – Mortgage insurance for members of the Armed Forces, including the Coast Guard. The MIP premium is waived as long as the borrower remains in the military.

Section 235 – Mortgage insurance and interest subsidies for low-to-moderate-income families.

Section 236 – Mortgage insurance and interest subsidies on apartment houses for low-to-moderate-income tenants. FHA controls the rent.

Most FHA loans are made to borrowers who are required to occupy the property being financed. However, occasionally the FHA will agree to insure a loan for a non-owner occupant borrower. Since the lending industry generally feels that the risk is greater when a borrower will not reside in the property he or she is purchasing, the FHA restricts a non-owner occupant loan amount to 75% of the value of the property or the purchase price, whichever is less. This forces the investor/borrower to make more substantial cash investment in the property and reduces the lender's risk factor accordingly.

Section 203b – The Standard FHA Program. The Department of Housing and Urban Development limits the maximum loan amount for Section 203b loans, the major portion of the mortgages issued by the FHA. The maximum loan amount depends upon the medium range housing costs for the area. Except for homes appraised by FHA (or being sold for) not more than $50,000, which commands the FHA's loan-to-value ratio of 97% of the total home value (or cost), the maximum loan amount is 95% of the median home price in the area, subject to overall FHA maximums (for example, the current maximum for a single-family home is $124,875). This results in varying maximum mortgage amounts from one area of the country to another.

The loan-to-value formula for homes costing more than $50,000 involves two steps, with two percentages:

Step 1. Compute 97% of the first $25,000 of the sale price

Step 2. Add 95% of that portion of the sales price which exceeds $25,000.

Example: Sales price of $66,000

Step 1: $25,000
                   x.97
                 $24.250

Step 2 $41,000 ($66,000 - $25,000)

                              x.95

                         $38.950

Step 3 $24,250

                 +38,950

                 $63,200 loan amount

Thus, for a home priced at $66,000, the FHA will finance only $63,200.

One unusual feature of FHA loan computations, is that a borrower is allowed to have his closing costs added to the sales price, and the maximum allowable loan is then calculated based on the total. That is, the buyer is able to finance part of the closing costs, rather than being required to pay up-front, all of the closing costs in cash at the time of closing, as would be true with most other types of loans. This further reduces the buyer's cash requirements for FHA financing in comparison to conventional financing. FHA offices maintain a table for use by lenders in the area, which specifies the amount of closing costs which can be added to a purchase price when calculating a loan amount.

NOTE: For information about availability of FHA mortgages, contact a Federal Housing Administration office (usually located in a HUD office) in the nearest large city. Or, write the Washington D.C. office at: FHA, Washington D.C. 20410. List of the regional offices for the HUD is on p. 44.

G. THE PROCEDURES OF THE VA-GUARANTEED LOAN PROGRAM

The Veterans Administration guarantees repayment of certain residential loans made to eligible veterans. VA loans are available to purchase single-family homes or multiple-family residences containing one to four units. There are no investor loans guaranteed by the VA, and for single-family dwelling homes the veteran must intend to occupy it as his or her residence; if the property is a multiple-family dwelling, the veteran must occupy one of the units. Unlike the FHA, the VA does occasionally make loans itself directly to eligible veterans. However, it will do this only when there are no private lenders willing to make the loan. This situation develops from time to time in very rural areas.

H. VA LOAN CHARACTERISTICS

The VA-guaranteed loans have many characteristics which are highly attractive to borrowers. Unlike most loans, VA loans may be obtained with no downpayment.[3] However, if a downpayment is used in a VA loan, VA regulations permit the buyer to finance part or all of the downpayment (secondary financing). VA loans are freely **assumable** by qualified buyers (a credit check is required) and contain no **prepayment penalty**. For loans issued after March 1, 1988, however, the person assuming the mortgage must be approved by the VA or its authorized agent, and the person must usually pay a funding fee of 0.5 percent to the government. The **interest rate** on VA loans may not exceed the maximum allowable rate determined by the Veterans Administration. The maximum VA rate is normally below the prevailing market rate for conventional loans. VA loans have **no mortgage insurance** (either private mortgage insurance or FHA-style mutual mortgage insurance). **Discount points** are paid by the seller, and not by the buyer. Finally, secondary financing is permitted in conjunction with most VA loans.

Veterans who obtain loans guaranteed by the Veterans Administration are legally obligated to indemnify the United States government for any claim paid by the Veterans Administration under the guaranty. The indemnity liability continues for the life of the loan even though the property is transferred to another owner and

---

[3] The exceptions to the no down payment rule are worth noting. Mortgages of more than the threshold amount (recently $184,000) do require a down payment. The down payment must be at least 25% of the amount by which the purchase price will exceed the threshold amount. For example, if you are buying a $200,000 house, your down payment must be at least $4,000 – i.e., the purchase price ($200,000) exceeds the threshold ($184,000) by $16,000, and 25% of the $16,000 excess is $4,000. Another exception, might be to note that VA loans to purchase mobile homes do require a down payment of 5%.

the foreclosure occurs because the default of a subsequent owner. *So, the advantage of a VA loan is not that it relieves you of the normal responsibilities associated with a mortgage, but merely that it makes a mortgage easier to obtain.*

It is, therefore, important that veterans who sell or transfer their homes in transactions where the VA loan will not be paid off at closing, be made aware that they are not necessarily released from liability on that loan, but may be released only if the following three conditions are met:

1. The loan must be current.
2. The purchaser must be an acceptable credit risk.
3. The purchaser must assume the obligations and liabilities of the veteran on the loan, including having to demnity the VA for any loss incurred by any lender or for default. The assumption of obligations must be evidenced by a written agreement as specified by the Veterans Administration. (The person assuming the loan does not have to be a veteran).

In addition to being released from liability on the loan, the veteran seller may, under the proper circumstances, have his or her loan entitlement restored. In order to accomplish this, the buyer must be a veteran who has an unused entitlement which is at least equal to the veteran seller's initial entitlement, and the buyer must consent to substitute his or her entitlement for the seller's. Provisions to this effect should be included in the purchase and sale agreement. The veteran buyer must also satisfy the conditions set out just above.

ELIGIBILITY. Eligibility for VA loans is based on the length of continuous active service in the U.S. armed forces. The minimum requirement varies depending upon when the veteran served.

90 days continuous active duty, any part of which occurred:

1. September 16, 1940 through July 25, 1947 (WWII)
2. June 27, 1950 through January 31, 1955 (Korea)
3. August 5, 1964 through May 7, 1975 (Vietnam)

181 days continuous active duty, any part of which occurred:

1. July 26, 1947 through June 26, 1950
2. February 1, 1955 through August 4, 1964
3. May 8, 1975 through September 7, 1980

24 months continuous active duty for veterans who enlisted after September 7, 1980, except:

1. individual discharged for disability;
2. individual discharged for hardship; or
3. any case in which it is established that the person is suffering from a service-connected disability not the result of willful misconduct and not incurred during a period of unauthorized absence.

For persons who fall into one of the exceptions to the 24-month service requirement, the 181-day service requirement applies. Veterans who are discharged for hardship or for a non-service connected disability, are eligible only if they have served a minimum of 181-days. Persons who have served six months active duty for training purposes only, are not eligible. There is no minimum active duty service requirement for veterans discharged for a service-connected disability. Veterans who received a dishonorable discharge are not eligible.

A **veteran's spouse** may be eligible for a VA loan if:

1. the vet was killed in action or is a possible prisoner of war because of service during the Vietnam era; or
2. the vet died of service-related injuries and the spouse has not remarried.

> **NOTE:** Your local VA office can always help you determine the length-of-service requirements in your specific case. If you think you may be qualified, visit your VA office and apply to be given a *"Certificate of Eligibility."* This certificate is what you'll need to present to a qualifying mortgage lender in order to get a VA mortgage. If you can't readily find your local VA office, contact the VA at: Department of Veterans Affairs, 810 Vermont Avenue N.W., Washington D.C. 20420. Telephone number (202) 233-2044. (While you are at it, you may request, as well, a copy of this excellent pamphlet titled, *"VA Guaranteed Home Loans for Veterans."*)

AMOUNT OF GUARANTY

The amount of mortgage which the VA will guarantee will depend on two factors — the VA appraisal, called a *Certificate of Reasonable Value* (CRV), and the size of the loan. Only a portion of the loan will be guaranteed by the VA. The maximum zero-down loan amount is calculated based on the VA guaranty amount available to that veteran. The maximum VA guaranty amount has been increased periodically since WWII. Current guaranty amounts are:

LOAN	GUARANTY
up to $45,000	50% of loan amount
$45,000-$56,250	$22,500
$56,251-$144,000	40% of loan amount or $36,000, whichever is less

In certain cases, the VA will guarantee loans larger than $144,000. On those, the guarantee is 25%, up to a maximum of $46,000.[4] On loans for manufactured or Mobil homes, the guarantee for these is 40% of the loan amount.

Lenders usually will issue a VA mortgage up to four times the guaranty amount and the downpayment (if any) that you make. Thus, if you qualify, you can get a VA mortgage for up to $184,000 without a down payment (i.e., $46,000 x 4). And with a $5,000 downpayment, you might get a VA loan of up to $204,000 (i.e., four times $51,000 or $46,000 plus the $5,000 down payment).

In cases where a vet has unused entitlement, the remaining eligibility may be used for a new loan.

EXAMPLE:

A vet purchased a home with a VA loan in 1964 for $19,000. His entitlement of $7,500 was used in full. Since the present entitlement is up to $36,000, the vet has $28,500 partial entitlement remaining ($36,000-7,500 = $28,500).

Partial eligibility is normally used only when the vet has sold the property for which the original loan was obtained, since VA loans require owner occupancy.

If the original VA loan is paid in full, and the vet has sold the house for which the original loan was made, then full entitlement is restored. However, the vet must demonstrate a need for new housing in order to obtain a new VA loan. Unused entitlement may be applied to refinancing the vet's current home, regardless of whether a VA loan was originally used to purchase the home.

---

[4] Why in the world, you might wonder, would a lender make an $184,000 loan when the VA's guarantee is for only $46,000? Well, it may still make economic sense to the lender for a couple of reasons: it still has the traditional collateral to fall back on, after all, namely, the home itself; under the VA rules and policies, if you default on a VA loan, the lender will move promptly to repossess the home and to resell it to someone else, and if the lender were to take any loss on the sale, the VA will reimburse the lender for that loss – up to $46,000.

By and large, the VA will guarantee fixed-rate mortgages, but it does not currently guarantee adjustable-rate or balloon mortgages. VA loans cannot be obtained for coops, but can be obtained for condominiums, providing certain conditions are met: construction of the development must be complete; the development must contain a certain number of units; the VA must examine and approve the condominium documents; and the individual condo unit you plan to purchase must be appraised.

I. VA CLOSING COSTS

As is the case with any mortgage, you'll have to incur some closing costs with a VA loan. VA loan regulations do place a limit on how high such closing costs can go for a VA-backed mortgage. Analysts contend, however, that in practice, such limits are often not quite effective or enforced. Analysts note, for example, that lenders sometimes try to add other closing costs to VA loans to make up for their below-market interest rates, such as charging up to three to six points.

Federal regulations generally prohibit a lender from charging "points" to buyers applying for a VA loan. Yet, in practice in the market place, because the lenders want the points, what usually happens is that they will have the home seller pay them, and then raise the price of the home enough to make up for their payment to the lender. At other times, the buyers and sellers would arrange to split the points; a seller, for example, might raise the price of the home only enough to cover just half the cost of the points. Again, although, in theory, the VA regulations prohibit sellers from raising the selling price of a home to compensate for or to offset his selling costs or charges, such regulations are hardly ever enforced. The regulation is hardly ever enforced because, as one analyst put it, "it countermands the laws of economics. If this regulation were enforced, sellers would refrain from selling to people who were getting VA mortgages. The person getting a VA mortgage will often end up indirectly footing the bill for the points after all."[5]

In addition to points, the VA mortgage borrower can expect to pay an assortment of other closing costs, such as the following: a VA "funding fee" payable at the closing designed to help pay the cost of the upkeep of the VA mortgage program (comes out to about 1.25 percent of the loan value); a one percent loan "origination fee"; and charges for survey of the home, title search, title insurance, recording fees, and the like. Added together, direct and indirect closing costs for the VA mortgage, like those for the FHA mortgages, tend to be on the high side. Indeed, quite often (though not always) they are higher than those incurred in conventional financing. Nevertheless, in the opinion of many home mortgage experts, *all things considered, the below-market interest rate associated with the VA loans would often still make paying these closing costs worthwhile for you as a mortgage seeker.*

J. SUMMARY AND CONCLUSIONS

To summarize, the chief advantages of VA an FHA loans are:

- a more lenient financial standard in qualifying for a loan
- a smaller downpayment
- a more favorable interest rate

The disadvantages and problems of these loans are:

- higher closing costs
- limits on the size of the loan amount that can be obtained
- increased red tape

---

[5] John R. Dorfman, *The Mortgage Book*, p. 132

As a general rule, VA and FHA mortgages are best suited for families and people just starting out and purchasing their first home. The central attraction of the VA and FHA mortgages to the average home buyer, lies in the fact that *it resolves the main obstacle that often stands in the way of home ownership for many families in America: namely, the inability to come up with the downpayment of some 20 percent of the home value*. Consequently, if you happen to be one of those Americans who lack enough money to make a sizeable downpayment, a VA or FHA mortgage is most likely the best choice for you. Or, even more realistically, it may be your ONLY choice; conventional lenders are unlikely to issue you a mortgage without a substantial downpayment (20 percent or so). And while you'll have to endure the usual disadvantages of these loan programs (delays, red tape, high closing costs, etc.), these are often offset, in part or totally, by the required small downpayment and the lower interest rate you'll need to pay for the loan.

HUD's REGIONAL OFFICES

The Department of Housing and Urban Development (HUD) is the agency responsible for administering federal programs concerned with the nation's housing needs. HUD is divided into two sections: the Office of Fair Housing and Equal Opportunity, and the Office of Neighborhoods, Voluntary Associations and Consumer Protection. The Fair Housing office administers the fair housing program authorized by the Civil Rights Act of 1968, and is chiefly concerned with the housing problems of lower-income and minority groups. The Office of Neighborhoods exists to protect consumer interests in all housing and community development activities, and to enforce the laws regarding interstate land sales, mobile home safety standards, and real estate settlement procedures. For information, publications, advice, referrals, or complaints about local housing practices, contact the regional office nearest you.

Region I
(Conn., Maine, Mass., N.H., R.I., Vt.)
Tel. (617) 223-4066
Dept. of Housing and Urban Development • John F. Kennedy Bldg., Room 800 • Boston, Mass. 02203

Region 11
(N.J,N.Y., Puerto Rico, Virgin Islands)
Tel. (212) 264-8068
Dept. of Housing and Urban Development • 26 Federal Plaza • New York, N.Y. 10007

Region III
(Del. Md., Pa., Va., W. Va.)
Tel. (215) 597-2560
Dept. of Housing and Urban Development • Curtis Bldg.• 6th and Walnut Sts. • Philadelphia, Pa. 19106

Region IV
(Ala., Fla., Ga., Ky., Miss., N.C., S.C., Tenn.)
Tel. (404) 526-5585
Dept. of Housing and Urban Development • 1371-1375 Peachtree St., N.E. • Atlanta, Ga. 30309

Region V
(Ill., Ind., Mich., Minn., Ohio, Wis.)
Tel. (312) 353-5680
Dept. of Housing and Urban Development • 300 South Wacker Dr. • Chicago, Ill. 60606

Region VI
(Ark., La., N.M., Okla., Texas)
Tel. (214) 749-7401
Dept. of Housing and Urban Development • 1100 Commerce St. • Dallas, Texas 75242

Region VII
(Iowa, Kan., Mo., Neb.)
Tel. (816) 374-2661
Dept. of Housing and Urban Development Federal office Bldg. • 911 Walnut St., Room 300 • Kansas City, Mo. 64106

Region VIII
(Colo., Mont., N.D., S.D., Utah, Wyo.)
Tel. (303) 837-4513
Dept. of Housing and Urban Development•Executive Tower Bldg. • 1405 Curtis St. • Denver, Colo. 80202

Region IX
(Ariz., Calif., Guam, Hawaii, Nev.)
Tel. (415) 556-4752
Dept. of Housing and Urban Development • 450 Golden Gate Ave. • P.O. Box 36003 • San Francisco, Ca. 94102

Region X
(Alaska, Idaho, Ore., Wash.)
Tel. (206) 442-5414
Dept. of Housing and Urban Development•3003 Arcade Plaza Bldg. • 1321 Second Ave. • Seattle, wash. 98101

For General information
Office of Public Affairs • HUD • 451 7th St., S.W., Room 10132 • Washington, D.C. 20410

CHAPTER 6

SELLER-ASSISTED HOME FINANCING

This type of home financing goes by different names — "owner financing," "taking back a mortgage, " "seller-assisted financing," etc. Whatever the label used, however, the concept remains the same: it always involves the seller (the homeowner) issuing the buyer a mortgage to enable the prospective buyer make the purchase.

In the traditional house-purchase transaction, the usual process is for the buyer to use his own savings to pay for the downpayment, normally about 20 percent of the purchase price, and the remainder of the purchase price, the 80 percent, is then obtained as a bank mortgage loan. This way, the seller receives full payment for the house at the closing — part (the 20 percent) from the buyer's own resources, and the rest (the 80 percent) from the bank.

Ideally, it would, of course, be nice to be always able to have buyers who would be able to have the 20 percent cash at hand, and also be able to qualify for a bank loan for the 80 percent balance. But what if, as is often the case, you have a situation where the seller finds a serious and desirable buyer, but who does not quite have the full 20 percent downpayment? Or, who has the downpayment but can only qualify for part of the balance, say 60 percent, rather than the 80 percent?

In such a case, the seller may elect to serve as a bank for the buyer, for part of the money he'd need to effectuate the purchase. In effect, the seller makes a conclusion that, to make the sale, he'll have to help the buyer with the financing.

THE 'SECOND MORTGAGE' OR SELLER TAKE-BACK

The most common form of seller-assisted financing is the "SECOND MORTGAGE" FINANCING. It's a form of seller-takeback because here, instead of the seller getting all cash, he takes back a mortgage for a part of the sale price. For example, let's say the buyer has only 10 percent cash to put down but can qualify only for an 80 percent bank mortgage. So, the seller will agree to carry the remaining balance for 10 percent.

80% mortgage from a bank	10% take-back or 2nd mortgage	10% cash

It's also a "second mortgage" because any such mortgage loan is a mortgage which will begin to be protected (with the property serving as collateral) **only after** a previous mortgage is first satisfied and retired. For this reason, a lender making a second mortgage will likely want a higher interest rate, and usually does offer less money for a shorter period of time.

The need for a second mortgage arises usually when, as a purchaser, you find there's a gap between the amount of mortgage money the conventional lender (a bank) grants you and what you actually need to fully meet the purchase price of the house (including the settlement costs). The seller, then, not wanting the deal to fall apart for want of a relatively small extra amount of money, may agree to become a source of a "second mortgage" money to you; he "lends" you (i.e., he lets you owe him) the shortfall amount you need, and gets you to sign a Promissory Note promising to pay him the amount over a period of time (usually a short period, such as a few months or years), and, as his security in the event that you don't, he'll also have you sign a "second" mortgage document for him (meaning merely that this mortgage is 'second' to or behind the first, original mortgage for the main purchase money). [See Chapter 3 for more on seller-oriented types of mortgage loans].

> **EXAMPLE:** The seller agrees to sell his house for $100,000. Thus, the total price will come from the following sources:

Buyer's out-of-pocket cash	$ 10,000
Buyer's first mortgage (e.g., loan from bank)	$ 80,000
Second mortgage extended from seller to buyer	$ 10,000
Total house price	$100,000

This kind of second mortgage is also known as a *"purchase money mortgage"* because it is part of the total purchase price of the property. Sometimes brokers and sellers also refer to this arrangement as *"taking back paper,"* in that the seller (the mortgagee) is accepting (taking back) *"paper"* (the mortgage note) from the buyer (the mortgagor) for a certain amount of money in lieu of actual cash, and will be paid back over a period of time at the agreed terms and conditions.

The second mortgage, although the most common form of seller financing, is not the only kind of this type of mortgage. If the seller owns the property free and clear with no mortgage outstanding on it, he can handle the whole financing himself by giving the buyer a FIRST MORTGAGE. In this method, known as THE INSTALLMENT SALE OR LAND CONTRACT METHOD, the buyer will typically give the seller a down payment and make payments for the balance over a number of years.

ADVANTAGES AND DISADVANTAGES OF SELLER-ASSISTED FINANCING

There are certain advantages and disadvantages associated with seller-assisted financing. For the seller, the obvious advantage of the seller-assisted financing is that it would facilitate a sale, particularly in a soft real estate market environment. Furthermore, as a seller, you can often get a relatively higher interest rate for such a loan, as compared with putting the same money in the bank. The bank may, for example, pay only 4 percent, while the second mortgage might be set at an interest rate of say 9 or 10 percent — a far bigger return. On the other hand, the prime disadvantage for the seller is that, if the buyer should for any reason default on the mortgage and fail to make the payments, the seller's only recourse would be to foreclose on the second mortgage and take the property back — a move which would generally be economically practicable only in a robust real estate market where the value of the property shall have considerably appreciated over the original sale price to allow for the house to be disposed of at a high profit, since the costs and time factor associated with foreclosure are themselves often horrendous.

In general, seller financing is highly ADVANTAGEOUS FOR THE HOMEBUYER (the general rate is usually below the market rate, and you're likely to avoid certain closing costs, such as origination fee and points); and is said, on the other hand, to be *highly* DISADVANTAGEOUS FOR THE SELLER (it's difficult for the seller as a private individual to check the buyer's credit and to follow through with collecting the monthly payments and taking the steps necessary in the event of default on the loan). Certainly, for a buyer, if you can get such a mortgage from your homeowner, you should seriously go for it. As a rule, owner financing is prevalent usually during times when houses are difficult to sell (usually because interest rates are high), and that is when prospective home sellers are usually prompted to edge into the mortgage business themselves.

CHAPTER 7

How You Can Assess The Better Mortgage Deal
Using "Points" or Interest Rates to Compare

A. WHAT IS "POINT"?

Points (sometimes referred to as "discounts" or "loan fees"), are a one-time charge that is used to raise the lender's yield (his profit) on a loan. In addition to increasing the lender's yield, points are a tool that allows the lender to stabilize the effects of an ever-changing interest rate market. Lenders must take the current money market rates into consideration when determining the rates at which to give their loans, but the market rates change several times each day. Consequently, lenders feel it would be too confusing to change loan rates each day. Instead, what the lenders do is to adjust the yield on the loan by changing the number of "points" that will be charged. This then brings the yield for the lender on the loan in line with the current market rates.

B. WHAT IS THE VALUE OF A POINT?

A single point is equal to 1 percent of the loan amount. For example, on a $150,000 mortgage, one point would be $1,500, 2 points will be $3,000, and 3 point will be $4,500 ($150,000 x .03). Points may be paid by you (the borrower); or, the lender may subtract the points charged from the amount it lends you and give you the balance. The points charge is usually paid to the lender at settlement or closing. The number of points charged on a loan will vary according to market conditions at the time the loan is made. When credit is tight, the number of points (and the yield to the lender) will usually be higher. Other factors will also affect and change the number of points that will be charged. For instance, if the borrower is taking out the loan at a higher interest rate, the points will be lower. This is what is often done by mortgage lenders who will quote rates such as the following:

10% interest rate with 4 points
10% interest with 2 points
10% interest rate with 0 points

The yields on the above three quotes are basically the same for the lender (although the lower rate may allow a borrower to qualify more easily for the loan). It should be emphasized that one point is not equal to the yield that 1 percent of interest would bring over the life of a 30-year mortgage. In terms of interest rates, the rule of thumb is that one point is usually valued as one-eight of 1 percent over a 30-year fixed-rate loan. Thus, if a loan is taken out with a rate of 10 percent, for example, and the borrower pays 4 points, the actual yield on the loan is 10.5 percent (10% + 1/8% x 4, or .125% x 4). *Most buyers, however, do not keep their loans to the end of the 30-year term.* In fact, the average mortgage loan is held by the borrower for about 7 to 10 years. As a rule, under the concept of the 'time value of money' in economics (the fact that a dollar in hand today, is better than one to be received in 10 or 20 years), if the loan is not held for the full term, the yield on the loan will usually be higher since the points were **prepaid** at once at the start of the loan.

In our example of a 30-year fixed-rate loan at 10 percent, a loan paid after seven years would yield the lender 10.83 percent. If it were paid off after ten years, the yield would be less, at 10.67 percent. The sooner the loan is paid, the higher the yield is to the lender. Realizing that most loans will not be held to the end of their term, some lenders price the loan with fewer points. The number of points will depend on how long they expect the loan to stay on their books.

C. INTEREST RATE VERSUS POINTS

Is it better for you, as a borrower, to take a mortgage with a lower interest rate and more points, or one with a higher interest rate with fewer points? This question has been called "the central quandary" for the borrower who has to decide on a loan. It's a question a borrower must answer whenever he has to compare a lender's loan package. For some borrowers, there may be little or no choice because they may not be able to qualify for the loan any other way unless the lower interest rate is used. ***In most situations, however, in general the answer depends on how long the borrower intends to own the property and keep the loan.***

For example, a lender offers a 30-year $80,000 loan at 10 percent interest with 2 points, or a loan at a 10¼ percent interest with 1 point. Which one is the better loan deal for the borrower? The comparison of the two loans is listed in the table below. The 2 points here will come to $1,600 (2% of $80,000), while 1 point comes to $800.[1]

If you take the higher interest rate (10 ¼%), you'll pay 1 point <u>less</u>, or just $800 – i.e., you'll save $800 on "points." What you'll be losing in interest rate differential, is the difference between the monthly payment at 10 percent ($702) and at 10 ¼ percent ($717), which is $15 per month. It would take almost 54 months to make up the $800 difference in the "point" at the rate of $15 per month. Another consideration worth noting, is that by paying out the additional point money at closing, the borrower will lose the investment opportunity value (what could reasonably be expected to be earned on the money if it were invested) of the additional funds.

From this example, what it says is that if the borrower expects to keep the property <u>longer</u> <u>than</u> 54 months, the loan with the higher "points" would be more advantageous. However, if the borrower intends to keep the property <u>less</u> <u>than</u> 54 months, then the loan with the lower points would be better. *In general, the longer the period the loan is held, the cheaper the cost of the additional points.*

Table 7.1. Points vs. Interest

	Loan 1	Loan 2
Loan amount	$80,000	$80,000
Interest rate	10%	10¼%
Monthly payment	$702	$717
Extra monthly payment cost	—	$15
Number of points	2	1
Cash value of points	$1,600	$800
Extra cost for points	$800	—

D. A FEW METHODS FOR COMPARING POINTS RELATIVE TO INTEREST RATES

Let's say you are faced with the task of reviewing two loan packages offered you by two local banks. One bank offers the loan of $100,000 at ¼ percent lower than the other – a difference in monthly payment of about $9 on the loan amount. But that same bank also charges 1 point more than the other bank; so, getting the loan will cost you $1,000 more in up-front costs. Now, how do you decide which of the two options is better?

---

[1] More precisely, as reported in a recent U.S. Census report released in October 1998, the "medium" time Americans lived at one residence was 5.2 years (meaning that half moved sooner than that, and half remained in the nest longer). Homeowners, however, were reported to stay put somewhat longer, averaging 8.2 years, while renters relocate every 2.1 years.

Here are a few ways of comparing between two (or more) loans, which have differing interest rates and points:

1. Two Quick Formulas

One speedy way to evaluate the difference, is to make a comparison based on monthly payment as against the cost of a point; that is, to decide whether the small savings you get in monthly payments (such as in the example above), is worth paying the extra $1,000 to get the loan. To do this, you simply compute how many months the lower payments will take to make up. Thus, you divide the $1,000 loan point cost by the monthly saving, $1,000 ÷ $9 = 111 months, or just 9 years and 3 months. So, in this case, if you plan to live in the house for a relatively long time, for at least 9 years and 3 months, you'll do better by paying the higher point.

A second rough approximation you can do very quickly in one or two minutes, is this. First make a determination of the number of years you expect to live in the house. Take the number of points and divide it by the number of years you expect to stay in the home. Add the fraction of the stated interest rate. For example, let's say the simple interest rate you're charged is 9 percent, and that you are to pay 3 points. Assuming you plan to stay in the home for the entire duration of the 30-year mortgage (or to stay there indefinitely), you would just divide the 3 points by 30 to get 0.1 (3/30 = 0.1). You add that fraction to the original 9 percent interest rate, to get roughly 9.1 percent interest rate. If, on the other hand, you plan (or expect) to stay in the home for a short time, say for only 5 years, the effective interest rate would be roughly 9.6 percent. (Keep in mind, though, that these two quick formulas are merely a rough approximation for a number of reasons: the average American homebuyer stays in the house for 7 to 10 years; these formulas do not take into account the factors of compound interest and the "time value of money" – that is, the concept that a dollar in hand today, is worth far more than a dollar received in 10, 20 or 30 years from today.

2. Using The Points Equivalency Table to To Gauge

There is another method, a relatively more precise measure, of making a comparison between different lenders' terms on the interest rates and points issue. The method is by the use of the *Points Equivalency Table* (See Table 7-2 below). As the table is named, it gives the calculated equivalence of each interest rate in terms of points. The important advantage of this method is that it takes into account the "time value of money" factor – the economic concept that if you didn't have to pay an amount today up-front, you could be earning interest on that money, that a dollar in hand today is worth far more than a dollar received in 10, 20, or 30 years.

Table 7-2 below shows the "effective" interest rates equivalents for 30-year and 15-year mortgages in terms of "points," each carrying from 1 to 4 points. The figures in the table assume that you will stay in the home for the full term (15 or 30 years) of the mortgage.[2]

Table 7-2

---

[2] The tables and the exposition of the method herein, are excerpted from John R. Dorfman's *The Mortgage Book* (Consumer Report book: 1992), pp. 36, to whom the present writer is deeply indebted and grateful.

Table 7-2. *Point Equivalency Table*

30-Year Mortgage

Interest Rate (Percent)	Number of Points			
	1	2	3	4
6.00	6.09	6.19	6.29	6.39
6.25	6.35	6.44	6.54	6.64
6.50	6.60	6.70	6.80	6.90
6.75	6.85	6.95	7.05	7.15
7.00	7.10	7.20	7.30	7.41
7.25	7.35	7.45	7.56	7.67
7.50	7.60	7.71	7.81	7.92
7.75	7.85	7.96	8.07	8.18
8.00	8.11	8.21	8.32	8.44
8.25	8.36	8.47	8.58	8.69
8.50	8.61	8.72	8.83	8.95
8.75	8.86	8.97	9.09	9.21
9.00	9.11	9.23	9.34	9.46
9.25	9.36	9.48	9.60	9.72
9.50	9.62	9.73	9.85	9.98
9.75	9.87	9.99	10.11	10.23
10.00	10.12	10.24	10.37	10.49
10.25	10.37	10.50	10.62	10.75
10.50	10.62	10.75	10.88	11.01
10.75	10.88	11.00	11.13	11.26
11.00	11.13	11.26	11.39	11.52
11.25	11.38	11.51	11.64	11.78
11.50	11.63	11.76	11.90	12.04
11.75	11.88	12.02	12.16	12.30
12.00	12.13	12.27	12.41	12.55
12.25	12.39	12.53	12.67	12.81
12.50	12.64	12.78	12.92	13.07
12.75	12.89	13.03	13.18	13.33

15-Year Mortgage

Interest Rate (Percent)	Number of Points			
	1	2	3	4
6.00	6.16	6.32	6.48	6.64
6.25	6.41	6.57	6.73	6.90
6.50	6.66	6.82	6.99	7.15
6.75	6.91	7.07	7.24	7.41
7.00	7.16	7.33	7.49	7.66
7.25	7.41	7.58	7.75	7.92
7.50	7.66	7.83	8.00	8.17
7.75	7.92	8.08	8.25	8.43
8.00	8.17	8.34	8.51	8.68
8.25	8.42	8.59	8.76	8.94
8.50	8.67	8.84	9.02	9.19
8.75	8.92	9.09	9.27	9.45
9.00	9.17	9.35	9.52	9.70
9.25	9.42	9.60	9.78	9.96
9.50	9.67	9.85	10.03	10.21
9.75	10.18	10.36	10.54	10.72
10.00	10.18	10.36	10.54	10.72

Table 7-2 *Point Equivalency Table* (**continued**)

Interest Rate (Percent)	Number of Points			
	1	2	3	4
10.25	10.43	10.61	10.79	10.98
10.50	10.68	10.86	11.05	11.24
10.75	10.93	11.11	11.30	11.49
11.00	11.18	11.37	11.56	11.75
11.25	11.43	11.62	11.81	12.00
11.50	11.69	11.87	12.06	12.26
11.75	11.94	12.13	12.32	12.51
12.00	12.19	12.38	12.57	12.77
12.25	12.44	12.63	12.83	13.03
12.50	12.69	12.88	13.08	13.28
12.75	12.94	13.14	13.34	13.54

3. Using The Annual Percentage Rate (APR) To Gauge

Under the *Consumer Protection Act* of 1969 (generally known as the *"Truth-in-Lending law"*), lenders are required to inform, in advance, the non-business borrower of all the terms and conditions of a proposed loan so that the borrower will readily be able to compare various available credit options. Under this law, part of the information your lender is required to disclose to you, is what is known as the **Annual Percentage Rate (APR)** they'll charge on your loan, including points. The whole idea of the APR is to make it simpler for consumers to shop for loans. The APR (along with a host of other information) will be contained in a disclosure statement provided you by your lender. The great advantage of the use of the lender-provided APR, is that, because all lenders are required to calculate and to disclose the information in a *uniform manner*, it makes it easier for borrowers to do market comparison-shopping. Furthermore, the APR method is advantageous because it considers all loan fees and charges (or, at least, all the major ones), and not simply the interest rate or only a combination of the rate and the number of points. Thus, two lenders may each charge 10 percent interest rate, yet one may be a better deal because of the differences in points, or in mortgage insurance fees, or in methods of interest calculation.

Hence, an important figure to use in comparing one mortgage against another, is the APR.[3] [See sample copy of the *Disclosure Statement*, which contains the APR, on p. 78]. The APR is the sum of the interest charged on the loan and the total of all prepaid expenses. Another way of saying it, is that it represents the relationship between the total finance charge – all costs the borrower paid and that the lender required, such as interest, points, service charges, mortgage insurance premiums, but not including costs for credit reports, hazard insurance premiums, taxes, legal fees, and title insurance – and the total amount financed. In other words, beside the interest costs and points, the APR reflects most (though not all) closing costs, as well.

[3] By law, the APR information as contained in the Truth-in Lending Disclosure statement, must be furnished to you in writing by the lender when you attain a commitment of normal approval of your loan application from the lender. You can – and should – however, always ask for it from the outset so that you can start your study of it much earlier, and most lenders will often be glad to oblige you.

The APR is calculated by dividing the total finance charges by the net amount financed, to determine the finance charge per $100 financed. Then, the Federal Reserve System APR Tables are used to match the finance cost per $100 with the applicable APR (rounded to the nearest ¼ percent). The APR takes into account the difference between simple annual interest and monthly compound interest. (The stated interest rate is usually listed in simple annual interest rate terms; and the APR is generally a few tenths of a point higher than the stated interest rate). The APR also takes into account the fact that you pay interest monthly, not annually. For example, if the lender's stated annual interest rate is 12 percent, the monthly rate is 1.0 percent. On $100, the annual interest rate at 12 percent is equal to $12; but the monthly interest at one percent will equal $12.68 – the result of "daily compounding" factor. Also, because the APR calculation assumes that the points are "amortized" (spread out) over the full duration of the mortgage (often 30 years or so), a good rule-of-thumb is that each point adds roughly 0.125 percent to the APR on a 30-year mortgage with a 10 percent interest rate.

As we have seen from the above discussion, the APR has many virtues as a useful tool and piece of information in comparing and deciding between two mortgages with different interest rates and different numbers of points. Nevertheless, unfortunately, the APR is not perfect, however. One major drawback it has, is that *the APR calculation requires making certain assumptions*. The principal of these assumptions, is that you will stay in your home for the full term of the mortgage. This assumption, however, is a totally unrealistic one: most first-time homebuyers, for example, stay in their house for less than 5 years, and most buyers as a whole move well before their mortgages expire. Hence, you should take strict note that, as one analyst sums it up, "while the APR is certainly a useful shopping tool; it isn't the final word in choosing a mortgage"[4]

POINTER: The length of time you stay (or realistically expect to stay) in your home ultimately determines whether it's worth paying points to get a lower interest rate, or vice versa. If your realistic expectation is that you'll fare no better than the average American homebuyer (say, between 7 to 10 years of stay), you will probably do better going for a mortgage having a slightly higher interest rate, as opposed to paying a higher number of points. If, however, you think you will remain in your house for the next 20, 25, or 30 years, it might be better for you to pay the extra point and go for the lower interest rate on a long-term loan. In short, *your decision as to what option to take, will depend primarily on the circumstances in the case*. Furthermore, you need to make your comparisons on a long-term basis and on the basis of ALL fees and charges, not just on the basis of what your initial costs would be or what the interest rates (or a combination of the rate and the number of points) would work out to during the next few years. Finally, never ever make comparisons with two or more different programs offered by one lender, without also going to other lenders.

4. Using the Ten-Year Analysis Calculation to Gauge

Finally, another useful method that can be used in making a determination between two mortgages with different interest rate and different numbers of points, is the use of a calculation measure called *"The Ten-Year Analysis."* Here, you're assuming you don't really know how long you're going to stay in a house, and so you simply make the bold assumption of 10 years. It's a fair and somewhat realistic number: it isn't far from the average mortgage duration of most American homeowners, recently estimated to be at 8.2 years. For purposes of making the calculation, you assume, of course, that one of the two mortgages involved has a lower rate and more points (call it Mortgage "A", as in the Table 7-3 Worksheet below), while the other has higher interest rate and fewer points (Mortgage "B" in the Worksheet).

---

[4] John R. Dorfman, *The Mortgage Book*, p. 63.

Using the Table 7-3 Worksheet below, you can readily calculate the math for matching the mortgages you're considering.[5]

Table 7-3. 10-Year Analysis Worksheet

Ten-Year Analysis Worksheet

Mortgage A has a lower interest rate but higher points than Mortgage B. To compare them over the full length of the mortgage term, use the annual percentage rate, or APR (see chapter 7). To compare them over a 10-year period, use the worksheet below:

Mortgage A (the one with the lower interest rate)

1. Monthly payment: $_____

2. Multiply monthly payment × 120: $_____
There are 120 months in 10 years, so this is how much you would pay in principal and interest for the full 10-year period.

3. Prepayment penalty. If you pay your mortgage off early, there may be a prepayment penalty. If so, enter the amount here: $_____

4. Dollar amount of points: $ _____

5. Forgone interest: $ _____
To pay the points, you presumably have to take money out of your bank account. Therefore, you will lose some interest. Estimate the lost interest as follows:

(a) By what dollar amount do the points on this mortgage exceed those on mortgage B? $_____
(b) Take 63 percent of the amount in step (a) (multiply by .63). This is the approximate amount of interest you are giving up in personal savings, assuming that you can earn 5 percent after taxes on your savings and investments: $_____

6. Balance (principal remaining) at the end of 10 years: $_____

7. Total cost (add steps 2, 3, 4, 5, and 6): $ _____

Mortgage B (the one with fewer points)

1. Monthly payment: $ _____

2. Multiply monthly payment × 120: $ _____
There are 120 months in 10 years, so this is how much you would pay in principal and interest for the full 10-year period.

3. Prepayment penalty. If you pay your mortgage off early, there may be a prepayment penalty. If so, enter the amount here: $ _____

---

[5] This Worksheet is excerpted by courtesy of the authors, from *The Mortgage book*, by John R. Dorfman, et al (Consumer Reports Book: Yonkers, N. Y. 1995) pp. 39-41. The present writer is deeply indebted and grateful to the aforementioned parties for their consideration.

4. Dollar amount of points: _____

5. Forgone interest: $ _____
Because this mortgage requires you to make higher monthly payments than does Mortgage A, you presumably will have to take some extra money out of your bank account each month. Therefore, you lose some interest. Estimate the lost interest as follows:

(a) By how much does the monthly payment for Mortgage B exceed that for Mortgage A?: $ _____
(b) Multiply the amount in step 5(a) by 35: $ _____

This is the approximate amount of interest you are giving up in personal savings, assuming that you can earn 5 percent on your savings after taxes (around 6.4 percent before federal taxes for most taxpayers).

6. Balance (principal remaining) at end of 10 years: $ _____

7. Total cost (add steps 2, 3, 4, 5, and 6): $ _____

If the total cost for each of the two mortgages is reasonably close using this analysis, choose the one with the lower annual percentage rate (APR). However, if the APRs are close and there is a significant difference in the 10-year analysis, you are probably best off choosing the mortgage with the lower 10-year cost.

CHAPTER 8

Make An Honest Assessment of Your Current Financial Condition: Your Income, Expenses, and Net Worth

A. FIGURING OUT YOUR PRESENT FINANCES

In the whole process of applying for a mortgage loan, *and successfully getting one, the importance of first taking an honest, objective, up-to-date assessment of your current finances, cannot be overemphasized.* As a potential homebuyer – and, therefore, a potential applicant to lenders for a mortgage loan – it is most helpful that you have a fairly good idea of exactly where you personally stand financially BEFORE you ever begin to make the loan application. You must know, for example, the size and nature of your income; what amount of your income will be available to you which you can put towards your housing expense allowance; what your present various and total monthly financial obligations are; and what debts from among your present outstanding obligations will count against the mortgage amount you will need to borrow (or be able to borrow), and similar issues. And in order to do this, you'll need to have as your prerequisite a concrete assessment of just what you own and have personally, out of your own personal resources.

Hence, one of the very first acts you *should undertake in the mortgage application process, even before you ever find a mortgage source or make a formal application to any bank, is this*: TAKE A HARD, <u>HONEST</u>, <u>OBJECTIVE</u>, EVEN <u>HARSH</u>, LOOK AT YOUR PRESENT FINANCES AND FINANCIAL CONDITION.

Start by completing the following form, Figure 8-1, about yourself. [And, next, you should figure out your financial "Net Worth," as is figured in Figures 8-2 and 8-3 below]. If parties are married, the resources and obligations of both the husband and the wife are to be counted in making any calculations. Fill out the forms *completely* and *honestly*.

Figure 8-1. Figuring Your Present Financial Conditions.

Your Present Housing Expenses (What You Actually Spend Now for Housing)

Rent or mortgage payment	$_____
Electrical Costs	$_____
Heating Costs	$_____
Water and/or sewer cost	$_____
Renters/hazard insurance policy	$_____
Any other costs (parking, etc.)	$_____
Monthly total...$_____ **(A)**	

Income

Monthly – husband's salary	$_____
Wife's salary	$_____
Any other income	$_____
Monthly total income (gross)............................$_____ **(B)**	

Deductions

Federal income tax	$_____
Federal income tax	$_____
State income tax	$_____
State income tax	$_____
Social Security or other	$_____

Social Security or other	$_____
Insurance (health, life)	$_____
Insurance (other)	$_____
Any other deductions	$_____

Monthly total of deductions.............................$_____(C)

Total net monthly income (B) – (C)...................$_____(D)

Monthly Debts

Car payments	$_____	# of months left _____	Value of item if sold today $_____
Personal Obligations	$_____	# of months left _____	Value of item if sold today $_____
(Credit cards,	$_____	# of months left _____	Value of item if sold today $_____
Furniture payments, etc.)	$_____	# of months left _____	Value of item if sold today $_____
Other debts	$_____	# of months left _____	Value of item if sold today $_____

Monthly total (Debts)..$_____(E)

Other Monthly Obligations

Contributions/tithing	$_____
Child Care	$_____
Car expenses/gas	$_____
Car/parking	$_____
Other transportation costs	$_____
Life insurance	$_____
Health insurance	$_____
Car insurance	$_____
Medical Care	$_____
Monthly food costs	$_____
Meals eaten out	$_____
Clothing	$_____
Entertainment/recreation	$_____
Other	$_____

Monthly total of "other monthly obligations"............$_____(F)

Total debts & obligations **(E) + (F)**......................$_____(G)

Net Monthly Income   **(D)** $_____

Less: Total Debts & Obligations - **(G)** $_____ = $_____ **(H)**

ANY REMAINER LEFT ....$_____ **(I)**

Your Cash Reserve[1]

Checking Account #1	$_____
Checking Account #2	$_____
Savings Account	$_____
Whole life insurance (Cash value)	$_____
Bonds (current market value)	$_____
Boats, autos, etc. that are pd. for	$_____
Stocks (current market value)	$_____
Pension fund (actual cash value)	$_____
Other cash items	$_____

Total available cash......................$_____(J)

*Anticipated Housing Expense
** in the new home** $_____

Total monthly mortgage payment $_____

Monthly principal and interest,
  Insurance and taxes $_____

Electrical cost	$_____
Heating costs	$_____
Maintenance	$_____
Water/sewer costs	$_____
Other	$_____

Monthly total housing expense..........$_____(K)

Cash Needed*

---

[1] This should be anything that can be "liquidated" (turned into cash) without much trouble. When you include any items (boats, automobiles, antiques, jewelry, and the like), they must be items that are already paid for. Otherwise, they must be listed at liabilities and under "obligations."

*See "NOTE" ON P. 57

Anticipated down payment	$_____
Anticipated closing costs	$_____
Anticipated prepaid items	$_____
Anticipated discount points	$_____

Total cash needed to purchase
(i.e., exclusive of the mortgage money).$_____ **(L)**

> ***NOTE:** Refer to Chapter 10 for an idea of the array of other extra costs and charges you may have to pay, beside merely the home purchase money, in the home purchasing process. There are many ways and sources by which you can attempt to estimate or obtain an estimate of the essential housing cost of items (the monthly interest payable, insurance, taxes, utilities or maintenance costs, etc.), and your cash needs for a home purchase (anticipated down payment, closing costs, and the like). You can base an estimate of loan rates and terms on current market trends, and an estimate of non-mortgage housing expenses can be taken from comparable costs of an average home in the desired area. (Your local broker or banker can always help you with such information). Another good source, indeed an excellent one, is to take such information from the "The Truth-in-Lending Statement" and the *"Good Faith Estimate of Settlement Charges"* statement. Both statements are required by federal law to be given you by a lender upon your application for a loan. (See Exhibits 11-4 & 11-5 in Chapter 11, for samples of these forms).

B. ANALYZING YOUR FINANCES

Having completed Figure 8-1, just look over the form again.   Do the amounts listed under "Cash Needed" on the "Anticipated Down payment" line and the other lines for anticipated cash needs, more or less amount to the amount that is in the "Cash Reserve" section? Is the "Anticipated Housing Expense" section higher than the "Present Housing Expense" section? If so, is there enough to cover the additional monthly cost in the section "Other Monthly Obligations" on the line named "Any Remainder Left" for saving spurposes?

Perhaps these figures have brought a startling truth to light for you. Maybe the figures show that you will need to adjust your 'wants' in terms of the size of the house you have in mind buying, the locality you desire relative to the going market prices of the property in the area, etc. Maybe you can see that it looks like there are some debts that'll first need to be paid off, or more money that should be saved, or some assets that should be sold off to bring things into line. Either way, you now have a realistic picture of your financial condition. Taking a hard, realistic look at your gross and net income figures, and your total monthly debts, you can see from the figures on your Housing Expense items, just what you can possibly afford. If your cash appears to be a little short, you may perhaps want to try to find a home that already has some of the things on your "want" wish list: for example, a house where the seller leaves the stove and perhaps the drapes. Find out what has been the common practice concerning closing costs and points in the areas you're looking at. If you find that the sellers have been paying these costs in that area, this fact may save you money. [Remember, however, if that's the kind of loan you are looking for, that the FHA will usually add closing costs and finance this along with the loan as long as it does not exceed the maximum loan limits].

C. FIGURING OUT YOUR NET WORTH

Next, you'll need to work out, formally, your financial *net worth* – that is, the difference between the value of all your assets (everything you own), and all your liabilities (every debt or obligation you have). Working out your net worth is of great importance just as well, because to a lender attempting to evaluate your loan application, your financial strength includes assets that you have (i.e., things that you own, such as bank accounts, investments, automobiles, etc.), as well as your "net worth" – that is, what is left of your assets after your liabilities (the debts you have and things you owe) shall have been subtracted from that. *The higher your assets and the lower your liabilities, the better your financial condition to lenders.* Hence, just as your monthly debt payment burden (e.g. on credit card balances, store revolving account, car payments, etc.) affects your financial strength, your net worth condition, meaning what you own free and clear, also affects your financial strength in the eyes of your loan application appraisers.

To figure out your net worth, simply complete, *in full and honestly*, Figures 8-2 and 8-3 in that order. As outlined in Figure 8-3, the final computation in figure 8-3 gives you your NET WORTH.

Figure 8-2.
Worksheet For Figuring Your Net Worth

WHEN YOU GO TO A LENDER TO APPLY FOR A MORTGAGE LOAN, YOU SHOULD BE PREPARED TO ANSWER A NUMBER OF QUESTIONS ABOUT YOUR FINANCIAL SITUATION. THIS WORKSHEET WILL HELP PREPARE YOU TO ANSWER SOME OF THOSE QUESTIONS.

INFORMATION ON YOUR ASSETS

LIST ALL YOUR ASSETS.   Include any of the following:

Assets   VALUE

- Amount you now have in Savings Account(s) $_____

- Cash on hand (in cash or checking account) $_____

- Stocks, bonds, life insurance policies (give current market value or actual cash value) $_____

- Real Estate you now own (give assessed market value or price paid) $_____

- Automobile(s) (give the book value for make, model, and year of the car) $_____

- Household furnishings (give the value of all items including furniture, silverware, carpets, paintings, T.V.'s, stereo, other appliances) $_____

- Jewelry, antiques, furs (give appraised value) $_____

- Other items of value (for example, boat, trailer, bike, etc.) $_____

- Amount of money owed to you (IOU's, tax refunds, etc.) $_____

- Other $_____

TOTAL ASSETS $_____

WHEN YOU KNOW THE APPROXIMATE VALUE OF YOUR ASSETS YOU WILL ALSO WANT TO KNOW WHAT YOUR LIABILITIES ARE; THAT IS, ALL THE OUTSTANDING DEBTS YOU OWE TO OTHER PEOPLE. SEE THE NEXT PAGE.

Figure 8-3. Worscet For Figuring Your Liabilities

Figure 8-3. ## Worksheet For Figuring Your Liabilities

> YOU WILL WANT TO LIST THE *TOTAL AMOUNT OWED* TO AN INDIVIDUAL CREDITOR
> (BUT *NOT YOUR MONTHLY PAYMENT* TO THE CREDITOR).

<u>Liabilities</u>

PERSON OR INSTITUTION TO WHOM *MONEY IS OWED* (CREDITOR)	*TOTAL AMOUNT NOW OWED*
• Personal loans from Banks or Finance Companies	$_____
• Automobile loans	$_____
• Installment Accounts (charge accounts, credit cards, department stores, revolving accounts)	$_____
• Medical/dental bills due (including hospital)	$_____
• School (tuition, education loan)	$_____
• Real Estate loans	$_____
• Personal loan from relatives or friends	$_____
• Other debts now owed or bills not paid	$_____

TOTAL LIABILITIES | $ |

SUBTRACT THE AMOUNT OF YOUR *LIABILITIES* FROM YOUR TOTAL *ASSETS* (bottom
of preceding page) TO ARRIVE AT THE FIGURE FOR YOUR *NET WORTH*.

TOTAL ASSETS (Fig. *8.2*) | $ |

less TOTAL LIABILITIES (above) | $ |

equals NET WORTH | $ |

> THIS WILL GIVE YOU AN IDEA OF YOUR PRESENT INDEBTEDNESS,
> AND HELP YOU DETERMINE HOW MUCH MORE FINANCIAL BURDEN YOU
> CAN HANDLE.

CHAPTER 9

Determine First, in Advance, the Home Price Range You Can Actually Afford and Pre-Qualify Yourself For A Mortgage Loan

A. FIRST THINGS FIRST: FIRST, ESTIMATE THE HOME PRICE RANGE THAT'S RIGHT FOR YOUR INCOME BRACKET AND WHICH YOU CAN AFFORD.

Most people, unfortunately, go about the process of buying a home the wrong way, in a completely backward sequence: first, they find a real estate broker (or agent) and search through the local newspaper listings and begin looking at properties to buy. Next, they find a house they like and think they can afford, and they make the seller an offer. Now, if the offer is accepted, at this point they then go to a bank and start applying for a mortgage loan.

This approach, unfortunately, just happens to be dead wrong, however; A COMPLETELY WRONG WAY. Simply put, those steps are done completely backwards, in exactly the wrong sequence. Actually, the right sequence should have been in exactly the opposite and reverse order: *determining the home price range you can realistically afford and applying for financing, should be your very FIRST steps. Then, after that – and only after that – should you now start looking for the home to buy.*

There are a multitude of reasons why this sequence, rather than the one usually employed by the typical homebuyer, makes a far better sense for the prospective homebuyer. In the first place, this approach allows you yourself, the buyer, rather than the seller, or even the lender, to remain in control of the home-buying process because, since the process of getting approved for financing takes time and paperwork, any way, the faster you can get started on it and get approved, the better for you. The offer to buy a home often rests on the contingency of the buyer getting the lender's financial approval, and, in fact, most home deals that fall through do so primarily because a lender turns down the prospective buyer's loan application for the reason of not meeting the *lender's* (and not the buyer's) requirements and qualifications. Given that reality, if you were to have started out with applying for financing as your first step, you wouldn't then care much that the process is consuming that much time. Furthermore, as another dimension of keeping you in control of the home buying process, applying for financing as your first step saves you from otherwise wasting some valuable time and efforts in looking for the wrong home to buy in that, with an earlier knowledge and information of what kind and how much of a home you can realistically afford, you can simply limit yourself to seeking those properties you can reasonably afford, and not waste your precious time and money looking at those you can't possibly afford.

B. GETTING YOURSELF PRE-QUALIFIED WITH A LENDER BEFORE YOU EVEN LOCATE A HOUSE TO BUY

Indeed, the flip side of this approach – the approach of first determining, and in advance, the kind of home price range you can realistically afford even before you start looking for a house or looking at one – is what's known in the mortgage banking trade as "pre-qualification:" the advanced determination by a lender that you do, indeed, qualify for a given level of mortgage. Consequently, both concepts – the question of how large or what home price range you can afford, and the given mortgage size you do indeed qualify for – will be treated here as one and the same problem, since having an idea of how large a mortgage you can afford, will, in turn, directly determine what price of a home you can afford.

Loan-Making Actually Has TWO parts: The Pre-approval, and the Approval Phases

In reality, the process of obtaining a lender's financing approval for a loan, actually has two parts any way: The "pre-approval" and the actual "approval" phases. The pre-approval part is based only on issues of your financial and credit status, while the approval part, is related to issues concerning the specific property itself to be bought. And while the former takes relatively little time, it is with the latter (e.g. matters like home appraisal, home inspection, title search, etc.) that the real delays and difficulties in financing occur. Consequently, generally you would have lost not much time, any way, in getting yourself pre-qualified (pre-approved) for a loan by a lender.

The process should work roughly this way. First, you work out the calculations yourself. Try to pre-qualify yourself and see roughly, how much of a home and mortgage you can realistically afford, given your particular family income and financial circumstances. [See Section C below for some of the main rules-of-thumb to apply]. Then, you make a formal application to a lender and get officially pre-qualified for a loan by the lender in advance of even locating a house to purchase. [See Chapter 12 for how to locate the proper mortgage sources and to engage mortgage search services]. Your own pre-qualification calculations, though a rough estimation, is still a very useful tool for you, in that it will give you a rough approximation and idea of your standing. And the lender's own pre-qualification of you is even more helpful because it is the loan company itself who, after all, will make the final judgment on your loan qualification (or lack of it) in terms of its own particular standards and criteria. Hence, even though there are methods of more sophisticated or elaborate nature you can use to evaluate your chances for landing a loan [see Chapter 15], you need not, at this stage, do any more than you can do with the financial qualification formulas outlined in Section C below.

Whenever you're in a position where the lender has already pre-qualified you and you're able to have the lender's pre-approval already in your hands BEFORE you start looking at homes, it is a tremendous advantage for you; you now have a much greater leverage. The lender, because he has now looked at your financial and credit condition and has largely approved it, can now go about the reviewing and processing of your loan application without the pressures of a deadline written into your offer for a specific property. Secondly, having been pre-approved for a home of a certain price range, you now know exactly what you can afford, and that important knowledge narrows down your search considerably when you set about looking for a home to buy [Chapter 16].

Next, after having secured a loan pre-approval, you now commence the process of trying to locate a home to purchase [See Chapter 16]. And your task this time is simpler: all you'll have to do is locate properties that are within your price range. No more is your price range to be dictated by sentiments or your perceptions of what is a good bargain, or by your 'wants' in terms of the attractiveness of the amenities and facilities of a home or neighborhood you desire to live in. *Rather, the home price range you go for – and, consequently, the choice of homes you can look for – simply boil down to this: WHAT YOU CAN AFFORD! Indeed, this single piece of knowledge alone saves you as well as your real estate agents and lenders, a whole lot of time and troubles. You would not, for example, now make the mistake of allowing yourself to fall in love with a house of a price range you can't possibly afford!! And a real estate agent won't have to show you properties you just can't possibly afford.*

C. SOME QUICK RULES-OF-THUMB FORMULAS

How do you determine how much home value you can afford?

There are many so-called "rules of thumb" which loan agents use to officially pre-qualify (or even qualify buyers). And use of such rules here, though by not means definitive but only a rough guideline, could be helpful in giving you a fairly realistic idea of the kinds of houses you can possibly afford. Here in this section, our focus is on a speedy approximation and on quick, simple formulas that you can do in minutes on the back of an envelope, perhaps. [Elsewhere in Chapter 15, you'll find outlined a somewhat more sophisticated, more elaborate and focused methods of borrower qualification which are more specific to particular types of lenders – conventional, FHA and VA]

1. Method One

One rule-of-thumb by which lenders, housing financiers, and real estate professionals, have often attempted to determine the kind of house a buyer can afford, is this: a person can afford that kind of house which costs no more than 3 times the person's yearly gross (before tax) income. (Thus, for example, if you [or your household] were making a net income of $30,000 a year, the kind of house you could possibly afford, by this guideline, would be one priced $30,000 x 3, or $90,000).

2. Method Two

Another rule-of-thumb guideline is: the combined monthly payments on a house (the monthly mortgage payment, plus the monthly taxes, house insurance premium, and average insurance premium) should be less than 1 week's take home (after tax) income of the prospective home buyer.

EXAMPLE: say you required a $120,000 mortgage, and that your terms of borrowing at the time, are interest rate at 9 percent for a 30-year term. Hence, from the mortgage amortization payment tables (see Table 9.1 on p. 63) your monthly mortgage payment on $120,000 would be $866. Assume your projected or actual other expenses are as follows: yearly taxes on the house $960; monthly utilities average $100; and yearly home insurance premium $480. Your monthly expense picture on the house would be as follows.

Mortgage payment per month	$ 866.00
Taxes per month (960 divided by 12)	$ 80.00
Utilities average per month	$ 100.00
Insurance expense per month ($480 divided by 12)	$ 40.00
	$1,086.00

Thus, under this guideline, to be able to afford the $120,000 mortgage, you (the homebuyer) should be making a take-home income of $1,086.00 per week, or better.

Figure 9.1

**Mortgage Factor
Chart**

EQUAL MONTHLY PAYMENT TO AMORTIZE A LOAN OF $1,000

Term Rate %	10 Years	15 Years	20 Years	25 Years	30 Years
4	10.13	7.40	6.06	5.28	4.78
4⅛	10.19	7.46	6.13	5.35	4.85
4¼	10.25	7.53	6.20	5.42	4.92
4⅜	10.31	7.59	6.26	5.49	5.00
4½	10.37	7.65	6.33	5.56	5.07
4⅝	10.43	7.72	6.40	5.63	5.15
4¾	10.49	7.78	6.47	5.71	5.22
4⅞	10.55	7.85	6.54	5.78	5.30
5	10.61	7.91	6.60	5.85	5.37
5⅛	10.67	7.98	6.67	5.92	5.45
5¼	10.73	8.04	6.74	6.00	5.53
5⅜	10.80	8.11	6.81	6.07	5.60
5½	10.86	8.18	6.88	6.15	5.68
5⅝	10.92	8.24	6.95	6.22	5.76
5¾	10.98	8.31	7.03	6.30	5.84
5⅞	11.04	8.38	7.10	6.37	5.92
6	11.10	8.44	7.16	6.44	6.00
6⅛	11.16	8.51	7.24	6.52	6.08
6¼	11.23	8.57	7.31	6.60	6.16
6⅜	11.29	8.64	7.38	6.67	6.24
6½	11.35	8.71	7.46	6.75	6.32
6⅝	11.42	8.78	7.53	6.83	6.40
6¾	11.48	8.85	7.60	6.91	6.49
6⅞	11.55	8.92	7.68	6.99	6.57
7	11.61	8.98	7.75	7.06	6.65
7⅛	11.68	9.06	7.83	7.15	6.74
7¼	11.74	9.12	7.90	7.22	6.82
7⅜	11.81	9.20	7.98	7.31	6.91
7½	11.87	9.27	8.05	7.38	6.99
7⅝	11.94	9.34	8.13	7.47	7.08
7¾	12.00	9.41	8.20	7.55	7.16
7⅞	12.07	9.48	8.29	7.64	7.25
8	12.14	9.56	8.37	7.72	7.34
8⅛	12.20	9.63	8.45	7.81	7.43
8¼	12.27	9.71	8.53	7.89	7.52
8⅜	12.34	9.78	8.60	7.97	7.61
8½	12.40	9.85	8.68	8.06	7.69
8⅝	12.47	9.93	8.76	8.14	7.78
8¾	12.54	10.00	8.84	8.23	7.87
8⅞	12.61	10.07	8.92	8.31	7.96
9	12.67	10.15	9.00	8.40	8.05
9⅛	12.74	10.22	9.08	8.48	8.14
9¼	12.81	10.30	9.16	8.57	8.23
9⅜	12.88	10.37	9.24	8.66	8.32
9½	12.94	10.45	9.33	8.74	8.41
9⅝	13.01	10.52	9.41	8.83	8.50
9¾	13.08	10.60	9.49	8.92	8.60
9⅞	13.15	10.67	9.57	9.00	8.69
10	13.22	10.75	9.66	9.09	8.78
10⅛	13.29	10.83	9.74	9.18	8.87
10¼	13.36	10.90	9.82	9.27	8.97
10⅜	13.43	10.98	9.90	9.36	9.06
10½	13.50	11.06	9.99	9.45	9.15
10⅝	13.57	11.14	10.07	9.54	9.25
10¾	13.64	11.21	10.16	9.63	9.34

Figure 9.2

Buyer Qualification Computation Chart

Enter the Purchase Price:_____ Mortgage Interest Rate:_____

			YEARS TO REPAY LOAN		
			20	25	30
DOWN	1. In Percent				
PAYMENT	2. In Dollars				
3. Loan Total (Home price, less the down payment)					
4. Monthly Payment on loan: [Work out from Fig. 2.1]					
5. Monthly Taxes and Insurance (From Fig. 6.9)					
6. Utilities, Monthly Average (Get from Fig. 6.9)					
7. Total Monthly Expenses [Add columns 4, 5 and 6]					
8. Yearly Payment (Housing Cost) [Column 7 x 12]					
9. The Required Buyer's Minimum Yearly Salary [Column 8 x 4]*					

The first column heading is blank so you can insert any specific payment period you may desire.
*Column 8 multiplied by 4.

To apply this rule of thumb to any particular case (yours or anybody else's), first use the Fact Sheet (Figure 8.1 on p. 55) to assemble your figures on the relevant data (the tax expenses, utilities, insurance, etc…) on the house. Then simply use Figure 9.2 above to make the computation. From the mortgage amortization payment table (Figure 9.1 on p. 63), you find the amount a buyer must pay per month for each $1,000 of the loan amount, then multiply this amount by the number of thousands contained in Line 3 of Figure 9.2. Enter this in Line 4. Finally, the yearly payment on the house (Line 8) multiplied by 4, gives you the minimum yearly take-home income the buyer (borrower) must earn to be able to afford the house (line 9).

Note that this qualification method can also be worked in reverse. First, you start with the proposed borrower's (buyer's) yearly income on Line 9 and divide by 4, you have Line 8. Divide Line 8 by 12, giving you Line 7, which is the total monthly expenses the party can afford. By subtracting Lines 5 and 6 amounts from Line 7, you get Line 4 – the monthly payment this party can afford on a house.

You may repeat this procedure a number of different times with different down payments and loan repayment periods for your available interest rate. You'll get the maximum loan a buyer can make and be able to buy a particular house based on the person's specific salary. This then gives you the down payment the prospective buyer has to come up with to be able to buy the given house.

3. Method Three: Debt-to-Income Ratio

Another rule-of-thumb (guideline), probably the most common method used nowadays for roughly pre-qualifying or qualifying mortgage applicants, is something called the **"28/36 ratio" rule**. It's a debt-to-income ratio. This is the guideline set by the *Federal National Mortgage Association (Fannie Mae)* and generally followed by most lenders in the industry. Under this rule, the "28" figure refers to how much (what percentage) of your gross income may be spent on your mortgage payment; and the "36" figure refers to the percentage of your monthly gross income that your total debts may not exceed. To put in another way, basically, this rule says, first, that if you are a prospective homebuyer, your monthly mortgage payment should be ONLY 28% (no more than 28%) of your monthly gross income; and second, that your total, combined debts – the mortgage payment, plus all your other major debts[1] – may not exceed 36% of your monthly gross income. (Where you don't know what the real estate taxes and insurance expense costs are, simply ask a knowledgeable Realtor in the area).

To calculate the ratio for yourself, you are to complete two basic steps. First, you determine the amount of your monthly mortgage payment and other housing-related expenses (property insurance due each month, taxes, PITI payments, etc.) The total of these payments must be *no more than* 28 percent of your gross monthly income. Next, you look at the total of the above payments and add to that any other long-term debts payable. The sum total of all such payments must be *no more than* 36 percent of your monthly gross income. And after you've done these calculations, if you're below the stated 28 percent and 36 percent income-to-debt ratio threshold, then congratulations! You're probably in good financial condition to qualify for a mortgage – some given level of mortgage.

To figure out your 28/36 Debt-to-income Ratios, you can also simply use the Pre-qualifier Worksheet (Figure 9.3) below, and the table on p. 63 (Table 9.1) to make the computation.

PRE-QUALIFIER WORKSHEET – Figure 9.3
(All figures are estimates rounded to the nearest dollar amounts).

1. Monthly Real Estate Tax and Homeowners Insurance Payments (annual amount divided by 12). $_____

2. Monthly Installment Payments (auto loans, child support, alimony, student loans,
   but not monthly household costs). $_____

3. Monthly Gross Income (including alimony and dividends for party or parties). $_____

4. Multiply the Monthly Gross Income (Line 3) by 0.28 ———>   = $_____
   Subtract the Monthly Real Estate Tax and Homeowners Insurance Payments (Line 1)——-> = $_____

5. ....*Amount A* = $_____

6. Multiply the Monthly Gross Income (Line 3) by 0.36 ———>   = $_____
   Subtract the total of the Monthly Real Estate Tax and Homeowners Insurance Payments
   and the Monthly Installment Payments (Lines 1 & 2). —————>   = $_____

7. ....*Amount B* = $_____

The lesser of the above two amounts, Amount A and Amount B, is the approximate monthly mortgage payment for which you can qualify.

4. Method Four

Another rule-of-thumb guideline, attempts to gauge the house "affordability" for a given buyer – the approximate home purchase price that you (a would-be buyer) can afford. The formula is the same principle as the so-called "28/36" ratio employed in Method Three above, but with a slight twist.

To use this method to pre-qualify any particular case, simply use the Affordability Worksheet on p. 66 (figure 9.4), along with the table on p. 63 (Table 9.1) to make the computation. Line 16 in Figure 9.4 gives the approximate purchase price the buyer can afford.

---

[1] The other debts which are usually includable in calculating the "total" debt, apart from the principal and interest of the mortgage loan, are the following: property taxes and insurance, auto loans, student loans, child support, alimony, and debts that will have more than 10 months to run. Credit card debts are usually not counted with this category (unless the party has a lot of them), and regular household costs, such as household utility bills or rents, are also excluded.

FIGURE 9.4
The Affordability Worksheet

(1) Enter your monthly gross income (yours and a co-borrower's combined) $_____

(2) Multiply the amount from line 1 by 0.28 $_____

(3) Multiply the amount from line 1 by 0.36 $_____

(4) Enter estimated monthly real estate tax (may get from Fig. 6.8 or inquire with area realtor or local tax assesor's office) $_____

(5) Enter estimated monthly homeowners insurance payment (may discuss coverage needed with qualified insurance agents or get from Fig. 6.9) $_____

(6) Enter other monthly installment payments (debts with 6 or more months to run, e.g., auto loans, child support, major credit card or revolving credit balances. Exclude household costs (utilities, phone bills, etc.)

(7) Add lines 4 and 5 and round the result to nearest dollar amount $_____

(8) Add lines 6 and 7 and round the result to nearest dollar amount $_____

(9) Subtract line 7 from line 2 $_____

(10) Subtract line 8 from line 3 $_____

(11) Determine mortgage interest rates by asking your realtor, or lenders, $_____
    and then look at the Monthly payment table (Fig. 2.1). Use the interest rate
    in the Term Rate % column and follow across the page until you reach the
    Term that you prefer. Enter the monthly payment amount.

(12) Look at lines 9 and 10. Enter the amount of whichever line is less. $_____
    This is the approximate monthly payment that you can qualify for.

(13) Divide line 12 by line 11. Enter the number. $_____

(14) Multiply line 13 by 1000.00 and round the result to the nearest dollar amount $_____
    This is the approximate mortgage amount your lender will allow you to borrow.

(15) Enter amount available for down payment. $_____

(16) Add lines 14 and 15. The result is the approximate purchase price you can $_____
    afford.

NOTE: Bear in mind that the results of these calculations, whichever of the above three methods used, is only a rough estimate. The final judgment and qualification must usually be made by a loan company to whom the prospective home buyer ultimately applies. The point of this "pre-qualification" calculation is primarily to have some idea, a reasonable measure, of your (the prospective buyer's) ability to borrow, how large a mortgage you can afford, at what rate, and how long. This way, the dreamers who cannot possibly qualify financially and have no business bidding on a house of a given value can be eliminated before hand!

Can you afford it?

CHAPTER 10

Know the Totality of All the Financial Costs That's Involved in Making A Home Purchase: the Closing Costs and Other Costs

When you purchase a home, and/or take out a mortgage to purchase one, one thing you can surely count on, is that, quite apart from the home purchase price money, there are an array of other significant fees and charges you will further need to pay in order to be able to make the purchase. The majority of such fees and charges will be paid or payable at the closing of the house – that is, at the final meeting at which you formally buy the home, and the home seller hands you the legal title of transfer in exchange for your final payments and the signing of the final papers and agreement by the parties. Hence, such extra fees and charges, because they are typically paid and payable at the closing, are often called the *"closing costs."*

From your standpoint as a prospective homebuyer, *the important thing for you to know, is that such fees and charges—the closing costs—are going to be primarily YOUR responsibility, that they are additional costs and expenses you'd have to budget for and to have in hand over and above the direct price of the home.* Furthermore, another important thing that is relevant for you to know in this connection is that, as in almost everything else connected with purchasing a home, many of these closing costs are not necessarily cast in stone but are matters which are still subject to negotiation and amendments. Thus, even though a loan officer or a service provider might have expressed some specific closing costs to you as though they are final and not subject to negotiation, nothing should stop you from trying for a lower price; you might still be able to bargain for a lower amount, nevertheless. You should recognize that typically, many of the services for which you're charged closing costs (appraisal, credit reports, home inspections, title insurance, title search, etc.) are not performed by the lender, but by a separate firm or service provider totally independent of the lender. Nor are the dollar amounts of the typical closing costs insignificant or minor matters. Not at all! Indeed, quite to the contrary, *the value of the closing costs for a home could typically be substantial. Experts estimate, for example, that the average closing costs for a home purchase often run between 7 to 10 percent of the mortgage amount.* Thus, using such estimate as a rough rule-of-thumb, the closing costs for a $100,000 home mortgage amount will typically cost you roughly $7,000-$10,000 in closing costs alone!

A. *Here are a brief summary of some of the closing costs you may need to pay:*

1. Points or Loan Origination Fee. The loan origination fee is a fee you pay the lender for the privilege of getting a mortgage; and points are a regular fee imposed by the lender beyond the regular interest rate, and is paid in advance. One "point" equals one percent of the loan amount. The loan origination fee may be expressed in terms of points (see Chapter 7 for fuller treatment of points). The points charges will vary from one to three points, and even higher, depending upon various factors, such as the borrower's credit rating, loan-to-value ratio, whether property is owner occupied or not, etc. Some lenders will charge the origination fee at a flat fee completely separate and apart from any points you may pay; others will call one point a loan "origination fee" and refer to additional points as "discount points."

As a rule, in housing markets when mortgages are plentiful and competition to initiate mortgage loans is keen, buyers will often escape paying points or origination fees; however, in tight mortgage markets when mortgages are scarce and interest rates are high, buyers have been known to pay discount points of up to four or more points – that is, some $4,000 or more on a mortgage of $100,000. Points, therefore, could potentially be one of your biggest closing costs, if not the biggest. [See Chapter 7 for a fuller discussion on points and interest rates].

2. *Application Fee.* Some lenders charge a non-refundable fee, often called a loan application fee, at the time you apply for the mortgage loan. Lenders who charge this fee, assert it is necessary to cover their costs for processing the application. Lenders may charge this as a flat amount, such as $75 or $100 or $300, or they may fix it at a percentage of the mortgage amount, such as one-half of one percent.

POINTERS: Be sure to check in advance on the practice of the lender you are considering; try to find out, for example, in your first contact with the lender even before you make a formal application to them for a mortgage, whether it is the policy of the lender to refund the application fee if in the end you don't qualify for a mortgage, and if the lender will apply the fee towards your closing costs if the mortgage is issued. Also, you can try to assess whether you are likely to qualify for a mortgage under the lender's requirements. This way, other things considered, you can decide to avoid any lenders who charge an application fee even when the mortgage is not approved, or those who charge on a percentage basis.

3. *Assumption Fee.* This fee, also known as a transfer fee, is charged only if you are "assuming" – that is, taking over – a mortgage that had been previously held by the selling party.

4. *Attorney's Fees.* Not only your own attorney's fees (if you use one), but in most cases your new lender's attorney's fees, as well. Figure about $300 to $600 for your attorney's fee, depending on your locale, and some $150 to $300 for your lender's attorney, his charge-back to you of some of the services he might have rendered to the lender.

5. *Title Insurance.* Your new lender will likely require you to obtain a new title insurance policy to protect the lender against the possibility that the title search may miss uncovering some impairment to your ownership. Depending on the size of the loan, this may cost you anywhere from $300-$1,000 in insurance premium, but is a single, one time-only premium which you pay at the closing. Be aware, that the costs of title insurance is sometimes paid by the seller, sometimes by the buyer, and sometimes split between the buyer and seller, depending on the understanding had by the parties.

6. *Title Search Costs.* Your new lender will still want to be assured that the present seller is truly the owner of the property. So, he will hire a title search agent to do the title checking to be sure that there are no claims, liens, attachments, and debts, outstanding on the property; and you will reimburse the lender for the cost of the agent's services.

7. *Credit Check*. The lender will run a credit check on you to check out your income and credit worthiness, and you'll be charged a small fee for the service. This is one fee that bears investigation and bargaining on the part of a borrower, because some lenders will charge it in advance, whether you get the loan or not, while others will not charge you such a fee unless they do, in fact, grant you the credit.

8. *Survey Fee.* Your new lender may require that you obtain a new survey map, at a cost of roughly $100 to $400, especially if the previous survey is a very old one. A survey shows the exact legal description, boundaries, and location, of the property. The cost may be borne by you or by the seller, depending on the locale and its particular custom.

9. *Escrow Fees.* Most lenders set up an account, called an "escrow account," for the deposit of monies that are paid by the home buyer for the property taxes, homeowner's insurance premiums, and so forth, that become due once a year. Lenders will prefer that you make a deposit of a year's worth of such payments into the escrow account, and they themselves will then be making the payments monthly out of this account for the home owner. This way, they (the lenders) will be in control of these payments since they can be assured that the payments will be made and that the value of the property will be maintained.

This arrangement, also called a *reserve account or impound account*, is usually mandatory for loans that finance 80% or more of the sale price of the home. Also, both the FHA and VA loans require escrow account. But the way this works in the FHA and VA system is that at the closing, the lender will require that you put an initial amount into the "escrow account" – generally enough to cover 6 to 12 months worth of property tax payments and homeowner's insurance premiums – the object of which is to protect your new home against fire, vandalism, and other casualties and liabilities. In addition, some lenders will charge you a fee for the work of actually setting up the escrow account. One expert,[1] warns that the cost of escrow charges varies widely in terms of the location and the area's property taxes, but estimates as reasonable some $300 to $600 for the homeowner's insurance escrow charge, and $1,200 to $3,000 for taxes.

10. Appraisal Fee. The lender, in order to make sure that the house you plan to buy is worth enough to provide adequate collateral for the loan value, will usually appraise the property to determine its current appraised value. And for this, it will usually use one of its own appraisers and then charge you the cost of the appraisal fee. The appraisal fee will run anywhere from $150 to $400.

11. Transfer Tax. Some states, counties, cities, and towns, assess a tax when real estate changes hands. Often called a stamp charge or stamp tax in many areas for the reason that the local government rules often require that an official stamp be affixed to the documents ore receipts of payment, the tax often runs about $250 but varies widely from state to state depending on the value of the property, and can run anywhere from $75 to $1,125. Depending on the custom in the state, it may be the buyer who is required to pay the transfer tax, or it may be the seller.

12. Mortgage Registration Tax. In those states that charge a mortgage tax for taking out a home mortgage, you may have to pay a state or county mortgage tax since you're getting a new mortgage. Mortgage registration tax is assessed according to the size of your mortgage, not according to the value of the property being transferred.

13. Mortgage Insurance. Let there be no confusion on this; let us be clear on one thing: there are TWO totally different types of housing-related "mortgage insurance" – the mortgage default insurance, and the mortgage life insurance. Mortgage default insurance, is insurance you purchase meant to protect the lender should you fall behind on your monthly mortgage payments; while mortgage life insurance is a life insurance policy you (the homebuyer) take out on your own life with the lender as the beneficiary, meant to ensure that the lender gets its money back in the event that you (the mortgage borrower) die unexpectedly. Mortgage default insurance is sometimes referred to as the private mortgage insurance or PMI.

As a mortgage borrower, you will be the one responsible for the payment of the insurance premiums. However, unless you are taking a mortgage that is more than 80 percent of the home's purchase price, lenders will generally not require that you purchase mortgage default insurance. The cost for mortgage default insurance is roughly 0.3 percent to 1 percent of the loan amount, depending on the amount of your down payment. The insurance premiums are usually structured so that the premium payments are added to your monthly mortgage payments. With respect to life insurance, the option of which company you may buy the life insurance policy from is generally the homebuyer's, and the lender may not dictate that. Hence, be sure to shop around with various insurance companies as costs vary greatly from one company to another.

14. Mortgage Lock-in Fee. Some lenders may charge borrowers what is known as a "lock-in" fee. A lock-in is also known as a rate lock or a rate commitment. This fee is said to be for the privilege of allowing a borrower

---

[1] John R. Dorfman, *The Mortgage book*, p. 46.

to "lock-in" a specified interest rate he'll have to pay on his mortgage. Hence, the interest rate for your mortgage will remain at the stated level no matter the level of the interest rate (and the number of points) the lender happens to be charging at the time you go to closing. The clock-in fee could be as much as 0.5 percent, or one percent of the loan amount. Some lenders, however, offer borrowers a lock-in privilege without a separate charge for it.

15. Other Costs. Other costs and charges which could be payable by a homebuyer, whether at closing or otherwise, include the following: *document preparation fee* chargeable by the escrow company for preparation of certain documents, *recording fees* for the recording of the required documents with the county records office, *termite and home inspection fees*, (averages $175 to $350), *brokerage commission* (this is normally paid by the home seller), the *first mortgage payment* (not generally the case, but depending on the term of your mortgage, the lender may require that you make your first regular monthly mortgage payments at the closing), *notary fees*, etc.

B. SUMMARY AND CONCLUSIONS

The points of this chapter are simply these: **(1)** to emphasize that the closing costs involved in the purchasing of a house are no ordinary matter but are a matter that could constitute a substantial expense for the home buyer; **(2)** that the closing costs are of such substantial size and magnitude that you must, as a prudent homebuyer, be sure to gather the facts by which to estimate and to make full provision for the anticipated closing costs in your overall budgeting for your home purchase; and **(3)** that though closing costs may well be a necessary evil in home buying, not every closing cost is either inevitable or necessarily needs to be paid by the home buyer in the specific amount charged or demanded. *In sum, the point is that at least some closing costs, though seeming to be final and cast in stone, can often be negotiated with the lender or service provider, and can be modified or even eliminated.*

Indeed, one of the biggest closing costs, are points charges on the mortgage loan. And if all you can accomplish is to get a good bargain on just the points alone in your mortgage shopping, you shall have probably done one of the biggest things you could do in helping to hold down your closing costs by that single action alone. Hence, as a prospective homebuyer, you had better be prepared to make it your conscious duty always to engage your lender – and the many service providers that are often involved in the home buying process – in negotiations and bargaining on the terms, prices, and other charges they propose.

SAMPLE CLOSING COST

TABLE 10.1

The sample closing costs shown below are based on the purchase of a $125,000 home, with a 20 percent ($25,000) down payment and a $100,000 mortgage. Not all of the fees and charges are charged by all lenders. And costs vary widely from area to area, and even from one lender to another. So treat these costs as examples only.

Application fee	$ 150
Appraisal of home by lender	200
Attorney's fees:	
Your own attorney	250
Lender's attorney	125
Credit report fee	75
Escrow payments:	
For homeowner's insurance	400
For property taxes	2,000
First monthly payment on mortgage	878
Inspection of home by buyer	250
Lock-in fee	250
Mortgage default insurance	*
Mortgage life insurance	*
Mortgage origination fee	300
Notary fees	50
Points (1.5)	1,500
Recording fees	50
Survey of property	200
Title search and title insurance	600
Transfer tax	250
Total Closing Costs	**$7,528**

*This insurance may not be required. Negotiate to see if the lender will waive it. If charged, mortgage default insurance and mortgage life insurance might run approximately $300 to $500 each.

---

*Reproduction courtesy of John R. Dorfman's *The Mortgage Book*, p. 51

CHAPTER 11

The Typical Procedures For Applying For a Mortgage Loan, Processing a Loan, and Qualifying a Borrower For a Loan

How does a borrower physically apply for a mortgage loan? Let's say that, a borrower has undertaken all the efforts and research work essential for finding a suitable mortgage source and lender (Chapters 2 and 12), and that he has finally made his choice and settled on the lending institution or institutions he wants to borrow from. Now, how does he – by what procedure does he – typically go about the process of applying for the loan, and, even more important, how does the lender undertake the processing of his application and their evaluation, and their determination of whether or not the borrower is qualified to be granted a loan, and just how much loan he may be approved for?

To be sure, every lender uses its own peculiar methods of borrower analysis, evaluation, and scoring system, to determine the credit worthiness of a borrower. However, there are still some rules and procedures generally common to, and followed by lenders. And here in this chapter, we try simply to outline some of the general procedures.

A. BORROWER'S LOAN APPLICATION AND OTHER PRIMARY DOCUMENTATIONS

Typically, upon your finding the lending institution or institutions you wish to borrow from, you will contact the institution(s) and ask for their loan application forms. The lender, in the course of trying to arrive at some determination of whether to loan you (to invest in you) the money being requested, will usually begin its loan processing work by reviewing and analyzing several key documents. Generally, this will commence after the sales contract has been signed between the buyer and the seller, although it need not necessarily go in that sequential order. For a residential home application,[1] the key documents the lender will use in its analysis, include: **(1)** loan application form; **(2)** verification of deposit; **(3)** verification of employment; **(4)** Truth-in-Lending disclosure statement (an estimate of home-buying costs that is to be provided by the lender); and **(5)** credit report.

The loan application form is the first document that your lender will process. The application form is the primary and most important source that your loan underwriter (the loan officer who rates your acceptability for the loan) uses to judge your ability and willingness, as a prospective property buyer, to live up to the terms and conditions of the mortgage loan agreement with the lender. Indeed, just from the loan underwriter's detailed analyses of this document alone, the underwriter shall have been pretty able to ascertain whether the prospects of extending the loan are good, or simply marginal, or totally unpromising.

---

[1] For the most part, the process of analyzing the borrower also applies to loan requests for other types of real estate beside residential homes. Except that, when the applicant is a partnership or a corporation, additional documents may usually be required.

B. LENDER'S LOAN APPLICATION ANALYSIS PROCESS –
PROPERTY SURVEY, APPRAISAL, INSPECTION, ETC.

What happens next, after you've completed your loan application form and filed it with the lending institution you've picked? It's mortgage loan officer will set about the task of collecting detailed information about you (and about the property, if you've picked one yet), and analyzing such information in order to make a decision as to whether, in the loan officer's or loan committee's estimation, you fit the institution's "profile" for a borrower whose loan is likely to be both secure and trouble-free — whether you have, in other words, the ability and willingness to meet the monthly payments of the loan in the lender's estimation.

What is on the loan officer's (or committee's) mind as he considers your application? First and foremost, he wants to assure himself that if it were ever to come to the point where you can't keep up with your mortgage payments and the lender has to take the property back ("foreclosure"), the lender will be able to resell the property for at least as much money as you'll owe them on it. So, even before they set up a meeting with you, the institution arranges for a survey of the property (assuming you've picked out one yet) and gets the property officially appraised; it sets its own "appraised price" on the property to be sure that it is worth what you're paying for it. At the same time, the lender will arrange for inspection of the property to prove that it is structurally sound: independent inspectors will check the structure and it's various systems (plumbing, septic, electric, etc.). Then he wants to know about your present financial status, your credit history, and all of the personal aspects of your life that will potentially affect your ability to meet the monthly payments: do you earn enough steady income in the household? Do you already owe other significant debts and have significant obligations to others that will eat into your monthly income and, thus, make it more difficult for you to be able to make the mortgage payments? (See Figures 8.2 and 8.3 on pp.58 & 59). What other property or assets (real estate, automobile, bank savings, jewelry, antiques, furs, stocks, bonds, other securities, etc.) do you have, if any, which you could sell, tap, or fall back on, in the event of an emergency? He wants badly to know about any assets (items and property of value) you may have because, in case of your default on the mortgage, the lender may have to claim some of those assets (through the proper legal actions) that may have been pledged against the loan. He is very much interested in knowing: Are you a good credit risk, and is there a past record of "willingness to pay" on your part – your credit rating? The lending officers want to find out what reading they can make of your "character" – are you part of a growing, stable family, for example, and what is your relationship (your salary, length of stay, position, etc.) to your career or employer?

Exhibit 11-1 (pp.77-78) is a sample standardized loan application form of the kind used for conventional mortgages.[2] (Usually, a lender will use the standardized forms and follow the standard underwriting policies if it anticipates participating in the so-called *secondary mortgage market*). As can be seen from Exhibit 11-1, the loan application is comprehensive and provides the underwriter a complete and detailed financial and other data about the borrower, including a profile of who you are, the property you want to buy, the terms of the mortgage you want, and the assets and means of income you have available to pay for it, among other information. *Through the underwriter's careful analysis of various aspects of the data supplied in the application form alone, he is immediately able to draw some preliminary judgments.* For example, just from the Exhibit 11-1 sample form, the underwriter can immediately draw some preliminary conclusions, already, and make out the following relevant information about the applicants involved in this instance: Mr. Will Carter and his wife, Tammy carter, have a relatively stable monthly income and employment situation (both have been with their current

[2] All sample forms employed in this chapter, namely, Exhibits 11-1, 11-2, 11-3, 11-4A/B., and 11-5, are reproduced herein by courtesy of the author and publisher of *Real Estate Finance* by C.F. Sirmans (McGraw-Hill Book company: New York 1989 ed.). The present author and publisher are deeply indebted to the aforementioned for the great worth and value of these samples as excellent illustrative tools.

employers since graduation from college for 3 years)[3]; they'll be able to have available a down payment money of $20,000 from inheritance from Will's father; the monthly expenses they currently make on housing ($450) will more than double with the new home (at $956.46); they have a stable married family background; they have a combined monthly income of $3,117 and will need an additional $19,285 to close the loan; there are no court judgments, litigations, or other legal obligations or issues outstanding against them; and the Carters have modest financial assets and their liabilities are a relatively small amount.

C. THE TRUTH-IN-LENDING DISCLOSURE STATEMENT &
THE GOOD FAITH ESTIMATE OF SETTLEMENT CHARGES

As part of the whole effort of the government to make it simpler for American consumers to shop for loans, Congress passed the *Federal Truth-in-Lending Act of 1969* which requires mortgage lenders (and lenders in general) to disclose to their borrowers in advance, all terms and conditions and cost items of the loan so as to enable the borrower to readily compare various available credit terms. BUT WITH THIS BIG DIFFERENCE AND ADVANTAGE FOR YOU, THIS TIME: *the lenders can still set the prices they wish to charge you on various mortgage items; but now, they must compute those charges, and disclose those charges to you, in a uniform manner common to all banks and mortgage lenders so that you can comparison-shop among different lenders.*

Therefore, shortly after you have picked up the loan application forms from your lender, and often immediately upon your returning the completed application to the lending institution, you should expect to be given a document known as the *Truth-in-Lending Disclosure Statement* by the lending institution. This document (see Exhibit 11-4A on p. 81 *for a sample) is a very important element in your whole mortgage borrowing process: because, not only is this document required by law to be issued you, but its calculation of the lender's mortgage charges is to be standardized and uniform for all lenders such that you are able to compare different lenders mortgage and cost items (different interest rates, numbers of points, etc.) in an essentially uniform basis.*

The Truth-in-Lending Disclosure Statement (see sample copy on p. 81) will tell you the terms of the mortgage, how it calculated the components of the finance charge, an estimate of the costs, fees and charges you'll pay, your legal rights and obligations, and so on. It will, for example, tell you the annualized percentage rate (APR) of the loan you are contemplating – that is, what the total cost of the loan (interest, points, closing costs, etc.) is on an "annualized" basis, which is then expressed as an interest rate, thus enabling you to compare "apples with apples."

The important point to make about the disclosure statement is that this is a document you will want to study; it will familiarize you with all of the loan's features, and will be highly useful to you in deciding between two or more mortgages with different interest rates, numbers of points, and other terms. And you should keep it handy for future reference.

NOTE: It's important that you press the lenders you propose to do business with to be given the
disclosure statement immediately at the time you pick up the application, and not a minute after. This way, you will be able to verify the terms and various finance components of the mortgage even BEFORE you apply. Why? Because it may have been too late already after you applied.
Note also, that under the federal law called the *Real Estate Settlement Procedure Act (RESPA)*, at the very time that you take the application, one of the papers the lender is supposed to give you, is something called **Good Faith Estimate of Settlement Charges** (see sample copy, Exhibit 11-5, on p. 83), which is to detail the costs the borrower will be charged when the loan is consummated or closed. The primary reason for this legally mandated document, is to provide you, the borrower, with sufficiently detailed information (especially when,

---

[3] A stable monthly income is the borrower's gross monthly income from primary employment base earnings, plus any recognized secondary income: commission, bonuses, overtime or part-time employment income that is stable (it is considered stable, if it is typical for the occupation and is substantiated by the borrower's previous one year's earnings, and its continuation is probable, based on foreseeable circumstances).

combined with the Truth-in-Lending Disclosure Statement) to allow you to effectively compare the terms of a loan being offered you. So, be sure, as well, to carefully study this document and all the supporting documents accompanying it (it comes with a booklet and a Settlement Costs Guide, among other information); it can provide you some very useful help in attempting to compare with other loans the terms of the loan being considered.

D. CREDIT CHECK, EMPLOYMENT VERIFICATION, DOWN PAYMENT VERIFICATION, ETC.

At the same time that the other processing activities are going on, the lender's credit department will draw, usually at your expense, a full credit report on you from a professional credit information storage agency. (You have a legal right to ask for, and to see a summary of this report, though not the actual report itself, and to protest any contents of the report that you consider factually inaccurate). *Indeed, as a smart shopper, you should already have ordered your own credit report from a credit-reporting agency so as to make sure that no unanticipated problems would arise with your loan application.* The credit report will give your lender information about your debt-repayment history with those creditors you listed on the application form, as well as others. The report may include the date of your employment, position, job security, annual salary, and net worth. It may also include data from other creditors and any information from public records that reveal any pending suits against you.

At the time you submitted the loan application, the loan officer may have had you sign the request forms to have your down payment deposit and employment verified. See Exhibits 11-2 and 11-3. These forms authorize the disclosure of such information to your lenders by those depositories (banks) you listed on your application form. Or, alternatively, some lenders will simply have their loan officers call the applicant's bank to verify the claimed balance, and probably check the court records in the counties where you live or have lived, to establish that you've left no trail of unpaid debts. Then, to verify your statements concerning your employment, salary, or other income items, the lender may require a verification of employment from your employer.[4] [See Exhibit 11-3 on Tammy Carter's employment, for a sample]

Meanwhile, the lender is conducting a title search on the prospective home (assuming you have located one yet) – a historical check of all the records showing the past ownerships of the property – so as to assure that if you were to buy the property, you will, indeed, own it with a free and clear title. [See p. 68 for more on the title search process]. The lender also arranges for title insurance, an insurance policy to protect the lender, not you, the buyer, against unforeseen problems that might affect your ownership. (Note that the policy is the lender's policy; it protects the **lender**, not you. Yet, you pay for it, however).

E. EVALUATING YOUR ABILITY TO PAY

Once the lender has received all the necessary documents, the lender is in a position to make a determination on whether you are worth the risk of being granted a loan, or not. Remember, this is a long-term loan commitment (most real estate loans are), and in the professional, investment-minded head of the loan underwriter, he's thinking caution and security; his major concern is: 'How do I minimize the risk associated with this loan?' This, to him, is what they call the *'default'* type of risk in the field of financial analysis. And he is, first and foremost, trying to determine this primary question in all of his present analyses of you: What is your apparent or probable ability and willingness to meet the debt obligations on your requested loan?

---

[4] For a self-employed borrower, the necessary income verification documents would be profit and loss statements and the balances of the business for the past 2 or more years, or completed federal income tax returns. Income verification for a borrower retired or about to retire, are based on the retirement income and the financial reserves accumulated for living expenses and debt service.

In assessing your qualification for a loan, and determining how big a mortgage you should be granted, lenders look at several factors, not just one or two. *But, all things considered, it is fair to say that the size of your income is probably the most important criterion and consideration.* However, highly important and relevant, as well, are job stability and the steadiness of your income, the amount of your debt (or lack of debt), the value of the home you want to buy relative to your income and financial resources.

Job stability is especially important to a prospective lender because you'll need to be making mortgage payments for a long time – year after year, after year for some 15, 20, or 30 years. So, if you are, for example, a free-lance writer or a new self-employed typist who just set up shop only 6 months ago or so, you'll certainly have a far less receptive mortgage application experience or prospects than you would if you were a corporate vice-president with some 10 to 15 years tenure at a company!

Next, having dealt with the concern of minimizing the risk factor, your mortgage lender's underwriter will now shift attention to evaluating *the loan's yield for the lender, and its yield on the lender's entire mortgage portfolio.* Here, the underwriter basically wants to evaluate whether you will be able to afford the monthly payments involved, and if so, how well you will be able to handle them. To put it another way, he wants to determine, looking at it from the lender's own perspective, what "quality" of loan this might fall under – whether the loan is a "high quality" loan for the lender, or a "bad" (or very bad) loan, or simply a questionable one. To do this, he sits down with a worksheet or ledger (or a plain old calculator or simple computer) to work out some key **financial ratios**.

There are many ratios and industry standards that are used in the real estate industry to evaluate the borrower and his assets (See Chapter 9 and 15, for example, for more elaborate calculation of ratio analysis). But, for our purposes here, to summarize it in the interest of simplicity and brevity, here are some of the more common ones. Here's what your underwriter will probably do. If your loan is a 'conventional' type of mortgage, your underwriter may look at the ratio of your total monthly long-term debt (your PITIUM, plus other debts that will take 10 or more months to pay off, such as car loans, credit card balances, alimony, etc.) to your net income. To meet the lender's requirement, the calculated total monthly debt payments *may not exceed* 50 to 55 percent of your stable monthly net income (or, if the gross income is used, it may not exceed 33 percent, or up to 40 percent with some lenders, of your gross monthly income).[5] Or, if you happen to have little or no long-term debt, the underwriter will simply apply what is know as your **PITI Debt ratio** to assess how much monthly housing debt you can afford – that is, the ratio between your principal, interest, taxes, and insurance (PITI) costs, and your gross income. Conventional loan industry standards usually requires that the total monthly housing expense (i.e., the ratio of the PITI to your monthly gross income) should not exceed 25 to 30 percent of the borrower's stable monthly gross income. These formulas will vary somewhat if you are seeking an FHA or a VA type of loan. (See chapter 15 at pp. 118 & 122 respectively, for the applicable standards).[6]

Finally, in addition to the use of qualifying ratios and their analyses, your underwriter may also (only some lenders do) use *a point scoring system* to evaluate your general credit worthiness. Thus, while the use of ratio analysis will tell the lender whether you can afford the monthly mortgage payments, the use of the point scoring system is meant to give the lender a general overview of your past credit history, and your past approach and attitude to debt handling and repayment, and your potentials for repaying your debts. (See Chapter 15 at p. 125 for the procedures of the point scoring system).

---

[5] The ratios cited here assume you are borrowing 80 percent or less of the purchase prize of the home. You should note that, in certain cases, a lender will let you borrow more than 80%, but in that case the lender will usually be stricter in determining how much you can afford for monthly payments.
[6] The more elaborate calculations of the various ratio analyses are outlined in Chapter 15 of the manual.

F. LOAN APPROVAL AND COMMITMENT

After having evaluated all your documentations, reports, and information on your application, the loan underwriter (the loan officer who oversees your case) will make a final determination and recommendation on your application. And if your loan is approved, you qualify for the mortgage; subject only to legal requirements and completion of remaining required documentations.

The lender then sends you a loan commitment letter, or contract, to make you the loan under certain enumerated terms and conditions – the specific amount at a specific interest rate, the charges and fees you'll pay, the closing requirements and documents needed to close, etc. The loan commitment documents will state that the lender is willing to lend you a specific amount of money to be repaid over a set number of years for a particular piece of property or kind of property.

The commitment may also list some specific conditions that are to be met before the loan can be made. For example, you may be required to pay off some outstanding bills in order to qualify, or that you meet other requirements. The commitment stays in force for a certain period of time, typically 30 to 90 days. [The lender will, at this stage, also furnish you a written notification of the annual percentage rate (APR) – a document which takes into account the difference between simple annual interest and monthly compound interest, as well as points and some closing costs, as more elaborately explained in Chapter 10].

The commitment is not final; it is subject to negotiations and change by either party. The lender, for example, may alter the mortgage terms if they have changed since you submitted your application, and in that case you are welcome to look that over and make your "counter-offer." And on your own part, you can, for example, seek a "lock in" agreement with the lender to hold ("lock in") the interest rate to *the same* initially agreed level over the period covered by the commitment letter, until the actual closing when you finalize the buying of the home. A "lock in" will ensure that if the interest rates were to fluctuate between the time of the loan's approval and the time the home purchase is actually finalized, you will not be charged the higher rate. You can either sign or return the commitment, or you may make your own counter-offer by physically making changes on it. Your counter-offer becomes a contract, however, only when (and if) the lender accepts it with the changes and signs it. In the end, after you review the commitment, and assuming you agree with the terms, you sign and return it. At that point you have a MORTGAGE CONTRACT with the lender. The mortgage lender issues you a note and mortgage.

Exhibit 11-1.   **Standard Loan Application Form for Conventional Mortgage**

RESIDENTIAL LOAN APPLICATION

MORTGAGE APPLIED FOR	[X] Conventional [ ] FHA [ ] VA	Amount $ 68,000	Interest Rate 12 %	No of Months 360	Monthly Payment Principal & Interest $ 699.46	Escrow/Impounds (to be collected monthly) [X] Taxes [ ] Hazard Ins. [ ] Mtg. Ins.

Prepayment Option
No prepayment penalty

Property Street Address: 209 Boweevil Street   City: Crete   County: Pike   State: Any State   Zip: No Units:

Legal Description (Attach description if necessary)
Lot 10, Block B, Cotton Hills Estates   Year Built 19xx

Purpose of Loan: [x] Purchase [ ] Construction-Permanent [ ] Construction [ ] Refinance [ ] Other (Explain)

Complete this line if Construction-Permanent or Construction Loan	Lot Value Data		Original Cost $	Present Value (a) $	Cost of Imps. (b) $	Total (a + b) $	ENTER TOTAL AS PURCHASE PRICE IN DETAILS OF PURCHASE
	Year Acquired N/A						

Complete this line if a Refinance Loan N/A   Purpose of Refinance   Describe Improvements [ ] made [ ] to be made

Year Acquired; Original Cost $; Amt. Existing Liens $ Cost: $

Title Will Be Held In What Name(s)
Will C. and Tammy Carter

Manner In Which Title Will Be Held
Joint Tenancy

Source of Down Payment and Settlement Charges
Savings Account and Inheritance

This application is designed to be completed by the borrower(s) with the lender's assistance. The Co-Borrower Section and all other Co-Borrower questions must be completed and the appropriate box(es) checked if [ ] another person will be jointly obligated with the Borrower on the loan, or [ ] the Borrower is relying on income from alimony, child support or separate maintenance or on the income or assets of another person as a basis for repayment of the loan, or [ ] the Borrower is married and resides, or the property is located, in a community property state.

BORROWER			CO-BORROWER		
Name Tammy Carter	Age 26	School Yrs 16	Name Will C. Carter	Age 26	School Yrs 16
Present Address No. Years [ ]Own [ ]Rent			Present Address No. Years [ ]Own [ ]Rent		
Street 5665 College Avenue			Street 5665 College Avenue		
City/State/Zip Crete, Any State 00000			City/State/Zip Crete, Any State 00000		
Former address if less than 2 years at present address			Former address if less than 2 years at present address		
Street N/A			Street N/A		
City/State/Zip			City/State/Zip		
Years at former address [ ]Own [ ]Rent			Years at former address [ ]Own [ ]Rent		
Marital Status [x]Married [ ]Separated [ ]Unmarried (incl. single, divorced, widowed)			Marital Status [x]Married [ ]Separated [ ]Unmarried (incl. single, divorced, widowed)		
Name and Address of Employer Dependable Electric Co. 135 Industry Drive Crete, Any State 00000	Years employed in this line of work or profession? 3 years Years on this job 3 [ ] Self Employed*		Name and Address of Employer American Monitor Corp. 127 Work Street Crete, Any State 00000	Years employed in this line of work or profession? 3 years Years on this job 3 [ ] Self Employed*	
Position/Title Hard Worker	Type of Business Electric Motors		Position/Title Hard Worker	Type of Business Monitor Products	
Social Security Number*** 004-06-8967	Home Phone 556-1865	Business Phone 555-1279	Social Security Number*** 005-06-8968	Home Phone 556-1865	Business Phone 556-2000

GROSS MONTHLY INCOME				MONTHLY HOUSING EXPENSE **		DETAILS OF PURCHASE	
Item	Borrower	Co Borrower	Total	Rent $ 350.		Do Not Complete If Refinance	
Base Empl. Income	$ 1500	$ 1417	$ 2933	First Mortgage (P&I)	$ 699.46	a Purchase Price	$ 85,000
Overtime				Other Financing (P&I)	--	b Total Closing Costs (Est.)	2,730
Bonuses	100	100	200	Hazard Insurance	25.00	c Prepaid Escrows (Est.)	555
Commissions				Real Estate Taxes	85.00	d Total (a + b + c)	$ 88,285
Dividends/Interest				Mortgage Insurance	--	e Amount This Mortgage	(68,000)
Net Rental Income				Homeowner Assn Dues	--	f Other Financing	(--)
Other† (Before completing, see notice under Describe Other Income below.)				Other		g Other Equity	(--)
				Total Monthly Pmt	$ 809.46	h Amount of Cash Deposit	(1,000)
				Utilities	100. 150.00	i Closing Costs Paid by Seller	(--)
Total	$ 1600	$ 1517	$ 3117	Total $ 450	$ 956.46	j Cash Reqd. For Closing (Est.)	$ 19,285

DESCRIBE OTHER INCOME

▷ B Borrower C Co Borrower	NOTICE: † Alimony, child support, or separate maintenance income need not be revealed if the Borrower or Co Borrower does not choose to have it considered as a basis for repaying this loan.	Monthly Amount $
B None		
C None		

IF EMPLOYED IN CURRENT POSITION FOR LESS THAN TWO YEARS COMPLETE THE FOLLOWING

B/C	Previous Employer/School	City/State	Type of Business	Position/Title	Dates From/To	Monthly Income $

THESE QUESTIONS APPLY TO BOTH BORROWER AND CO-BORROWER

If a "yes" answer is given to a question in this column, explain on an attached sheet.	Borrower Yes or No	Co-Borrower Yes or No	If applicable, explain Other Financing or Other Equity (provide addendum if more space is needed)
Have you any outstanding judgments? In the last 7 years, have you been declared bankrupt?	No	No	
Have you had property foreclosed upon or given title or deed in lieu thereof?	No	No	
Are you a co maker or endorser on a note?	No	No	
Are you a party in a law suit?	No	No	
Are you obligated to pay alimony, child support, or separate maintenance?	No	No	
Is any part of the down payment borrowed?	No	No	

* FHLMC/FNMA require business credit report, signed Federal Income Tax returns for last two years, and, if available, audited Profit and Loss Statements plus balance sheet for same period.

** All Present Monthly Housing Expenses of Borrower and Co-Borrower should be listed on a combined basis.

*** Neither FHLMC nor FNMA requires this information

FHLMC 65 Rev. 8/78   FNMA 1003 Rev. 8/78

RESIDENTIAL LOAN APPLICATION

Exhibit 11-1.

This Statement and any applicable supporting schedules may be completed jointly by both married and unmarried co-borrowers if their assets and liabilities are sufficiently joined so that the Statement can be meaningfully and fairly presented on a combined basis; otherwise separate Statements and Schedules are required (FHLMC 65A/FNMA 1003A). If the co-borrower section was completed about a spouse, this statement and supporting schedules must be completed about that spouse also. ☐ Completed Jointly ☐ Not Completed Jointly

ASSETS		LIABILITIES AND PLEDGED ASSETS				
Description	Cash or Market Value	Creditors' Name, Address and Account Number	Acct. Name if Not Borrower's	Mo. Pmt. and Mos. left to pay		Unpaid Balance
				$ Pmt./Mos.		$
Cash Deposit Toward Purchase Held By	$	Installment Debts (include "revolving" charge accts)		/		
Homes Realty	1,000	Mastercharge		/		85.00
Checking and Savings Accounts (Show Names of Institutions/Acct. Nos.)				/		
Pike County Savings & Loan				/		
21-5579	19,450			/		
Stocks and Bonds (No./Description)				/		
None	None			/		
Life Insurance Net Cash Value Face Amount ($)	None	Other Debts Including Stock Pledges		/		
SUBTOTAL LIQUID ASSETS	$20,450					
Real Estate Owned (Enter Market Value from Schedule of Real Estate Owned)	None	Real Estate Loans		╳		
Vested Interest in Retirement Fund	None					
Net Worth of Business Owned (ATTACH FINANCIAL STATEMENT)	None					
Automobiles (Make and Year)		Automobile Loans				
1982 Dodge Charger	6,500	Ajax Credit Association		145/24		6,000
1974 Datsun 610	1,800	111-11111				
Furniture and Personal Property	3,800	Alimony, Child Support and Separate Maintenance Payments Owed To				
Other Assets (Itemize)				/		
		TOTAL MONTHLY PAYMENTS		$		
TOTAL ASSETS	A $ 32,550	NET WORTH (A minus B) $ 26,465		TOTAL LIABILITIES		B $ 6,085

SCHEDULE OF REAL ESTATE OWNED (If Additional Properties Owned Attach Separate Schedule)

Address of Property (Indicate S if Sold, PS if Pending Sale or R if Rental being held for income)	Type of Property	Present Market Value	Amount of Mortgages & Liens	Gross Rental Income	Mortgage Payments	Taxes, Ins. Maintenance and Misc.	Net Rental Income
None		$	$	$	$	$	$
TOTALS →		$	$	$	$	$	$

LIST PREVIOUS CREDIT REFERENCES

B - Borrower C - Co Borrower	Creditor's Name and Address	Account Number	Purpose	Highest Balance	Date Paid
B&C	First Citizens Bank, Crete, Any State	311-60142	Auto	$ 2,600	7-10-xx
B&C	Warsaw Furniture, Crete, Any State	011-3164	Furniture	4,500	8-24-xx
B&C	Buy Cheap Furniture, Crete, Any State	299-1492	Furniture	1,800	7-15-xx
		None			

List any additional names under which credit has previously been received

AGREEMENT   The undersigned applies for the loan indicated in this application to be secured by a first mortgage or deed of trust on the property described herein, and represents that the property will not be used for any illegal or restricted purpose, and that all statements made in this application are true and are made for the purpose of obtaining the loan. Verification may be obtained from any source named in this application. The original or a copy of this application will be retained by the lender, even if the loan is not granted. The undersigned ☐ intend or ☐ do not intend to occupy the property as their primary residence.

I/we fully understand that it is a federal crime punishable by fine or imprisonment, or both, to knowingly make any false statements concerning any of the above facts as applicable under the provisions of Title 18, United States Code, Section 1014.

_____ Date 9-15-xx   _____ Date 9-15-xx
Borrower's Signature   Co Borrower's Signature

INFORMATION FOR GOVERNMENT MONITORING PURPOSES

Instructions: Lenders must insert in this space, or on an attached addendum, a provision for furnishing the monitoring information required or requested under present Federal and/or present state law or regulation. For most lenders, the inserts provided in FHLMC Form 65-B/FNMA Form 1003-B can be used.

FOR LENDER S USE ONLY

(FNMA REQUIREMENT ONLY) This application was taken by ☐ face to face interview ☐ by mail ☐ by telephone

_____   _____
(Interviewer)   Name of Employer of Interviewer

FHLMC 65 Rev. 8/78   REVERSE   FNMA 1003 Rev. 8/78

Exhibit 11-2.   *Down Payment Deposit Verification*

Federal National Mortgage Association
REQUEST FOR VERIFICATION OF DEPOSIT

FNMA

INSTRUCTIONS: LENDER - Complete Items 1 thru 8. Have applicant(s) complete Item 9. Forward directly to depository named in Item 1.
DEPOSITORY - Please complete Items 10 thru 15 and return DIRECTLY to lender named in Item 2.

PART I - REQUEST

1 TO (Name and address of depository)	2 FROM (Name and address of lender)
Pike County Savings & Loan 129 Deposit Boulevard Crete, Any State 00000	Larry Lender 1234 Dollar Avenue Crete, Any State 00000

3 SIGNATURE OF LENDER	4 TITLE	5 DATE	6 LENDER'S NUMBER (Optional)
	Loan Officer		1717

7 INFORMATION TO BE VERIFIED

TYPE OF ACCOUNT	ACCOUNT IN NAME OF	ACCOUNT NUMBER	BALANCE
Now		21732983	$ 19,450
			$
			$
			$

TO DEPOSITORY I have applied for a mortgage loan and stated in my financial statement that the balance on deposit with you is as shown above. You are authorized to verify this information and to supply the lender identified above with the information requested in Items 10 thru 12. Your response is solely a matter of courtesy for which no responsibility is attached to your institution or any of your officers.

8 NAME AND ADDRESS OF APPLICANT(S)	9 SIGNATURE OF APPLICANT(S)
Will C. Carter 5665 College Avenue Crete, Any State 00000	

TO BE COMPLETED BY DEPOSITORY

PART II - VERIFICATION OF DEPOSITORY

10 DEPOSIT ACCOUNTS OF APPLICANT(S)

TYPE OF ACCOUNT	ACCOUNT NUMBER	CURRENT BALANCE	AVERAGE BALANCE FOR PREVIOUS TWO MONTHS	DATE OPENED
		$	$	
		$	$	
		$	$	
		$	$	

11 LOANS OUTSTANDING TO APPLICANT(S)

LOAN NUMBER	DATE OF LOAN	ORIGINAL AMOUNT	CURRENT BALANCE	INSTALLMENTS (Monthly/Quarterly)	SECURED BY	NUMBER OF LATE PAYMENTS
		$	$	$ per		
		$	$	$ per		
		$	$	$ per		

12 ADDITIONAL INFORMATION WHICH MAY BE OF ASSISTANCE IN DETERMINATION OF CREDIT WORTHINESS
(Please include information on loans paid-in-full as in Item 11 above)

13 SIGNATURE OF DEPOSITORY	14 TITLE	15 DATE

The confidentiality of the information you have furnished will be preserved except where disclosure of this information is required by applicable law. The form is to be transmitted directly to the lender and is not to be transmitted through the applicant or any other party.

PREVIOUS EDITION WILL BE USED UNTIL STOCK IS EXHAUSTED

FNMA Form 1006
Rev. June 78

VERIFICATION OF DEPOSIT FORM

Exhibit 11-3.   *Employment Verification*

Federal National Mortgage Association

REQUEST FOR VERIFICATION OF EMPLOYMENT

FNMA

INSTRUCTIONS: LENDER- Complete items 1 thru 7. Have applicant complete item 8. Forward directly to employer named in item 1.

EMPLOYER-Please complete either Part II or Part III as applicable. Sign and return directly to lender named in item 2.

PART I - REQUEST

1 TO *(Name and address of employer)*	2 FROM *(Name and address of lender)*
Dependable Electric Co. 135 Industry Drive Crete, Any State 00000	Peak Federal Savings & Loan 1234 Dollar Avenue Crete, Any State 00000

3. SIGNATURE OF LENDER	4. TITLE Loan Officer	5. DATE 10-19-xx	6. LENDER'S NUMBER *(optional)* 1717

I have applied for a mortgage loan and stated that I am now or was formerly employed by you. My signature below authorizes verification of this information.

7. NAME AND ADDRESS OF APPLICANT *(Include employee or badge number)* Tammy Carter 5665 College Avenue Crete, Any State 00000	8. SIGNATURE OF APPLICANT

PART II - VERIFICATION OF PRESENT EMPLOYMENT

EMPLOYMENT DATA	PAY DATA		
9. APPLICANT'S DATE OF EMPLOYMENT July 5, 19xx	12A. CURRENT BASE PAY (Enter Amount and Check Period) ☐ ANNUAL ☐ HOURLY ☒ MONTHLY ☐ OTHER ☐ WEEKLY *(Specify)* $ _____	12C. FOR MILITARY PERSONNEL ONLY	
10. PRESENT POSITION		PAY GRADE	

11. PROBABILITY OF CONTINUED EMPLOYMENT Good	12B. EARNINGS			TYPE	MONTHLY AMOUNT
	TYPE	YEAR TO DATE	PAST YEAR	BASE PAY	$
13 IF OVERTIME OR BONUS IS APPLICABLE, IS ITS CONTINUANCE LIKELY?	BASE PAY	$ 18,000	$ 17,500	RATIONS	$
	OVERTIME	$	$	FLIGHT OR HAZARD	$
				CLOTHING	$
	COMMISSIONS	$	$	QUARTERS	$
OVERTIME ☐ YES ☐ NO BONUS ☒ YES ☐ NO				PRO PAY	$
	BONUS	$ 1,000	$ 900	OVER SEAS OR COMBAT	$

14 REMARKS *(if paid hourly, please indicate average hours worked each week during current and past year)*

PART III - VERIFICATION OF PREVIOUS EMPLOYMENT

15. DATES OF EMPLOYMENT	16. SALARY/WAGE AT TERMINATION PER (Year) (Month) (Week) BASE _____ OVERTIME _____ COMMISSIONS _____ BONUS _____
17. REASON FOR LEAVING	18. POSITION HELD

19. SIGNATURE OF EMPLOYER	20. TITLE	21. DATE

The confidentiality of the information you have furnished will be preserved except where disclosure of this information is required by applicable law. The form is to be transmitted directly to the lender and is not to be transmitted through the applicant or any other party.

PREVIOUS EDITION WILL BE USED UNTIL STOCK IS EXHAUSTED

FNMA Form 1005
 Rev. June 78

VERIFICATION OF EMPLOYMENT FORM

Exhibit 11-4A.   The Truth-in-Lending Disclosure Statement

Date: October 6   , 19 XX   Loan No.:_____

Borrowers: Will C. & Tammy Carter

Address.   209 Boweevil Street

Lot 10, Block B, Cotton Hill Estates

Crete Peak, Any State

ANNUAL PERCENTAGE RATE	FINANCE CHARGE	Amount Financed	Total of Payments
The cost of your credit as a yearly rate.	The dollar amount the credit will cost you	The amount of credit provided to you or on your behalf.	The amount you will have paid after you have made all payments as scheduled
12.4 maturity 12.7 7 years %	$	$68,000	$251,805.60

You have the right to receive at this time an itemization of the Amount Financed
☐ I want an itemization.   ☐ I do not want an itemization.

Your payment schedule will be:

Number of Payments	Amount of Payments	When Payments are Due
360	$ 699.46	1st of each month, beginning Dec. 1, 19xx
	$	
	$	

☐ This obligation has a demand Feature.

Insurance: Credit life insurance and credit disability insurance are not required to obtain credit, and will not be provided unless you sign and agree to pay the additional cost. No such insurance will be in force until you have completed an application, the insurance company has issued the policy, the effective date of that policy has arrived and the required premium has been paid

Type	Premium	Term	Signature
Credit Life	$		I want to apply for credit life insurance.
Credit Disability	$		I want to apply for credit disability insurance.
Credit Life and Credit Disability	$		I want to apply for credit life and disability insurance.

You may obtain property insurance from anyone you want that is acceptable to this institution. If you get the insurance from _____
_____ you will pay $_____ for a term of_____

Security: You are giving a security interest in:
☐ the goods or property being purchased
☐ _____
Filing fees $_____ Non-filing insurance $_____

Late Charge: If payment is _____ late, you will be charged $_____ % of the payment.

Prepayment: If you pay off early, you
☐ may ☒ will not   have to pay a penalty.
☐ may ☒ will not   be entitled to a refund of part of the finance charge.

☐ **Required Deposit:** The annual percentage rate does not take into account your required deposit

See your contract documents for any additional information about nonpayment, default, any required repayment in full before the scheduled date, and prepayment refunds and penalties.
e means an estimate

I/We hereby acknowledge receipt of this disclosure.

_____   _____
                                    DATE
_____   _____
                                    DATE

TRUTH-IN-LENDING DISCLOSURE

Exhibit 11-4B. Settlement Statement

A.	U.S. DEPARTMENT OF HOUSING AND URBAN DEVELOPMENT SETTLEMENT STATEMENT.		B. TYPE OF LOAN	

Peak Federal Savings and Loan Association
202 College Avenue
Crete, Any State 30601

B. TYPE OF LOAN

Conventional Single Family

6. FILE NUMBER	7. LOAN NUMBER
021-315	57-311

8. MORT. INS. CASE NO.
N/A

C. NOTE: This form is furnished to give you a statement of actual settlement costs. Amounts paid to and by the settlement agent are shown. Items marked "(p.o.c.)" were paid outside the closing; they are shown here for informational purposes and are not included in the totals.

D. NAME OF BORROWER:	E. NAME OF SELLER:	F. NAME OF LENDER:
Will and Tammy Carter	H. O. Mowner	Peak Federal Savings and Loans

G. PROPERTY LOCATION:	H. SETTLEMENT AGENT:	I. SETTLEMENT DATE:
209 Boweevil Street 108 Cotton Hills Estates Crete, Any State	PLACE OF SETTLEMENT.	29 Oct. 19xx

J. SUMMARY OF BORROWER'S TRANSACTION		K. SUMMARY OF SELLER'S TRANSACTION	
100. GROSS AMOUNT DUE FROM BORROWER		400. GROSS AMOUNT DUE TO SELLER	
101. Contract sales price	85,000	401. Contract sales price	85,000
102. Personal property	--	402. Personal property	
103. Settlement charges to borrower (line 1400)	2,985	403.	
104.		404.	
105.		405.	
Adjustments for items paid by seller in advance		Adjustments for items paid by seller in advance	
106. City/town taxes to		406. City/town taxes to	
107. County taxes to		407. County taxes to	
108. Assessments to		408. Assessments to	
109.		409.	
110.		410.	
111.		411.	
112.		412.	
120. GROSS AMOUNT DUE FROM BORROWER	87,985	420. GROSS AMOUNT DUE TO SELLER	85,000
200. AMOUNTS PAID BY OR IN BEHALF OF BORROWER		500. REDUCTIONS IN AMOUNT DUE TO SELLER	
201. Deposit or earnest money	1,000	501. Excess deposit (see instructions)	
202. Principal amount of new loan(s)	68,000	502. Settlement charges to seller (line 1400)	5,105
203. Existing loan(s) taken subject to		503. Existing loan(s) taken subject to	
204.		504. Payoff of first mortgage loan	36,675
205.		505. Payoff of second mortgage loan	12,500
206.		506.	
207.		507.	
208.		508.	
209.		509.	
Adjustments for items unpaid by seller		Adjustments for items unpaid by seller	
210. City/town taxes to		510. City/town taxes to	
211. County taxes 1-1-xx to 12-1-xx	935	511. County taxes 1-1-xx to 12-1-xx	935
212. Assessments to		512. Assessments to	
213.		513.	
214.		514.	
215.		515.	
216.		516.	
217.		517.	
218.		518.	
219.		519.	
220. TOTAL PAID BY FOR BORROWER	69,935	520. TOTAL REDUCTION AMOUNT DUE SELLER	55,215
300. CASH AT SETTLEMENT FROM OR TO BORROWER		600. CASH AT SETTLEMENT TO OR FROM SELLER	
301. Gross amount due from borrower (line 120)	87,985	601. Gross amount due to seller (line 420)	85,000
302. Less amounts paid by for borrower (line 220)	69,935	602. Less reduction amount due seller (line 520)	55,215
303. CASH BORROWER	18,050	603. CASH SELLER	29,785

HUD-1A   REV. 10/77

Exhibit 11-5.   Good Faith Estimate of Settlement Charges

GOOD FAITH ESTIMATE
OF SETTLEMENT CHARGES

Listed below is the Good Faith Estimate of Settlement Charges made pursuant to the requirements of the Real Estate Settlement Procedures Act (RESPA). These figures are only estimates and the actual charges due at settlement, may be different. This is not a commitment.

		Estimated Charge	or	Range	of	Charges
801	Loan Origination Fee	$ 680.00			to	
	(Includes Item No.)					
802	Loan Discount	$1,360.00			to	
803	Appraisal Fee	$ 100.00			to	
804	Credit Report	$ 15.00			to	
805	Lender's Inspection Fee	$ --			to	
806	Mortgage Insurance Application Fee	$ --			to	
807	Assumption Fee	$ --			to	
901	Interest	$ --			to	
902	Mortgage Insurance Premium	$ --			to	
1101	Settlement or Closing Fee	$ --			to	
1102	Abstract or Title Search	$ --			to	
1105	Document Preparation	$ 25.00			to	
1106	Notary Fees	$ --			to	
1107	Attorney Fees	$ 175.00			to	
	(Includes Item No.)					
1108	Title Insurance	$ 250.00			to	
	(Includes Item No.)					
1201	Recording Fees	$ 35.00			to	
1301	Survey	$ 90.00			to	
1302	Pest Inspection	$			to	
		$			to	
	Total	$2,730.00			to	

In lieu of individual settlement charges, the lender at its option may elect to absorb all settlement charges and charge a fixed amount. If so, instead of amounts, all of the services and items checked above are included in the following fixed amount, in accordance with Section 3500.7(f) and 3500.8(d)(2), of the Real Estate Settlement Procedures Act. $ ————

This form does not cover all items you will be required to pay in cash at settlement, for example, deposits in escrow for real estate taxes and insurance. You may wish to inquire as to the amounts of such other items, as you may be required to pay other additional amounts at settlement.

THIS SECTION TO BE COMPLETED BY LENDER ONLY IF A PARTICULAR PROVIDER OF SERVICE IS REQUIRED

Listed below are providers of service which we require you use. The charges or range indicated in the Good Faith Estimate above are based upon the corresponding charge of the below designated providers.

Designated Charge Item No.	Phone No.	Item No.	Phone No.
Service Provided			
Providers Name			
Address			

We (☐ do), (☐ do not), have a business relationship with the above named provider.   We (☐ do), (☐ do not), have a business relationship with the above named provider.

Delivery of the above Good Faith Estimate and the booklet entitled "Settlement Costs and You" is hereby acknowledged.

Applicant's Signature,
or Mailed By: Date

Address of Subject Property

GOOD FAITH ESTIMATE

CHAPTER 12

The Sure-fire System to Seek out the Best Available Mortgage Lenders, and to Comparison-shop for the Best Loan for You

A. FOLLOW THESE GUIDELINES TO SEEK OUT THE BEST POSSIBLE MORTGAGE SOURCE

A comprehensive listing of the major sources for mortgage loans in the banking industry, and the peculiar characteristics and attributes of each source, are fully set forth in Chapter 2. You should be sure to go through that chapter. Refer, also, to Chapter 3 for the different types of mortgages available. *In general, to find a lender (whether they be those falling within the categories listed in Chapter 2 or otherwise), follow the following guidelines:*

- Make a list of possible mortgage lenders in your area and in the area where you'll like to buy a home. Look in the phone book under "Mortgages", "Banks," "Savings and Loan Associations," "Mutual Savings Banks," "Mortgage Bankers/Brokers," and the like.

- Ask your real estate agents (see Chapter 16, especially at p. 130, for how to pick the right ones) for leads. A number of real estate agencies possess extensive data banks that list mortgage offerings.

- A good place to start, if you are a good customer there, is your own bank. Call your own bank first. If they are willing to give you the type of loan you need, then just check around with the other lenders merely to compare the interest rates and other costs and charges.

- Look in the local newspapers that provide home-for-sale information, and articles and advertisements about the latest mortgage rates from lenders.

- Seek referrals from friends and customers in the area, check to see whether your credit union, or your insurance company, if applicable, issues mortgages.

- Always find out, whenever possible, the present bank where the existing mortgage is placed for the house you are considering buying. Other than the seller himself, the mortgage-holding bank which presently has the money invested in the property, is often the best possibility for financing a purchase and such banks are often anxious to do business even if with a little monetary incentive.

- As an alternative to having to conduct an extensive search of the marketplace yourself for the best loan or loan source, you may consider simply contacting a "mortgage broker," and letting him do it for you – that is, a professional who specializes in finding and matching lenders with borrowers for a living. (He gets paid a commission, not by the borrower or the home seller, but by the lending institution, based on the loan amount he "places" with the lender). A great many real estate brokers (though not all) either qualify as, or function as mortgage brokers as well.

Indeed, in recent times, more and more Americans have been using mortgage brokers to find their mortgage loans for them. It has become quite a dramatic shift in role: according to recent government study report, the percentage of all home mortgage applications in the United States that are written by mortgage brokers has grown dramatically from only 20 percent in 1987, to the point where it's now about 50 percent of all home mortgage loans issued per year, today. [See Chapter 2, at p.16 for more on this].

Generally, a mortgage broker, especially the good and experienced ones, will keep up with the ups and downs of the local mortgage market, and would have developed an ongoing working relationship with some one dozen or so loan officers and mortgage lending institutions. And, in light of his need to preserve his "professional credibility" with his loan sources and the fact that he'd lose out on his commission unless he can place the loan, you can be certain that the mortgage broker will usually not take you on or steer you to a source, unless he's first certain that your loan application stands some fair chance. He will, if he is among the good and competent ones, instantly know the answers to the important basic questions: Where is mortgage money currently available? What lenders today are making loans and what different variations of loan? What size of loan? Is there a bargain loan available – a certain loan variation or long-term loan available at a smaller interest rate than others? Are there lenders whose approach towards property or credit analysis will tend to favor your own particular profile?

[The same criteria recommended in pp. 130 with respect to picking the right real estate broker, are equally applicable here, and should be followed in attempting to pick the right mortgage broker.]

- Some local newspapers in various parts of the country publish comparative information on mortgage rates and provisions. For example, for a weekly subscription cost, a publication called **The National Mortgage Weekly** (P.O. Box 18081, Cleveland, OH 44118, Phone: 216-371-2767), provides information on mortgages in selected metropolitan areas, such as Boston, Cleveland, Columbus and Detroit. Another specialized paper, **The Mortgage Journal** (Essay, Inc., Box 2776, Westport, CT 06880, Phone: 203-454-6480/226-1498), carries advertising but lists, weekly, a wide variety of mortgages available in Connecticut, New York, New Jersey and various parts of New England. In any case, you can always check the real estate section of your local newspaper, or phone the paper and inquire whether it runs such comparisons.

- Read advertisements and promotional materials of banks and lenders very carefully. They don't always tell you all you need to know; in fact, they can't, or there won't be room for the ad! Get all the information you need, independently, before you make a decision.

- Don't be too tempted or automatically persuaded simply by an interest rate that may be way below the market rate. How long is the rate good for? (Mortgages, especially adjustable-rate mortgages, can have "introductory" rates). Are there higher fees and/or points that will be incurred to make up for that low rate?

- Consider, quite seriously, taking advantage of a recent innovation that's becoming increasingly very popular among mortgage seekers, namely, using the services of a Computerized Mortgage Search Organization to find a suitable mortgage for you. These organizations specialize in comparing mortgage rates and terms on a regional or national basis, and for a modest fee will provide comparative information on mortgages offered by dozens of lenders in a designated area of the country.

In the past when borrowers wanted to find a loan with the best rate and terms to fit their situation, they would have to make laborious contact with, and collect information from, each lender. These problems are now alleviated with the development of computerized mortgage services. As a borrower, you can now collect and compare loan information on many lenders easily and quickly, including lenders in other parts of the country, by using these services. **These services, though very useful, are by no means a complete substitute for shopping around by you, however.** Nevertheless, the great advantage of such service is that this information can help you find available low-cost mortgage, and thereby save you time in your comparison-shopping work. YOU SHOULD BE AWARE, HOWEVER, OF THIS IMPORTANT FACT: *that not all services that call themselves computerized mortgage information service, are truly a mortgage search service* (some are run by only one particular lender, for example), nor would the information put out by every such organization be necessarily or always useful to you as a borrower (the data bank's information may not always be up-to-date, or cover a large enough number of lenders in your area).

The largest and best known of such mortgage search service companies in the United States, is an organization called **HSH Associates**. For a $20 fee, the HSH (1200 Route 23, Butler, New Jersey 07405, Phone 1-800-UPDATES) will provide you a printout of some 20 to 60 lenders and their lending policies for lenders operating in the purchase area you specify anywhere in the U.S., and will offer you weekly updates thereafter (at $18 additional for each week). Another organization, the *Seldin Organization* in New Hyde Park, New York, which is paid to offer the service by the participating bankers, offers a similar service free of charge to callers. Their phone number is 1-(516) 775-2200.

- For a $20 fee to cover the cost for a single city or for an entire state, you'll get a mortgage report from an organization, **Gary S. Meyers & Associates** (308 West Erie Street, Suite 300, Chicago, IL, 60610, Phone: 312-642-9000), which resembles information offered by HSH Associates. Its chief executive, Gary Meyers, writes a syndicated column about mortgages that appear in 200-newspaper nation-wide, including Chicago Sun Times and Houston Post. And **Peeke LoanFax Inc** (101Chestnut Avenue, Suite 200, Gaithersburg, MD 20877; Phone 301-840-5752), provides mortgage information on about 100 Washington, D.C., Maryland and Virginia area banks. The reports can be obtained at a cost of $20 for the first report, and $15 for updates.

- Finally, there is one computerized mortgage service which stands out among most others in that it offers borrowers a slightly different service. Unlike most other such services, it does not merely offer borrowers (or lenders) published mortgage information, reports or listings for their use. Rather, the way its service works is that information provided by you (the borrower) is entered into its computer system comprised of a network of lenders nationwide; this then produces a range of mortgage prices listing the ones you can best afford. You then review all of the loan options offered, each sorted out by loan type, interest rate, annual percentage rate, down payment requirements, or other variables. After reviewing all the loan options provided, you (the borrower) then select a mortgage that best suits your needs, and thereupon you fill out an application. Verification forms and supporting documents for your application are electronically transmitted by computer to the lender(s) you selected to speed up the loan processing, and the originals of the loan documents are then sent by messenger service. Among other advantages, this system has the advantage of allowing lenders to begin processing your loan *immediately*.

There are several computerized mortgage networks of this type operating in the country. One of them, is **Rennie Mae**, which is developed by the **National Association of Realtors** (NAR). To avail yourself of this service, simply ask your lender or real estate broker whether they have this service, since this service is marketed nationwide to the real estate industry by the NAR and is open to participating member lenders and brokers nationwide.

B. YOU MUST THEN DO SOME COMPARISON-SHOPPING AROUND BEFORE YOU SETTLE ON A FINAL MORTGAGE PICK

Perhaps, the single, most important factor essential for any prospective homebuyer in a search for a mortgage, is to be sure that he or she absolutely does some SHOPPING AROUND first, before eventually settling on a mortgage deal. This is so because, as one analyst rightly sums it up, "all loan terms are not the same. Some institutions charge higher rates or higher up-front costs than others. Without shopping around first, you might pay far too high a price to finance your house and not even know it. You can't know until you do some comparison shopping for yourself."[1]

Indeed, for a borrower, the potential savings from comparison-shopping for a mortgage could be quite large. Surveys of mortgage rates have found, for example, that the difference which exists between the most expensive and least expensive fixed-rate mortgages available in a given city, is often about 1 percentage point. This may not sound like much on the surface, but in reality it actually amounts to a huge sum of money over the years in terms of the interest cost. On a 30-year, $80,000 loan in Philadelphia, for example, the difference (additional cost to the borrower) was found to amount to $37,557; while the difference on a similar loan in New York, had amounted to a whopping $41,006![2] Consequently, you should be absolutely aware of one thing: *that comparison-shopping for your loan is probably the single most vital element in ensuring that you make a wise and cost-effective mortgage decision*.

The point to emphasize and reemphasize here, is that whatever method or source you ultimately settle on, or use, in finding your mortgage loans [Section A above], and whoever you use for that purpose, whether you made a direct personal application to the lending institution, or used a real estate broker, a mortgage broker, or a computerized mortgage network service as your source, *the one thing you still must always do in the end, is to "comparison shop around" independently before making a final choice*. Many loan applicants are so thrilled at being able to find a lender willing to "give" them a loan, that they jump at the first loan offer they get just because it's available and look no further. This needs not be the case. It would still pay to shop around, to call upon other lenders and compare costs and loan features—chances still are, that another lender down the street will find you just as worthy of a loan, and perhaps even at better terms! And, in line with that, just because the realtor, or the seller, "refers" you to or "recommends" a particular bank or mortgage company, don't just automatically accept its offer blindly. You should still do some independent searching and checking on your own, regardless. [Such referral or recommendation may not always be the best deal for you. In some instances, the recommender may – just may – be getting a commission ("finder's fees") from that particular lender for steering your loan to him, and if so, BEWARE: you may not be getting the most competitive terms available; the type of loan that may best suit you could be the last thing in his mind!!]

John R. Dorfman, a widely respected mortgage specialist and long-time writer for the Wall Street Journal, emphasizes, as most other experts in real estate finance industry frequently do, that "the potential savings from comparison shopping for a mortgage are quite large." Dorfman adds, "So, if you're going to pay attention to any single piece of advice in this book, make it this one: Shop around!

[1] Michael C. Thomsett, *Your Home Mortgage*, p. 38.
[2] Facts, as recounted by John R. Dorfman, p. 69.

Casting your net wide you're much more likely to make an attractive catch…get mortgage quotes from at least 10 lenders. Fifteen or twenty might be even better."[3]

A recent report by the HSH Associates, one of the nation's largest publishers of mortgage information, sums up its advice on the matter to aspiring home buyers, in these words:

> …There are a lot of lenders [who would be] competing for your business…savings and loans, savings banks, and other thrift institutions…commercial banks…mortgage banks…credit unions…and mortgage brokers…all of these types of lenders are vying for your business…Rates and terms vary widely from lender to lender.
>
> Don't hesitate to shop, you never know who might have your 'best' mortgage! Everyone has his own system for mortgage shopping …In general, the more thoroughly you shop, the best chances of finding just the right program, with the right terms, and at saving considerable amounts of money on your mortgage. Many consumers use HSH updates [which list mortgage bankers and institutions and their terms] to follow the market before applying. They watch for lenders who are consistently competitive with their chosen program, narrow down the choices to two or three lenders, and, when they are ready to apply, select the lender which best meets their needs.[4]

A CENTRAL QUESTION: HOW DO YOU COMPARISON-SHOP?

In Chapter 13, we outline a comprehensive but simple system of undertaking your mortgage comparison-shopping. In the meantime, though, there's one relatively uncomplicated and cheap method of comparison-shopping that you can almost always use: using the telephone to make a "phone poll" of lenders who advertise in the area's regional newspapers and to ask them all the right questions previously enumerated above.

---

[3] Dorfman, pp. 69-70

[4] Another expert voice, by Richard F. Gabriel, the real estate sales specialist and author, makes a similar point: "Shopping for a mortgage, contrary to popular opinion, does not mean getting a quote from one, two, or three local lending sources, but requires extensive systematic search for the best possible deal." Gabriel advises loan seekers: "Prepare a chart, and on the left side indicate all the items that you'd want to know concerning a possible mortgage being offered to you, such as interest rate, whether the rate is fixed or variable, the term of the mortgage, percentage of cash down required, the number of points required, any prepayment penalty conditions, and so on. Then visit as many banks or savings and loan associations…**Do not just talk to one, or two, or three possible lending sources and from that assume that all lending sources will have the same story to tell you. In order to get the best possible overall mortgage for yourself, you should contact, in person where possible, from five to ten lending sources.** Why so many? Because different lending sources have different changing needs at different times and there is no way that you can anticipate what kind of mortgage package and costs will be offered unless you make **direct contact**. What a lender was prepared to offer to do, mortgage-wise, 30 to 90 days ago, is different than what they're prepared to offer you today. Also, what a possible mortgage lender was willing to offer a friend, associate or acquaintance of yours, has little or nothing to do with what they might, or might not, be willing to offer you. Also, different lenders might perceive you differently as a security, risk and growth, etc…" ("How to Buy Your Own House When You Don't Have Enough Money!" pp. 87-88).

CHAPTER 13

You Can Secure Your Mortgage Loan 99 Percent of the Time! Here Ar the Complete, Sure-fire Formula to Accomplish This Almost Always

A. YES, BY FOLLOWING A FEW SIMPLE PROCEDURES, IT'S POSSIBLE TO SECURE FINANCING ALMOST ALWAYS!

Banks and bankers are in business to lend out money to customers. That, in fact, is their only business! I f they don't lend out their funds to customers like you, they don't earn the profits they need to earn in order to pay back their depositors or those from whom they have, themselves, borrowed the money they now re-lend to you. In short, they are anxious to find people they can lend monies to – people like you. And, as a rule, they generally have a lot of it (money) at hand ready and available to be lent out. SO, THE FUNDAMENTAL QUESTION BECOMES, THEN: "Why then should you even have any problem getting a mortgage?" The answer is simply this: *All mortgage lenders have a 'short list' of principles and requirements which, if only you were to be able to satisfy them, the bank will be more than ready and happy to grant you the mortgage loan you desire in no time*.

If the truth be told, the more probable reality is that you have probably been led all your life to believe otherwise; to believe that getting a mortgage is a complicated and difficult affair, perhaps even an impossible thing to do. But, you had better believed this here and now: *the fact, actually, is that you can get a mortgage in 24 hours – yes, an approval of your loan application the very next day after you've submitted your application to the lender.* And don't think, either, that we're talking about this happening only in a few select unique eases involving just exceptional occasions or circumstances. Not at all! Quite to the contrary, we're talking in terms of its being something that's ordinary and routine with the average loan applicant and loan application. Actually, the reality of the mortgage industry world is that real estate agents, mortgage brokers, bankers and real estate brokers, do precisely that same thing all the time. They, simply, happen to know what exactly is *the 'short list' of principles and requirements of their bankers* which their loan applicants need to satisfy in order to be instantaneously rewarded with a loan.

Here in this chapter, we outline, in a simple step-by-step format, the several steps and procedures you should take, and which, if taken, will almost guarantee that you'll get your mortgage request approval some 99 percent of the time within 24-hours – or that you will, at least, have the loan officer assure you that you've met the bank's criteria for a loan.

CAUTION: This Mortgage Qualification system works! We know that because we've tried and pre-tested the procedures over and over again. It sure will work for you. But don't expect magic. It can only work for you if you follow the instructions closely and comply with them, and employ some common sense and intelligence. *Let's emphasize once again*. TO BE ABLE TO GET THE LOAN APPROVAL WITH ALL EASE AND SIMPLICITY, THE CENTRAL KEY IS THIS: YOU MUST FOLLOW AND DO THE PROCEDURES OUTLINED BELOW, STEP-BY-STEP – IN EXACTLY THE SAME ORDER IN WHICH THEY ARE LISTED BELOW IN THIS CHAPTER. DON'T (REPEAT, DON'T) SKIP OR JUMP AROUND!

B. STEP-BY-STEP PROCEDURES FOR GETTING YOUR LOAN APPROVAL ALMOST EVERY TIME YOU APPLY.

To get your mortgage loan approval almost every time you apply for a loan, just follow these simple STEPS and guidelines systematically, in the EXACT order they are listed below:

STEP ❶ : COMPILE AN HONEST, COMPREHENSIVE, OBJECTIVE EVALUATION OF YOUR PRESENT FINANCIAL CONDITION

Refer to Chapter 8 on pp. 55-9. Figure out your cash needs for a home purchase, as well as your current income, expenses and net worth

STEP ❷ : STUDY THE VARIOUS TYPES OF MORTGAGES AVAILABLE AND DETERMINE WHICH SPECIFIC TYPE IS BEST TO CHOOSE

In Chapter 3, we have outlined the different types of mortgages which are available in the home financing industry, setting forth the special characteristics of each type, how each works, and the advantages and disadvantages of each. For your maximum benefit, you should study the different types of mortgages outlined in Chapter 3, as well as the related matters covered in Chapters 4, 5, and 6. Then, you should zero in on that particular type of mortgage you'd prefer which best suits your needs and can best work for you.

Nevertheless, for our purposes here in the interest of practicality and simplicity, we wish to remind you of this: that *of these 16 or so different varieties of mortgage types, the type of mortgages most used and best preferred by the overwhelming majority of homebuyers, historically as well as today, still remains the FIXED-RATE Mortgages.* (The other commonly used mortgage types, in their order of "popularity" and preference with home buyers, are as follows: Adjustable Rate Mortgage (ARM), and the *Home Equity Mortgage* loans, which are not really a mortgage in the 'pure' sense of the term in that it merely provides cash to persons who already own a house).[1] *OUR SUGGESTION SIMPLY IS THIS*: in light of the long-standing preference for the fixed-rate mortgage by American homebuyers, and because of the fact that for most homebuyers it still remains the best choice relative to all other types of mortgages, just to keep it simple and practicable, simply go for a fixed-rate mortgage. Study,

---

[1] The other types of mortgages covered in Chapter 3 – balloon mortgage, growing-equity mortgages, share appreciation mortgages, etc. – are comparatively rare these days. However, homebuyers who may be interested in any of these types of mortgages may inquire with their banks or lenders for more information or details about those.

thoroughly, Chapters 4 and 7. Chapter 7 will help you in the area of making a determination on some of the basic factors that are relevant in making a choice of a mortgage, such as the term (length or duration) of a mortgage loan, the interest rate, the foregone interest on the borrower's savings, and taxes payable.

If you qualify for, and are interest in, the *Veteran Administration* (VA) and *Federal Housing Administration* (FHA) mortgages (Chapter 5), you should, of course, still go for it. VA loans, you should recall from Chapter 5, are always a fixed-rate mortgage, and FHA loans are overwhelmingly fixed-rate mortgages.

STEP ❸ : DETERMINE THE HOME PRICE RANGE YOU CAN AFFORD

Experts tells us that only 1 out of every 3 prospects who go looking at a particular house to purchase, can really afford to buy it. Consequently, one of the best ways to survey your chances for being able to secure a specific mortgage loan is to assume the role of the mortgage lender itself. Here's what you do. DETERMINE, OF YOURSELF, OBJECTIVELY AND CRITICALLY, THIS QUESTION: *Would you lend mortgage money to yourself?* You do this primarily by physically working out some numbers to determine what kind of home price range you can realistically afford.

Refer to Chapter 9, especially Section C thereof, for some quick rule-of-thumb formulas used in the real estate industry for doing this.

STEP ❹ : SEEK OUT THE BEST LENDERS, AND THEN 'COMPARISON SHOP' TO SELECT THE BEST LOAN FOR YOU

The Mortgage Shopping and Selection System (Fixed-rate Mortgages). To put it in a summarized form, here is a mortgage search and comparison-shopping system that can help you narrow down your mortgage financing possibilities and ensure an excellent final pick for you. The example used here, is for a fixed-rate mortgage, but the procedures are just as applicable for all other types of mortgages. You can modify this list and procedures to fit your individual priorities and circumstances. [Most of the concepts and provisions, such as APR, lock-in, prepayment penalty, etc., have been discussed in previous chapters].

    1. Get basic information from as many lenders as you can find on the mortgages they offer. To do this, simply use Figure 13-1, *"Mortgage Information Form: Questions to Ask the Mortgage Company"* (pp.103 or 104). You may send a copy of the form to each mortgage source or lender you select and request that it fill in the information for you. Or, you may simply phone the lender or mortgage source and take the information over the phone. Use any of the mortgage sources and methods you prefer from among all those outlined in Chapter 12 to select the lenders to send the form to. Use of the Mortgage Information Form makes it easier for you to compare one lender's mortgage against another. Collect mortgage information and details widely and extensively – from some 20, 30, or more lenders scattered across different geographical areas.

    2. Decide on the loan terms you want. Do you want it to be a 15-year loan term, 30 years, or some other term? Just remember (Chapter 1) that stretching out your mortgage for a long period of time lowers the monthly payment you'll need to be making on the loan; but, on the other hand, it means you pay (it would cost you) far more overall in total interest. [See Chapter 1 at p. 10 and Chapter 7, for some insights on this]. Once you decide on the term, you can compare different lenders' offerings on an equal basis.

3. To begin the comparison-shopping for the loans, compare the Annual Percentage Rate (APR). For each loan you're evaluating, be sure to look at the APR. This tells you the effective interest rate after adding in certain charges, notably points, that aren't in the specifically stated rate. The extra charges are spread over the life of the loan, so the APR gives you an accurate gauge of the cost if the loan is held for its full 15, 20, or 30-year or so term. (See Chapter 7). Now, to begin to narrow down your choice of mortgages under consideration, eliminate approximately half of the mortgages you have seen at this point – those that have higher APRs.

4. Focus on points. From among the remaining mortgages with similar or identical APRs, discard those that charge the most points up front. The reason? Because, as a rule, these loans will prove the most costly if you should live in the home for only a few years, or fail to finish out the loan term.

5. Look at the other loan provisions. Now, from among those mortgages that are similar in APR and points charged, identify any that have favorable provisions on other loan features – such as on prepayment (no prepayment penalty), assumability of the mortgage from the preexisting borrower, and lock-in of interest rate. Remember that while – ideally – you would like the loan to be assumable, it is not too common to find an assumability feature on a fixed-rate loan, and would actually be a pleasant surprise to find one that has that feature.

6. Do a 10-year analysis. Once you've narrowed down your list of candidates to only two, three, four, or five mortgages, do a 10-year analysis (using the Worksheet on page 53). The specific purpose for which this analysis is designed, is to see which mortgage would be cheaper if you were to stay in the home for 10 years. The APR computation is made based on the assumption that the new home buyer would keep the mortgage for its entire 15, 25, or 30-year term. And so, since many home buyers take out 30 year mortgages, and most of them don't, in fact, stay in the home for the full 30 years (the average for American homeowners as of 1998 Census Report is 8.2 years), it is considered that a 10-year analysis such as this, provides a somewhat realistic perspective for comparing between different mortgages with differentials in the interest rates and number of points being charged by the lenders.

7. Consider the reputation of the lender. Ask your real estate agents (both those you might have used, as well as others), mortgage bankers or brokers, friends, acquaintances, the lender's other customers and previous borrowers, etc., what they know concerning the reputation of the lenders you're still considering. For example, do the lenders serve their customers in a prompt, helpful manner? Do they impose charges or fees that aren't clearly spelled out in advance? To answer these questions, you may also want to consult the local Better Business Bureau in your area, or to check newspaper and magazine articles about the lender through a library or computer database.

8. If you're still in doubt, at this stage, here are some tiebreakers.
   (a). Choose from the two best mortgages with the lowest APRs.
   (b). If the final candidates you're considering have the same APR, choose from the two lenders that are more conveniently located, or the ones that appear likely to process your loan application more quickly.

9. Other general principles of comparison-shopping:
In comparing between different lenders' mortgage packages, consider ALL the fees and charges, and consider that other options which are built into a mortgage contract (such as assumability or the right to convert a loan from an adjustable-rate to a fixed-rate, etc.) have some economic value

all the same; don't simply confine your review to only the interest rate, or only a combination of the rate and number of points.

• Evaluate fees charged (interest, points, closing costs, other one-time costs, etc.) *based primarily on the length of time you realistically think you will own the house.* If you're pretty certain that you will move to a bigger or more expensive home in 5 years or less, you should pretty much go for the loan with the lowest up-front fees and charges, even if that means paying a higher interest rate.

• Always make your comparisons of the different loan programs offered by lenders with two, three or more lenders. That is, don't simply compare different programs offered by one lender, without also comparing them to the packages offered by several other lenders. It's much like buying a new car and wanting to compare features between two, three or more dealers.

• ALWAYS NEGOTIATE! The borrowing of money is no different from any other business: everything is still subject to negotiations. No matter what the loan officer tells you about his lender's offer and about the conditions for a loan in terms of the interest rate, the number of points, and other features, never, ever consider that it's final and cast in concrete and is no more negotiable. Not at all! Quite to the contrary, you can still negotiate on any terms and conditions of the loan offer. One good way to negotiate is by comparing the terms offered you to a competitor's terms. For example, by knowing the mortgage market thoroughly and knowing what other competitors offer, you can go to the lender and simply ask for a match to the terms offered by another bank. You might, for example, ask a lender to match the rates and points of a competitor, or to leave in a prepayment, or assumability or conversion priviledge, or to include a no-charge line of credit for, say, $4,000 with the loan.

STEP ⑤: DO NOT EVER FILE A LOAN APPLICATION UNLESS YOU FIRST HAVE CERTAIN IDEAL CONDITIONS AND DON'T HAVE CERTAIN PROBLEMS

To be in the strongest position possible, it's always advisable not to file an application for a mortgage loan unless you have, FIRST, CERTAIN IDEAL CONDITIONS PREVAILING:

    1. *Do not start an application if you've only had a short period at your job or if you are just starting on a new job, or there have been sudden layoffs, within your department or company:* Accepting a higher-paying position at another company with a better career outlook may be good, but changing jobs for any other reason is another matter altogether.

    2. *Do not start an application if you lack savings and/or are not even contributing to your employee-sponsored retirement plan at work:* To lenders, this might be a "red flag" that you are living from paycheck to paycheck, and that you may have difficulty paying your monthly mortgage loan. If you were to become sick or disabled for a few months and cannot work, wait a few months, or even a year, if necessary, and build up a reasonable cash reserve. Besides, you'll need to have available a down payment fund, as well as extra money for the closing costs.

    3. *Do not start an application if there is trouble in paradise:* If you (a husband or wife) have been having problems, don't just choose to believe it will go away by simply deciding that buying that new home (or having a new child) is what you really need; that this is what is really going to change things for you financially. They usually don't. Quite to the contrary, sooner or later, everything comes crashing down like a wave and one spouse or the other decides to leave while the other is stuck with mortgage payments that are now unaffordable. Better believe it, buying a house and getting a big home loan is not the remedy to a troubled marriage. Further more, as a rule, lenders have a special liking and preference for applicants who exhibit some promise of "stability" – persons who are in the same job and the same house and town for years and years, and are in the same marriage for long.

4. *Do not start any application if you still have large credit card balances:* this apparently happens many more times than can be imagined, say the experts. "I cannot begin to count the number of times I have sat down across the table from an applicant with $20,000 or $30,000 in accumulated credit card debt who wants to buy a house and hardly has any money for a down payment," states one exasperated financial analyst and loan consultant[2] with over 2000 successful loan transactions. "Now," he adds, "how much sense does that make?" As far as a lender is concerned, the size of your existing debts will directly affect your ability to service a new one – the mortgage loan. Hence, experts generally advise that as much as possible, before you ever apply for a mortgage, you should pay down a large portion of your credit card and personal loan debts. *If you are to be paying down these debts, however, you must do so at least a month or two prior to applying for the loan*: it takes credit card companies that much time to update your current balances in your credit files. (Your recently discharged debts may still show up on the credit report drawn on you by your lender. However, once a debt has been paid off, you need not list it thereafter on your mortgage application form. You merely should be prepared, however, to show the lender some proof that the debts have indeed been fully paid).

5. *Close down most of your credit cards.* If you carry several credit cards, consider closing down some (indeed, most) of the accounts. This is well worth doing by you just as well, even if you're fully paid up on the cards and the outstanding balance is plain zero: to a lender, an applicant with a large borrowing power (a large amount of revolving credit cards and open lines of credit) is still a big risk because you could potentially run up substantial balances (up to your credit limit on the card) if you wanted to. A better strategy: *cancel all but one or two of all your charge cards*; allow at least 30 or 60 days for the information about closure of your accounts to reach the credit reporting bureaus so that the report the lender will get, prior to your filing for loan, is accurate and current by then. To a lender who reads the new credit report, what it shows is a pattern of good risk for a number of accounts that have since been closed. That reduces the lender's perception of risks as far as you are concerned.

6. *Make sure you have cleaned up your credit profile as much as possible*. Your files should be accurate, up-to-date, and as clean as you can get them, BEFORE you ever apply for the loan. You know already that the lender will certainly order and obtain a credit report on you, anyway, as part of its decision-making process when you apply for your loan. So, it's always a wise move on your part: obtain your own credit report from two or three credit reporting agencies (see list below) even BEFORE you ever formally apply for a mortgage loan. The objective? So that you can update any potentially outdated information on you, and/or to check to make sure that the report on you is accurate.[3]

Under the law, for a modest fee you can order from a credit bureau a copy of its report on you. (If, however, you have been denied a loan or credit, or a job, within the past 30-days based on an adverse information contained in a credit report, then that credit reporting bureau must, upon request, send you a copy of that report free of charge). Here's the most important fact of reference here for you: if you find any adverse but inaccurate information in your credit report, the law allows you the right to write up and have the reporting bureau put in your credit file a statement of up to 100 words regarding such information, offering any explanation, corrections and clarifications, you may wish.

---

[2] Shaun Aghili, *The No-Nonsense Credit Manual*, p. 64.
[3] Substantial number of credit reports produced by credit reporting agencies, have been shown by various investigations to contain numerous errors. Indeed, each year about 3 million consumers are known to ask to have their credit reports changed or corrected because of incorrect or outdated information contained therein about them. Serious errors, such as the mixing of credit information for two or more people with similar names, frequently occur.

[LIST OF CREDIT BUREAUS]

How to obtain your credit reports directly from the credit bureaus:

Experian (TRW):   *P.O. Box 949*
Allen, TX 75013
(800) 643-3334
www.experian.com

TRW Complimentary Report
P. O. Box 2350
Chatsworth, CA 91313

Transunion (TU):   *P.O. Box 390*
Springfield, PA 19064
(800) 916-8800
$8.00/report
www.tuc.com

Equifax (CBI/EFX):   *P.O. Box 740241*
Atlanta, GA 30374
(800) 685-1111
One FREE report a year.
www.equifax.com/consumer.html

7. Avoid applying for any type of credit at least 90 days prior to applying for a home loan. Whenever you apply for any type of credit, the lender runs a credit check on you and the credit reporting bureau registers that inquiry on its computers for duration of some 18 months. An excessive number of inquiries (over 1 or 2 inquiries every 30 days) is said to constitute a "red flag" to lenders that the applicant is engaged in too much credit hunting and credit dealings.

8. Avoid shifting money around. To show proof that the required down payment portion of your home purchase money is truly from your own personal resources, your down-payment money will need to be fully documented. Hence, it's mightily helpful to you, as well as to your loan officer, that you avoid shifting large sums of money around between your bank accounts. Postpone large cash expenditures until much later in the buying process, that is, after the close of escrow.

9. Get yourself PRE-QUALIFIED for the loan first BEFORE you ever go out to look at properties: This will allow you to know just how much you can afford for a house, and the price range of a property to shop for. [See p. 96 for the pre-qualifying or pre-approval procedures]

STEP 6 : SUBMIT YOUR LOAN APPLICATION TO YOUR FIRST CHOICE OF LENDERS AND FILE FOR A LOAN PRE APPROVAL BEFORE YOU EVER PICK A HOME TO BUY.

A. FIRST AND LAST RULE: MAKE THE LENDER'S JOB EASIER FOR HIM OR HER

HERE IS A LITTLE KNOWN, NO-FAIL SECRET OF SUCCESSFUL LOAN PROCESSING: *Lenders simply love loan applicants who make their job easier! As a rule, if you make the lender's (his underwriter's) job easier for him – in terms, basically, of being frank and forth right with him about yourself and furnishing him all the necessary information about you up-front – you are far more likely to win the lender's heart and his approval for credit.* And how do you do this? It's simple. You take the first big step in this process by first securing the lender's *"pre-approval"* of the loan, his conditional or contingent loan approval in advance, BEFORE you even find a house to buy.

In attempting to determine whether to grant you a loan or not, there are, actually, two[4] basic types of financial *"risk factors"* that the lender is interested in. [See Chapters 9 and 15 for a more comprehensive treatment of this issue.] For him, the first risk factor is summed up simply by the question: Are you, as a borrower, seemingly capable of repaying the mortgage debt you are asking for based on your verified income, your net worth, and credit record and history? And the SECOND risk factor of interest to the lender is related, not to you as the borrower, but primarily to the property you're buying: What is its true price, condition, quality and location?

Loan Processing Really Has TWO Parts To it: "pre-approval" and "Approval"

In practice, it is really with regard to the lender's review of the SECOND risk factor, the property risk aspects, that the delays and complexity in loan processing generally occur. For, it is with the assessment of the risk factor concerning the property that an unusual array and varieties of time-consuming operations, as well as different cost factors, come into play – matters ranging from appraisal of the home, to home inspection, title search, survey of the property, and so forth. In contrast to the second risk element, review and consideration of the FIRST risk factor is a relatively easy matter for which the essential information for its determination (applicant's employment, income, expenses, assets, liabilities, and the like) can be quickly assembled, and for which a determination can quickly be made. Consequently, here's how to understand this: Simply view the "pre-approval" (or "pre-qualification") part of your loan application process as relating merely to the getting of the lender's review and approval for matters concerning your financial condition and credit status; while the second part, the "approval" (or "qualification") phase, concerns the next and finalizing phase of the loan application process and relates to the review of the quality and security of the property, and the more involved, more time consuming aspects of the mortgage loan processing.

The trick here is to file for the loan in TWO parts – the "pre-approval" part, followed thereafter by the "approval" part. This approach of filing first for a pre-approval, is very much beloved by lenders because doing it that way makes the lender's job much easier for him: you make it practicable for the loan underwriter to separate the two evaluations into two parts – one centering on your financial and credit qualification, and the other, centering on the quality and properties of the specific house you are to buy. Thus, he is enabled to execute these evaluations separately at different times. The two-part loan application evaluation process makes the job of the loan officer a lot easier for him, and the prospects of

---

[4] To be sure, there is a third risk factor that a bank will make in deciding on a loan, namely, determining whether it will be profitable for it to make the loan. However, this is an internal matter for the bank alone to decide on, and is not something you can, as a potential borrower, influence or help them with, one way or the other.

the applicant a lot better for her, in several ways and for several reasons: once the loan applicant has passed the personal financial and credit evaluation, that then makes the second part, the part dealing with the evaluation of the property, also easier. That becomes easier because, once the issues of the applicant's financial ability are already decided upon and it's clear that he can afford a house of a certain price range, the lender can now concentrate his evaluations solely on the property itself.

B. PREPARATION FOR THE PRE-APPROVAL OR FINANCE-BASED EVALUATION OF YOUR LOAN REQUEST

Briefly summarized, here are the procedures you take in securing the pre-approval (or pre-qualification) of your lender.

1. Pick up your loan application form and papers from the lender after you have carefully selected a lender (Chapter 12, and Step 4 of this Chapter); complete the application, attach the required supporting documentations, then submit them to the lender. Your lender's requirements may include, as well, that you complete a *Verification of Deposit* form, or a *Verification of Employment* form, or other forms. (See Chapter 11 for a complete discussion of the loan application documentations typically required).

NOTE: Under the federal Truth-in-lending Act, lenders must provide you with a *Truth-in-Lending Disclosure Statement* (see sample on p. 81) at the time of your loan application. And under another federal law called the *Real Estate Settlement Procedures Act (RESPA)*, one of the papers the lender should give you at the very time you pick up your application forms, is a document called a *Good Faith Estimate of Settlement Charges* (see sample on p. 83).

Both of these documents (along with the supporting papers that accompany them), will give you a pretty good idea of the terms of the mortgage you seek, and will give you the estimated fees and charges you'll pay in sufficiently detailed manner as to allow you to effectively compare the terms of the loan being offered you. The lender is mandated to give you the *Good Faith Estimate* right away at the time you're given the application forms; with respect to the *Disclosure Statement*, however, depending on the lender, a lender may give the applicant this document shortly after the applicant has picked up the loan application, or often immediately upon returning the completed application form to the lender. Nevertheless, for reasons outlined in Chapter 11 (see pp. 73-74), it is important that you press your lender and request a copy of the statement <u>immediately</u>, at the very time you pick up the application form, and not a minute thereafter. IN ANY EVENT, YOU MUST READ AND STUDY THESE TWO DOCUMENTS – AND THOROUGHLY.

2. After you've completed your application forms – and assembled all the required documentations and supporting papers [see Items 3 and 4 below] – you should first call and make an appointment with the selected lender's loan officer. Let him/her know that you are now ready with your papers and would like to come in with your application papers personally. (You get more prompt action and better results that way, by personal, face-to-face dealings than by phone or through the mail).

3. *Selling yourself to your lender*. A brief, written, "loan proposal" of some sort makes a favorable impression on bankers and reasonably ensures prospective success. Such a proposal helps establish you as a responsible person with whom the bank can do business.

The first step in making a proposal is to write a short COVER LETTER. This need not be anything more than a short description of how much money you estimate you'll need and what (the kind of property price range) you plan to buy. You could also mention in a general way, the steadiness or permanence of your employment, and the reliability of your future income with which to meet your mortgage payment obligations. If there are any serious negative or extenuating circumstances (e.g. about your credit, or past filing of bankruptcy or past debt repayment problems), you may also mention them in this letter in a general and brief way, and explain how you may have rectified the problem by now. (Full and timely disclosure is the best policy; lenders don't like surprises!). The cover letter should be short (no more than one or two pages), and should be simple, written in clear English and easily readable and understandable by the bank loan officer. [See sample model Cover Letter below.

NOTE: This is not a place for you to go into a boring plea or some sales pitch about how you so desperately need this money or feel you're too qualified for the loan. No details or long descriptions. Simply write a kind of "introduction" note of yourself – simple, short, modest. Not every lender subscribes to every kind of mortgage, of course. So, having first inquired and found out the different possibilities that exist with this particular bank, you are also to make a request that fits within the specific framework of what is offered there.

COVER LETTER (A SAMPLE)

(Borrower's name, address, and
phone numbers)

To:
 Mr. Joe Brown, Mortgage Officer
American National Bank
60 Bank Street
Newark, New Jersey 07102
Dear Mr. Brown:

This is to thank you for the time you have shared with me explaining the loan policy of your bank and the different types of mortgages you have available. At this time, my wife and I would like to follow up on the discussions with a formal proposal for a mortgage.

First, we wish to request an 80% mortgage loan in the amount of $104,000 at an interest rate of 8 1/2% for a term of 25 years. We have in mind buying a home in the price range of $125,000 to $130,000. With your $104,000 mortgage constituting 80% of that amount, we intend to put down the remaining 20% balance, namely, $26,000 (20% of $130,000 purchase price), in cash; $21,000 of our own funds will be added to an amount of $5,000 we are borrowing from the wife's father.

We wish to condition our proposal, however, upon a few minor requests. They will make a difference for us in being sure that this mortgage arrangement is a fair and wise one for our family and us. As you know from the preliminary discussions with you, it is the understanding that if we pay two-percentage point at the house closing, you will reduce your customary interest rate of 9 ¼% to 8 ½%. We wish to accept that option and to pay the 8 ½% interest rate. We also request that your prepayment penalty of 3% of the loan balance due the bank at the time of sale, be reduced to 1% after 3 years, with no fee charged after we've had ownership for 7 years. We have not located any particular property to buy at this time. We would like to get financially pre-qualified for a mortgage first, before we commence searching for a property to buy.

We hereby enclose a detailed record of our income and expenses and a full disclosure of our assets, liabilities, and net worth. We believe we can meet the required monthly payments on this mortgage easily and comfortably. Please be absolutely assured that we are always available to provide more information or clarifications, or to answer any questions you may have. Feel free to call at home or at the office at the numbers listed above, if you need to. Thank you.

Sincerely yours,

_____

4. MAKE NO MISTAKE ABOUT THIS: *good preparation, before hand and in advance, and providing detailed information about you, are the keys to getting a favorable mortgage commitment quickly. Because you shall have, by now (we should hope and expect)*, already gone through all the foregoing STEPS outlined above, you should already be more than prepared by now. You should have probably prepared or assembled, already, many (or most) of the documents that may be necessary.

Prepare the following documents, in advance, to bring with you to your loan appointment:

- Your cover letter, which should briefly introduce you to the bank, and formulate, as well, a brief loan request plan. [See a sample copy of cover letter on p. 98]. Retain a copy for yourself.

- A complete statement of your income and expenses (see Chapter 8 and Figure 8-1 therein); as well as a complete statement of your net worth listing all your assets and liabilities (see Figures 8-2 and 8-3). Together, these statements will give your lender an idea of your personal "financial profile."

- A listing of ALL current credit cards you have in active status, including the account number of each, the issuer and their addresses, the credit limits, and the outstanding current balances.

- A listing of all your bank accounts, including each bank's name, address and phone number, your account numbers, the type of account (whether its checking or savings), and the current balances.

- A summary of all investments and retirement plans you have, including the name of the institution or company where the funds are deposited, the account number of each, and the current balances.

- A letter from your employer, if you are an employee, stating the date you were employed, your job title, and your current salary. Or, if you are self-employed, simply include your business financial statement, including both the balance sheet and income statement of the latest month and for the last 2 or 3 years.

- Copies of your tax returns for the past 3 years.

STEP 7 : LENDERS' DECISION-MAKING PROCESS ON LOAN PRE-APPROVAL APPLICATION: WHAT AND WHAT WOULD MAKE THE LENDER DECIDE IN YOUR FAVOR.

What happens after you file your loan application with your selected lender? How does the loan officer decide on granting you a loan pre-approval?

The complete procedures of a full-scale evaluation of a loan application are outlined elsewhere in the manual (see Chapter 11). However, briefly summarized, the procedures for the lender's approval or rejection of a loan application at this pre-approval (or pre-qualification) stage, is pretty straightforward and predictable. *The bank loan officer's decision is made basically on the basis of THREE considerations: the state of your financial strength, of your income, and of your credit history.* For example, if you are able to show, from the review of your credit report, that you have a record of late payments or non-payment of past debts, that record hurts your qualification chances for a mortgage, and depending on the degree of seriousness of your debt delinquency record, this alone could result in a rejection of your application. (*SUGGESTION*: As explained in STEP 5 of this chapter, long BEFORE you ever apply for a mortgage loan, send away for your credit report to preview it to be sure that it does not contain a record of potentially serious debt repayment delinquencies, or even inaccurate information, that could cripple your mortgage approval prospects outright).

Another factor, the AMOUNT of your other existing debts, is one that the loan officer can view either as a positive or a negative consideration as loan officers are generally of the view that the amount of other debts you have will affect your ability to service a new one. These are two basic ways the loan officer considers the effect of your existing debt burden: firstly, in terms of the effect of the monthly debt payment burden you currently have on your present and future financial strength (your ability to service the new mortgage debt), and secondly, in terms of the effect of the accumulated debt and credit burden you now have on you — that is, in terms of whether or not you seem to carry an <u>excessive</u> number of charge accounts or lines of credit relative to your income and your other debts and financial obligations. (*SUGGESTION*: long BEFORE you ever apply for a mortgage, cancel all but one or two of your credit cards and keep your payments timely on just those few). If, for example, the loan officer sees that you are committed to paying out several hundreds (or thousands) of dollars each month on old, existing credit card balances, car payments, or store revolving accounts, he or she may very well be less inclined, on account of this monthly payment burden, to let you take on additional debt, namely a long-term mortgage loan. On the other hand, let's say your records show that you have a good record of making timely payments even though you are committed to paying out several hundreds or thousands of dollars on your existing debt burden each month. That's a big plus for you that you have a good record of timely payments. But a serious minus for you, still, that you carry a big debt balances and/or many charge cards. If you merely carry too many credit charge accounts and lines of credit – a seemingly excessive number of them – the loan officer would likely react negatively to that just as well: to lenders, borrowers who carry too many credit cards *today*, represent too much risk of potentially overusing and over-extending credit, *tomorrow*.

Your loan officer also reviews the statement of the assets you have as a future test of your financial strength: the higher your assets and the lower your liabilities, the stronger your financial strength. Your lender may also use some specific qualifying "ratios" to tell him whether you can afford the monthly payment on your proposed mortgage loan (see Chapters 9 and 15 for an elaborate treatment of ratio procedures). Each lender has its own formula.

Finally, your loan officer reviews your income and job history. He's looking to see how much job stability and security you (the party or parties applying for the loan) seem to show; whether you change jobs frequently or have, conversely, held jobs for relatively long stretches of time; the prospects that you'll still have a job – and, therefore, the income necessary to keep making the payments on the mortgage – some 2, 3 or 5 years or more from now. He wants to assess: do you make enough money such that the mortgage, if granted you, is not likely to be a heavy burden on you which you would not reasonably be able to afford to pay back? To answer these questions, the loan officer may again resort to applying some of the same formulas we've previously mentioned – the qualifying financial ratios (see Chapters 9 and 15). Your conventional lender's ratio policy may be, for example, that for a borrower to qualify, the amount of the proposed monthly payment cannot be greater than a specified percentage [generally 28% for conventional lenders][6] of the borrower's monthly gross income. In addition to the ratios that tell the lender whether you can afford a certain monthly payment, your lender may, perhaps, also use a "point scoring" system to judge your general credit worthiness [see Section K of Chapter 15 for full treatment of this system]. You gain points, for example, if you've held your job for a long time

---

[6] As fully explained in Chapters 9 (Section C), 11 and 15, each lender has its own specific formula for ratio analysis and qualification. Also, the formulas are slightly different for mortgages guaranteed or insured by the FHA or the VA (see Chapter 5).

or if your job seems reasonably steady or secure. And you lose points, if you're a new comer to your current job or your past employment history is spotty.

Lender's Pre-approval, Rate Commitment, and Loan Commitment

If you get the lender's pre-approval of financing at this preliminary phase of the loan granting process – that is, when the initial approval is gotten before a specific house is located – it's as good as a full loan approval. The only difference will be that, in a financing approval offered BEFORE a house is located, the lender makes the approval but with some conditions attached. For example, the lender may grant a loan approval, but based on the condition that the house you eventually select has to pass certain inspections and reviews, and fall within a given price range.

Thus, upon the initial pre-approval of the loan for you, the lender will usually offer you what is known as a **RATE COMMITMENT**. Not to be confused with the other type of commitment, known as *"Loan Commitment,"* this is simply a promise by the lender, in writing, to grant you a loan at a specific interest rate, not a promise to grant the loan. That is, the promise is with respect only to the "rate"; that in the event your application is approved, the loan will bear a designated interest rate only specified, and you are guaranteed that specified rate. Then, once you locate the right house you wish to purchase (see chapter 16 for the procedures for doing this), the lender will require a title search of the house to ensure that the title you'll be getting will be a legally valid one, and a title insurance policy. The lender will also want an appraisal of the house to determine the quality of the property, and whether its appraisers think it's worth what you're proposing to pay the seller for it.

Many steps and complexities, a lot other paperwork and requirements, follow in this phase, which is why this phase of loan processing is noted for being time-consuming: the home appraiser may recommend to the lender that a further evaluation, such as a structural and pest control inspection of the house, be made. Conditions discovered from the inspections may require that some repair work be done on the house before you may buy it; the home appraiser may appraise the home's value as being worth a lot less than the purchase price, which will mean that the lender probably won't approve the full loan amount, and so on. In any event, what is important to know is that once such requirements and conditions, to the extent that they are required by the lender, are met and satisfied by the home buyer (the loan applicant), the lender will be obligated, by virtue of the "rate commitment" agreement, to release the mortgage loan funds needed to buy the house.

The lender, upon completing its review of your finances as well as its substantial review of the property's value and quality, will at this point give you a document called a **LOAN COMMITMENT**, which is very different from the RATE COMMITMENT described earlier above. The important benefits that a loan commitment confers upon you: it will essentially specify the maximum loan amount the lender has pre-approved for you, at what interest rate, the loan's repayment term (duration), the type of mortgage you're offered (whether it is a fixed-rate type, for example, or an adjustable-rate type, etc.), the deadline within which you are to exercise the commitment, and whether or not there could be an extended deadline for that.

> **IMPORTANT**: Be conscious of the fact that, if the loan commitment deadline should expire, none of the above stated terms and conditions will continue to apply (unless, of course, there's a provision for an extension contained in the commitment). Hence, be vigilant, and if you find that the deadline is approaching, ask for acceleration of events so as to ensure that escrow on your house will close by the lender's deadline, or that you will be able to get an extension, if necessary. Indeed, many a time the delays in closing or the inability to close on the house, are caused by the lenders themselves. For example, escrow may not be possible to close because the lender has so far failed to review a required inspection report.

Terms of the Approved Mortgages

Finally, you should note that, as part of the lender's application loan evaluation process, when you are given the loan commitment offer, you might probably be given a number of loan choices. You may, for example, be offered some fixed-rate loans; others may be adjustable-rate type of loan, etc. Some offered loans might have conversion privileges within a limited number of years (e.g., a mortgage that begins with a fixed rate, then reverts to an adjustable after 3 years, but converts to a long-term fixed rate within the 30-year term), and so on. The possible variations are endless. [See Chapter 3 for some of the major varieties of mortgages available].

In sum, the point of significance for you to note here is that you'll be confronted with having to make choices, you'll need to do a comparison-shopping among different loans. [See Chapters 4, 5, 6 and 7, for some pointers on mortgage choice-making].

What if, by any chance, your application for a loan is not approved?

Turn to the next Chapter, Chapter 14, for some pointers on what you can do to reverse the lender's decision or to secure a loan with another lender.

A BRIEF SUMMARY: WHAT QUALITIES MAKE YOU GET A LENDER'S LOAN APPROVAL.

The central pillar for any workable and successful loan pre-approval (or approval) process is simply this: Make the loan officer's job easier for him or her, and you'll most likely get a loan approval. Thus, basically, if you have done the advance homework of what you're supposed to do BEFORE you ever file a loan application (STEP 5 of this Chapter), and if you've done the essential things you need to do to make the lender's job easier when you file your loan application (essentially by undertaking the STEPS outlined above, ranging from breaking out the loan reviewing process into two parts, to readily being open and forthcoming in providing the lender the necessary information and documentation about yourself and your finances), you will very likely win the loan officer's loan pre-approval and approval.

A key point is this: FULL DISCLOSURE. **Full and complete disclosure by the loan applicant, is the very best policy with lenders**. Lenders look favorably upon applicants who are forthright and forthcoming with essential facts and information, even if of adverse nature in content. Anticipate the questions the lender is likely to ask or want answers to; then provide them with the answers *beforehand*, along with the necessary supporting and verification documents and information. Any negative items about your credit or personal history? You filed for bankruptcy or had a judgment against you in the past few years, for example? Any repayment problem in your recent credit past? Simply volunteer the information, any way; disclose them to the loan officer in advance at the very beginning before the lender discovers them himself. Then that'll give you the opportunity to offer an explanation as to the special circumstances, if any, and how you might have rectified the problem. *The point is, don't wait for the loan officer to ask you. Rather, give the information about you up front, even if it's not all good. In the eyes of the lender, such an attitude makes a most helpful favorable impression that you are the kind of reliable person the bank can do business with. **And, gaining credibility with your lender, is the surest way to getting the approval (or pre-approval) for a mortgage loan**.*

Figure 13-1

Mortgage Information Form

Questions to Ask the Mortgage Company

(On Conventional Fixed-Rate Mortgage Loans (FRM)

Name of Lender_____

Address of Lender_____

Telephone Number_____ FAX # _____ Contact Person _____

Length of Loan (in years) _____ Annual Percentage Rate (APR) _____

What is the size of loan (Loans-to-value) you will make: 95% ☐   90% ☐ Other _____

Interest rate _____ %. Is loan discounted? If so, by how many points? _____

How much down payment do you require? $ _____ % _____

Loan origination fee _____ %

Is there a lock-in fee? If so, how much _____

Any limits on seller contributions? _____ If so, what do you count as seller contributions

_____

Do you have buy downs costs on 3-2-1? _____ 2-1 _____ Other _____

Can interest be increased to remove discount points? _____ If so, interest rate _____

PMI due at closing   95% _____ %   90% _____ %   Others _____ %

PMI monthly premium   95% _____ %   90% _____ %   Others _____ %

Any other PMI payment plan   95% _____ %   90% _____ %   Others _____ %

Approximate Charges for Closing Costs

The estimated total of closing costs and other fees you charge:

Amount $ _____ or _____ % of loan amount

Which of these one-time fees do you charge the borrower, and how much: Application $ _____

Credit report $ _____ Property appraisal $ _____ Attorney's $ _____ Escrow $ _____ Survey $ _____

Title Search $ _____ Title Insurance $ _____ Transfer (stamp) Tax $ _____ Others not yet Listed $ _____

If I Sell This House, Is the Loan

Assumable   Yes ☐ or No ☐ Non-qualifying ☐ or qualifying ☐

Non-escalating ☐ or Escalating ☐ If so, amount $ _____ or _____ %

Is there prepayment penalty? No ☐ Yes ☐ If so, amount _____ or _____ %

Any other features in this loan _____

Your qualification ratios? _____ / _____

What is the loan-to-income ratio required to qualify? _____

Housing costs figured against: Net Income ☐ or Gross income ☐

What makes up housing costs?

Principal and interest ☐ Monthly PMI premium ☐ Property Tax ☐

Hazard Insurance ☐ Estimated maintenance ☐ If so, costs used _____

Estimated utilities ☐ If so, costs used _____ Association fee ☐

Other _____

Could the PMI requirement be removed upon sufficiently paying down the principal? _____

What Counts as Debt

A debt ten months or less is counted: Yes ☐ No ☐ Six months or less counted Yes ☐ No ☐

Or other _____

How are credit cards viewed _____

Childcare counted as debt _____

Life insurance counted as debt _____

Car Insurance counted as debt _____

Anything else that would count as debt _____

Approximately how long does it take to get a loan approval? _____ How long will loan commitment be effective? _____

Do you have anything better in a fixed-rate loan — state, county, city or other? _____

_____

What documents will you need me (the borrower) to provide you?_____

_____

Could you provide me a copy of your Truth-in-Lending Disclosure Statement at the time I pick up the loan application, please? ☐ Yes ☐

No. If no, when will you provide it to me? _____

Figure 13-2
Mortgage Information Form

Questions to Ask the Mortgage Company
(On Conventional Adjustable-Rate Mortgage Loans (ARM))

Name of Lender_____

Address of Lender_____

Telephone Number_____ FAX # _____ Contact Person _____

Length of Loan (in years) _____ Annual Percentage Rate (APR) _____

What is the size of loan (Loans-to-value) you will make: 95% ☐ 90% ☐ Other _____

Starting (introductory) Interest rate _____ %. Is loan discounted? If so, by how many points?

_____

How much down payment do you require? $ _____ % _____

Loan origination fee _____ %

Is there a lock-in fee? If so, how much _____

Is accruing interest rate the same interest rate _____ If yes, what is the difference?

_____

How long will the initial interest rate be in effect?

_____

What is the loan indexed to? _____ Index rate now

_____ %

Do you have the highest _____ % (rate) and Lowest _____ % (rate) of index last five years?

_____

What is the margin rate on the ARM loan _____ %?

What is the interest rate cap? _____

Does the interest rate cap apply to: ☐ the introductory/initial (and lower) rate; or, ☐ the rate in effect after the introductory period is over? (Check one or the other).

What is the cap on monthly payment?

_____

How often can the adjustment be made in interest or payments? Is it every 6 months _____ or every year?

_____

Does this loan have adjustment interest cap? _____ % Or is it a payment cap?

_____

Does the loan have lifetime interest caps?

_____

What is the maximum adjustment that can be made in interest, or in payments, each adjustment period (max change at each adjustment)?

_____

Does loan have any negative amortization? _____. In the event of negative amortization, would the loan be "re-cast" after, say, 5 years to allow full amortizations?

_____

Any limits on seller contributions? _____ If so, what do you count as seller contributions. Do you have buy downs-costs on 3-2-1? _____ 2-1 _____ Other _____

Can interest be increased to remove discount points? _____ If so, interest rate _____

PMI due at closing 95% _____ % 90% _____ % Others _____ %

PMI monthly premium 95% _____ % 90% _____ % Others _____ %

Any other PMI payment plan 95% _____ % 90% _____ % Others _____ %

Approximate Charges for Closing Costs

The estimated total of closing costs and other fees you charge:

Amount $ _____ or _____ % of loan amount

Which of these one-time fees do you charge the borrower, and how much: Application $ _____

Credit report $ _____ Property appraisal $ _____ Attorney's $ _____ Escrow $ _____ Survey $ _____

Title Search $ _____ Title Insurance $ _____ Transfer (stamp) tax $ _____ Others not yet Listed $ _____

If I Sell This House, Is the Loan

Assumable Yes ☐ or No ☐ Non-qualifying ☐ or qualifying ☐

Non-escalating ☐ or Escalating ☐ If so, amount $ _____ or _____ %

Is there prepayment penalty? No ☐ Yes ☐ If so, amount _____ or _____ %

Any other features in this loan _____

Your qualification ratios? _____ / _____

What is the loan-to-income ratio required to qualify? _____

Housing costs figured against: Net Income ☐ or Gross income ☐

What makes up housing costs?

Principal and interest ☐   Monthly PMI premium ☐   Property Tax ☐

Hazard Insurance ☐   Estimated maintenance ☐   If so, costs used

_____

Estimated utilities ☐   If so, costs used _____ Association fee

☐
Other

_____

Could the PMI requirement be removed upon sufficiently paying down the principal?

_____

What Counts as Debt

A debt ten months or less is counted: Yes ☐   No ☐   Six months or less counted Yes ☐   No ☐

Or other _____

How are credit cards viewed _____

Childcare counted as debt _____

Life insurance counted as debt _____

Car Insurance counted as debt _____

Anything else that would count as debt _____

Approximately how long does it take to get a loan approval? _____ How long will loan commitment be effective?

_____

Do you have anything better in a fixed-rate loan — state, county, city or other? _____

_____

What documents will you need me (the borrower) to provide you?

_____

_____

Could you provide me a copy of your Truth-in-Lending Disclosure Statement at the time I pick up the loan application,

please? ☐ Yes ☐ No. If no, when will you provide it to me? _____

CHAPTER 14

Some Pointers on What to Do if Denied Your Application for a Mortgage

The following are some pointers on what to do if you've followed, even faithfully, all the rules and procedures prescribed in this manual but still got turned down for a mortgage loan.

1. Check With The Lender

Promptly after you've received your lender's letter of rejection, call the bank's loan officer and set up an appointment to meet with him or her in person. Make a visit with the loan officer and discuss in specific details the lender's reasons for turning you down. If possible, get those reasons from him in writing. Take copious written notes. Carefully study the reasons given; try to correct and rectify the legitimate deficiencies pointed out, then reapply to the same lender, or apply to another one.

2. Go Over The Sure-fire Loan Approval Checklist Again

At this point, and taking into account the explanations and reasons given you by the lender for your being rejected, go back once again to Chapter 13 of this manual. Systematically and deliberately run down the individual "STEPS" of that Chapter, and trace your way down, inspecting the steps one-by-one. DISCOVER THIS: *which specific steps, requirements, conditions, and/or recommendations therein, did you apparently skip or fail to follow?* (For example, if all you ever did were simply to follow the do's and don'ts recommended in STEP 5 of Chapter 13, that alone would have been sufficient to assure that you would not have possibly failed to qualify!) Jot down that information and remember that when you go back to apply again for a mortgage.

3. Consider Making a New Application Altogether to Another Lender

4. Consider Applying for the VA or FHA Mortgage

The Veteran Administration and Federal Housing Administration-backed loans [see Chapter 5] are generally easier to qualify for and to get than 'conventional' loans, and under their programs, you might, also, be able to qualify for a home with very little or no down payment.

5. Were You Possibly A Victim of Discrimination?

If you believe that you were the object of discrimination, for racial or whatever reason, here's what you are to do. Draft a letter of complaint and send it to the legal division at the lender's office. If your complaint is ignored, or is acted upon but you still think you have been discriminated against, you can make an appeal to various official banking and government agencies outlined below for their further review and action.

Under the Federal Equal Credit Opportunity Act (ECOA), it has been illegal and completely banned and impermissible for decades now, to deny a mortgage loan to a borrower because of his or her race, color, religion, national origin, sex, marital status, or receipt of income from public assistance. Other laws prohibit a practice called *"redlining,"* in which a mortgage loan is denied because of the location of the property. Unfortunately, however, although illegal and completely banned on paper for several decades now, such discriminatory practices still very much happen in America of today.

A 1991 study by the Association of Community Organizations for Reform Now (ACORN) based on Federal Reserve Bank data, found that *minority applicants' mortgage applications are rejected 4 times as often as those from white applicants with similar income*. Certainly, a substantial part of this wide gulf in loan approval rates is directly due to plain, old-fashioned racial discrimination! A 1992 computer analysis of the Federal Reserve data by the Wall Street Journal indicated that 85.3 percent of loan applicants from whites were approved, while only 66.6 percent of applications from blacks were approved – an average differential of 18.7 percentage points.[1] And, to cite just one more related report, a 1998 study by the Chicago Fair Housing Alliance, reports that lenders as well as real estate agents, discriminatorily direct a disproportionate number of minority home buyers to FHA loans thereby shutting minority home buyers out of higher valued loans and higher priced homes and neighborhoods.[2]

In short, discrimination is real; it does actually occur! You can argue as to how widespread or limited it may be. Certainly, however, it is a reality. So, if you are turned down for a mortgage loan and you have good cause to believe that it has something to do with discrimination against you, first contact the lending bank for a full explanation. Then, if the explanation is not satisfactory and you're still convinced that the loan rejection is unfair and discrimination-based, here's what you do: (1) send the lender that turned you down a formal written complaint (always retain a copy for yourself), always by certified mail with return receipt requested; (2) next, send a written complaint to the state or federal agency (or both) that regulates the lender who turned you down (see the addresses listed below), and ask for their investigation and action on your complaint; and (3) contact your State Attorney-General's office, your local Better Business Bureau, or your state consumer protection agency.

The following are agencies to send your complaint to which regulate federally chartered banks and savings institutions:

- For savings and loan associations or mutual savings banks, the main regulator is the Office of Thrift Supervision (formerly called the Federal Home Loan Bank Board); Consumer Affairs Division, Office of Thrift Supervision, 1700 G Street NW, Washington, DC 20552. Telephone: (202) 906-6237. From outside the Washington D.C. area, you can call toll-free 1-800-842-6929.

- The Comptroller of The Currency regulates the "national banks" (commercial banks, generally large, with the word "national" or the initials, "N.A.," somewhere in their names). Contact the director of Consumer Activities, Comptroller of the Currency, Department of the Treasury, 490 L'Enfant Plaza SW, Washington, DC 20219. Phone: (202) 287-4265.

- The Federal Reserve System regulates commercial banks that are state chartered but are members of the Federal Reserve System. Contact the Director, Division of Consumer and Community Affairs, Board of Governors of the Federal Reserve System, Washington, DC 20551, Phone: 202-452-3946.

- The Federal Deposit Insurance Corporation regulates almost all of the remaining commercial banks – namely, State-chartered banks that carry federal deposit insurance. Contact the Office of Consumer Affairs, Federal Deposit Insurance Corporation, 550 17th Street NW, Washington, DC 20429. Phone: (202) 898-3535. From outside the Washington, DC area, you can phone toll-free 1-800-424-5488.

- For federally insured credit unions: the National Credit Union Administration, 1776 G. Street NW, Washington, DC 20456. phone: (202) 682-9600.

---

[1] The first two studies cited, are cited by John R. Dorfman, in *The Mortgage Book*, pp. 179-180
[2] As reported in *The New York Times*, May 13, 1998, p. A16, "Home Loans Discriminate, Study Shows."

- If your mortgage lender is a bank that doesn't have federal deposit insurance, contact your State's Department of Banking in the state's capital. The Council of Better Business Bureaus, which is the national headquarters of all local BBBs in the United States, can give you the addresses and phone numbers of your local BBBs office. Contact: Council of Better Business Bureaus, Inc. (National Headquarters) 4200 Wilson Blvd., Arlington VA 22203, (703) 276-0100.

CHAPTER 15

The Process of Borrower Analysis For Mortgage Loan Financing: How Lenders Financially Qualify the Borrower

A. RATIO ANALYSIS

In evaluating whether or not to give an applicant a loan, a mortgage lender is concerned with minimizing risk while making certain that the lender's yield on each loan and on the lender's entire mortgage portfolio, is enhanced. To achieve these goals, the lender uses certain flexible but standard analytical techniques – FINANCIAL RATIO ANALYSIS AND STANDARDS. This process of analysis is called *financial qualification,* meaning an assessment or analysis of the prospective borrower's (or home buyer's) financial condition. In this chapter, we discuss some of the more common ratios and standards used by the real estate industry to evaluate the borrower.

Buyer qualification defines a buyer's purchasing capability in terms of cash equity and income. The following are among the underwriting standards used by analysts in determining the home purchasing capability of a buyer:

- The debt-to-income ratio
- The loan-to-value ratio (LTV)

The debt-to-income ratio aims at examining the ability to comfortably pay debt; the LTV ratio aims at determining how much cash a buyer will need in order to keep the value of the mortgage loan reasonably "safe" relative to the value of the property. A major part of the process of conventional financial qualification of the homebuyer centers on the application of these two ratios to the buyer's condition.

Income Qualification

Two principal factors govern income qualification for a buyer: the buyer's income level, and his long-term debt. *Basically, as a loan analyst, what you are looking for in income qualification is the level of a family's available monthly funds for housing*. This is expressed typically as: income, minus that portion of the long-term debt that is unrelated to housing.

The Two Basic Debt-to-Income Ratios

There are two rule-of-thumb ratios used by the mortgage industry which you can use in determining how much mortgage debt you can reasonably afford as a mortgage borrower: (1) the TOTAL long-term debt-to-income ratio – this we call here, the **LT Debt Ratio**; and (2) simply the mortgage debt-to-income ratio – this we call here, the **PITI debt ratio** for short, in that it is comprised of the loan principal, interest, taxes and, insurance premium.

LT Debt Ratio: this is especially applicable to you if you are a homebuyer with substantial LONG-TERM debts. LT Debt ratio is the ratio between long-term debt, including housing expenses, and the buyer's net effective income. Basically, what you do is determine your existing long-term debt (Chapter 8), and then apply the LT ratio to determine how large a mortgage you can afford given your effective income and resources.

PITI Debt Ratio: this is the ratio between your principal, interest, taxes and insurance (PITI) costs, and your gross income. This ratio is commonly used as a quick indicator of borrowing capability but is more specifically used where a borrower has little or no long-term debt. Like the LT debt ratio, the PITI debt ratio is used to identify how much monthly housing debt you can comfortably afford. (See the procedures on p. 111).

B. THE TOTAL LONG-TERM DEBT-TO-INCOME RATIO – THE LT DEBT RATIO

This ratio is commonly used by underwriters (loan officers) for VA and FHA loans, as well as conventional (i.e., non-governmental) loans. The long-term debt-to-income ratio is simply the ratio between your TOTAL long-term debt, including all housing expenses, and your net effective income (simply your gross income minus the withholding taxes). ("Long-term" debt is defined here as any debt that will last for at least another 6 months; and "housing expenses" here would include the mortgage principal and interest, taxes, insurance, utilities, and maintenance, or PITIUM for short).

This ratio is one rule by which determination can be made as to how much mortgage debt a borrower can reasonably afford; it measures the acceptable percentage of the homebuyer's net income he's allowed to spend on a house. In recent times, the underwriting ratio standard set by the real estate industry has been pegged at a maximum of 50 percent. However, you should note that this can at times fluctuate upwards or downwards, depending on the economic circumstances.[1] For instance, recent statistics continue to indicate that Americans are spending an increasing percentage of their net income on housing expenses. Hence, to be on the safe side, we shall, in the following illustration, simply use 55 percent.

Applying the LT Debt Ratio

Here is the formula for the LT Debt Ratio

Loan Principal?	P				
+ Loan Interest	I		Long-term debt	MUST BE	.55 x (gross income –
+ Taxes (Property):	T	+	(non-housing debts	LESS THAN:	withholding tax)
+ Insurance:	I		over 6 months)		
+ Utilities costs:	U				
+ Maintenance:	M				

We re-arrange this formula as follows:

[P+1+T+I+U+M+ Long-term (LT) Debt (non-housing)]   MUST BE   [.55 x (income – withholding tax)]
LESS THAN:

Now, remember that what we are after is the PI component of this formula, *which represents the monthly principal and interest the buyer can afford.* To determine this, we simply move the above equation around to solve the PI, as follows:

[1] You can always call the VA or FHA, or your broker or the lenders, to ascertain the current ratios.

$$P1 \text{ (that is affordable)} = .55 \text{ x (income - tax)} - T + 1 + U + M + LT \text{ debt)}$$

Once we solve for P1, we can use mortgage tables (see the Appendix) to determine the maximum available mortgage loan. THAT AMOUNT, PLUS THE DOWN PAYMENT, EQUALS THE PRICE OF THE HOME THE BUYER CAN AFFORD.

Illustrative Example:

Assume the following facts. Let's say you find a 3-bedroom home you'd like to buy and that you have some long-term debts (ones that will still last more than 6 months). Then, you'll need to use the LT debt ratio qualification. Your other assumptions and facts are:[2]

- going interest rate: 15 percent,
- loan term and type: 30 years, amortized,
- taxes: $50 per month (for a three-bedroom in that market)
- insurance: $50 per month,
- utilities: $75/month,
- maintenance: $40/month,
- buyer's monthly gross income: $30,000 divided by 12 = $2,500/month,
- buyer's withholding tax: 24 percent of monthly income, and
- buyer's monthly non-housing debt over six months - $300.

Then, using our above formula and plugging in the above facts, you'll get:

P1 (@ 15%, 30 years.)=55% x ($2,500 - 24% of $2500) - ($50 + $50 + $75 + $40) - $300

That is, P1 (@ 15%, 30 yrs.) = 55% x $2,500 - $600) – ($215) - $300.
Which is, P1 (@ 15%, 30 yrs.) = $1,045 - $215 - $300 = $530

Interpreted, using the long-term (LT) debt ratio with the same set of facts, what this is saying is that this buyer can afford making a mortgage payment of principal and interest (PI) of $530 per month. Now, using the loan amortization table (see appendix A), the mortgage amount that's affordable at $530 per month for a 15 percent, 30-year loan, is about $42,000.[3] Thus, applying this ratio, if you are this prospective borrower you can only qualify for no more than a $42,000 loan under this formula.

C. THE MORTGAGE DEBT-TO-INCOME RATIO – PITI DEBT RATIO

The PITI debt ratio is the ratio between a borrower's principal, interest, taxes and insurance (PITI) costs, and his or her gross income. This ratio is commonly used as a quick indicator of borrowing capability but is more specifically used where a borrower has little or no long-term debt. Like the foregoing total long-term debt-to-income ratio, the PITI debt ratio is used to identify how much monthly housing debt the buyer can comfortably afford. Traditionally, this ratio has stood at 25 percent with conventional lenders; that is, a home's PITI could not exceed 25 percent of gross income. Currently, however, under guidelines set by the Federal National

---

[2] As a general proposition, once a specific home has been selected, an estimate of the loan rates and terms can be made based simply on current market trends, and an estimate of the non-mortgage housing expenses (taxes, insurance costs, activities, etc.) can be taken from prevailing comparable costs of an average home in the desired area.

[3] This is calculated this way. Using the Amortization Table on Appendix A. You find that the calculated monthly payment to pay off $1,300 @ 15% interest over a 30 year term, is $12,6444. So, to find out how much the amount of $530 per month will carry at the $12.6444 rate, you simply divide the $12.6444 into $530, giving you as follows:

$$\frac{\$530.00}{\$12.6444} = \$41,915.79, \text{ which is rounded off to } \$42,000.$$

Mortgage Association (Fannie Mae), the acceptable PITI for a prospective homebuyer is set at a ratio of 28 percent of his or her gross income. For our purposes here, however, to use more stringent requirement, we will use a 30 percent PITI ratio. Thus, we have this simple formula:

> [P + I + T + I   must be   [30% of gross income]
> less than:

As we did with the previous debt ratio, we have to re-arrange the PITI debt ratio formula in order to find how much debt a borrower can afford. To do this, we move the taxes and insurance expenses to the other side of the equation as follows:

> [P + I]   must be   [30% of gross income – T – I]
> less than:

We apply the PITI ratio as follows: Assuming the same set of facts, rates, and terms as those used under the foregoing total long-term debt-to-income ratio, this formula becomes:

> [P + I]   must be   [30% of $2,500 – $50 - $50] = $650
> less than:

Interpreted, what this formula is saying, is that this buyer can afford making a mortgage payment of principal and interest (PI) of $650 per month. Now, using the loan amortization table (Appendix A), this buyer's capability of $650 per month in PI will enable him to qualify for no more than approximately $51,000[4] loan, assuming a 30-year mortgage at 15 percent interest.

D. THE TOTAL LONG-TERM DEBT (LT) RATIO vs THE PITI DEBT RATIO: WHICH ONE TO USE?

Here's the basic principle. The PITI debt ratio may be quickly applied to get your (a buyer's) approximate mortgage borrowing capability. However, to be on the safe side of caution, *whenever you have a substantial amount of LONG-TERM non-housing debt, then you should apply BOTH the LT (total long-term debt) and the PITI debt ratios and make a comparison.* Then, the ratio which yields the lesser PI capability, is the debt qualification figure you should use.

Take, for example, the computations made in the last two examples above. We determined, under the total long-term debt ratio, that what the prospective borrower could qualify for is a $42,000 mortgage, while under the PITI debt ratio, it is determined that what the prospective borrower could qualify for is a bigger amount, $51,000. In comparing the two estimates, the lesser amount, namely the $42,000 figure, is the amount of mortgage loan you're to pick as what you are qualified for – not the higher $51,000 figure. The point is that, by and large, it is better and more prudent for you to be on the side of thoroughness in your qualification process; you should generally use both ratios, then select the lesser figure (unless it is clear, however, that your long-term debt is minimal, in which case you should then simply use the PITI ratio).

---

[4] Simply calculated as follows: $\frac{\$650.00}{\$12.6444 \text{ (from the tables)}} = \$51,406.00$

E. CASH-ON-HAND QUALIFICATION

In addition to income (or debt) qualification, lenders also qualify a buyer for cash – that is, to determine that they have enough cash on hand to meet the minimum equity amounts that will be required for the particular loan sought, plus the cash needed for the house closing costs.

The LTV Ratio

How do you determine the minimum CASH that will be needed? Lenders determine this by what is known as the loan-to-value ratio, or the LTV ratio, for short. The loan-to-value (LTV) ratio for any mortgage is determined by this formula:

$$\frac{\text{The Mortgage Amount (L)}}{\text{The Home's market value (V)}} = \text{LTV}$$

Or, simply: $\dfrac{L}{V} = LTV$

For example, let's take a property that has an $80,000 mortgage on it and a current market value of $100,000. That property's LTV would be 80 percent as follows:

$$\frac{\$\,80,000}{\$100,000} = 80\%\ LTV$$

Usually, conventional lenders require a loan-to-value or LTV of 75 to 80 percent for their mortgage. Some may, however, agree to a higher figure with, say, the provision of a Private Mortgage Insurance (PMI) by the borrower, or other conditions.

The cash amount that a buyer will require in a home purchase – excluding the closing costs – is the price of the home, minus the mortgage amount. Viewed in terms of the LTV ratio, the cash required is:

$$\begin{array}{l}\text{Value} \quad\ \text{x} \quad\ (100\% - LTV) = \text{Cash}\\ \text{of property}\end{array}$$

Thus, to calculate the home purchase cash that is required to purchase a $110,000 home using a LTV limit of 80 percent, we see that $22,000 is required as a cash down payment, as follows:

($110,000)   x (100% - 80%) = Cash
which translates to, $110,000 x 20% = $22,000

Next, in other instances, a lender (or you) may want to calculate how much cash a buyer (or you) would have to have in order to buy a house of a particular price tag having a particular LTV ratio. Or, to put it another way, using the LTV ratio formula, you can calculate how much of a house you can afford with a given amount of available cash (down payment). This can be determined by the following formula:

$$\frac{\text{Cash down}}{(100\% - LTV\ \text{Ratio})} = \text{Price (Value)}$$

Thus, using the same figures and assuming you have $22,000 to put down and that your lenders are using an 80 percent LTV ratio, we see that you qualify to purchase a home of no more than $110,000, as follows:

$$\frac{\$22,000}{100-80} = \$110,000, \text{ or } \frac{\$22,000}{20} = \$110,000$$

NOTE: The last equation identifies the maximum housing cost you can afford based on how much equity you can command. You should note, however, that because the LTV can vary substantially even in ordinary circumstances, the equity qualification can render such a wide price range meaningless. Hence, what you should do as a potential borrower, is this: *Always perform the income qualification first, then determine, next, how much cash would be required at a given loan-to-value ratio for that particular income level. And, finally, you'll have to determine how much cash will be required, not just for the down payment requirement, but to complete the totality of a home purchase – by adding an estimate of the cash to be needed for the closing costs, to the cash needed for the down payment.*

Remember, also, when you qualify yourself and select the income and cash ratio amounts, to be most conservative. More specifically, the PITI debt ratio and LTV ratio you use should always be for the conservative side (or, at least, be based on what the institutional lenders themselves use at the current time). This way, though that may mean that you'll qualify for a much less expensive house, you'll be much more apt to be granted a loan by your lender and at more reasonable terms.

F. FINANCIALLY PRE-QUALIFYING YOURSELF IN A CONVENTIONAL LOAN SITUATION

Figure 15-1 at p. 116 is a handy worksheet you can use to work out a financial pre-qualification for a loan of conventional (i.e., not involving a government) type. Using this form, you can easily derive the realistic home price range for yourself (the range that you can reasonably afford) in terms of a particular interest rate and the LTV (loan-to-value) ratio. Now, once the appropriate range for you is established, all that will be left for you to do is to get matched with some real estate listings that have various down payment requirements and interest rates. When this form is completed, the exercise provides an income qualification; this is then adjusted by the amount of cash that is either available from you (the buyer) or required to be produced. The buyer's price range that is derived from the calculations (Section III of the Figure 15-1 form) can then be used in matching the buyer with listings having various down payment requirements and financial terms.

Assume These Facts about Yourself (the Buyer)
- The principal buyer, a mechanical engineer, has a gross income of $50,000 per year. Wife, a part-time clerk, earns gross income of $10,000. Parties' income is fairly stable (they have been at same job for 6 years), and goes up approximately 8 percent per year.

- Parties live currently in their home; they will invest in the proposed new home some $35,000 that they expect to realize from the sale of their present home.

- Couple pays $1,300 per month in income taxes.

- Total debts average out to $600 per month for debts that still have over 12 months duration to go.

- Taxes and insurance on the home is $200 per month

- Utilities and maintenance costs on the new home is about $100 per month.

- PITI debt ratio of 28 percent is assumed to be applicable because lenders in the area employ that ratio in their calculations.

- The long-term debt ratio to use with this loan, is 55 percent because a good part of this couple's long term debt still have about 3 years to go before they're paid off.

- This particular couple (the buyers) have a sizable amount of cash on hand, hence you figure that you can reasonably determine their purchasing power based on TWO loan-to-value ratios: 75 percent and 85 percent.

- The mortgage is for a 30-year term (amortized); you are to use a range of interest rates: 11 percent, 13 percent, and 15 percent.

- You decide to use the middle interest rate, 13 percent, and an 85 percent loan-to-value ratio in working out your cash analysis and adjustment section of the form (Section IV).

G. ANALYSIS AND EXPLANATION OF WHAT FIGURE 15-1's CALCULATIONS TELL US

From the within *Qualification Form (Figure 15-1) below, we learn the following:*

1. That these particular home buyers have an affordable home price range that runs from $105,600 at 15% interest rate (30-year term) and 85% LTV, to $158,700 at 11% interest rate and 75% LTV [Section 111(B) of the form]. That is, that given their income and the specified loan terms and conditions, they can afford (they can qualify for) a home of such price range.

2. That these particular buyers have a somewhat special circumstance in that they have more cash-on-hand than that required for the loans, thereby advantageously giving them some "cash-adjusted" higher price ranges for what they can qualify for. The higher price range they qualify for under these circumstances, are as follows: from $154,000 (comprised of the $119,000 mortgage, plus $35,000) at 11% interest, to $124,800 ($89,800 mortgage, plus $35,000) at 15%.

3. That cash-adjusted mid-range for the home price they can afford, at 13%, is $137,600.

4. That, in terms of rough qualification or estimate, this couple can afford a home priced anywhere between $124,800 and $154,000 (the two extreme figures), depending on what financing they can get.

5. That they can expect to get a mortgage loan that ranges anywhere from $89,800 at 15 percent interest rate, to $119,000 at 11% interest, with a mid range of $102,600 at 13% interest.

Figure 15-1

Quantitative Buyer Qualification Worksheet
(Conventional Loan Situation). An Illustration.

Buyer: _____

Essential Data
A. Monthly Income (Gross): $_____

B. Monthly taxes withheld: $_____

C. Projected change in annual income: _____ %

D. Cash available for down payment: $_____

E. Long-term debt: _____ /month

Assumptions
A. PITI ratio: _____ %

B. LT debt ratio: _____ %

C. Interest rate(s) used in analysis: _____ %

D. Loan term and type: _____ years; amortized/interest only (circle one)

E. Taxes (property) and insurance estimate: _____

F. Utilities estimate: _____; maintenance estimate: _____ /month

I. *Income (debt) qualification*

    A. *PITI debt ratio qualification*

        1. Income _____ /month x PITI debt ratio _____ %
            = _____ PITI affordability.

        2. PITI affordability _____ - Taxes (Property) and insurance = PI affordable _____

    B. *LT debt ratio qualification*

        1. Monthly income _____ - Monthly taxes withheld _____ = $ _____ (1) Net effective income

        2. Net effective income _____ x LT ratio_____ = $ _____

        3. Taxes + insurance _____ + Utilities _____ + Maintenance _____

            _____ + Long-term debt _____ = $ _____

        4. $ _____ (2) - $ _____ (3) = $ _____ PI affordable

    C. PI affordable: _____
                (enter here amount from box in Part A or Part B, whichever is less)

II. *Mortgage loan range*

    A. *Amortized vs. interest-only (circle one)*

        • If amortized, use loan tables
        • If interest only, use the following equation for mortgage amount:
              (PI affordable x 12) ÷ Rate = Mortgage amount

B. *Mortgage loan range (compute at desired rates):*[5]

     11%   12%   13%   14%   15%

III. Price range derivation

A. *Select LTV ratios to be applied to mortgage range:*

     75%   80%   85%   90%   95%

B. *Complete the buying range table below. To complete, divide each mortgage loan amount by each LTV ratio used.*

Price range   Assumptions: term _____   type _____

Interest Rate

     11%   12%   13%   14%   15%   Other %

    LTV

75% (25% down)

80% (20% down)

85% (15% down)

90% (10% down)

95% (5% down)

IV. Cash analysis and adjustment

A. *Cash Available:* _____

B. *Cash required at* _____ *interest,* _____% *LTV (Price - Mortgage)*

   1. If cash available <u>exceeds</u> required amount:[6]
      Cash available _____ + Mortgage amount _____ =
      Price qualified for _____

   2. If cash available is <u>less</u> than cash required:
      a. Cash available $ _____ + Mortgage amount $ _____ =
          Tentative price qualified to buy $ _____
      b. Compute new LTV: _____
      c. If acceptable, (a) is qualified amount
      d. If (b) is not acceptable, lower the mortgage amount until it is.

---

[5] Note that Paragraph II (B) represents the mortgage amounts the lender can grant under each interest rate, while paragraph III (B) represents the home price associated with each interest rate and downpayment.

[6] To figure out whether the cash available exceeds or is below the required amount, using the 13% interest and 85% LTV, for example, you simply subtract the applicable LTV figure ($120,700) from the applicable mortgage loan amount ($102,600), giving you $18,100. This amount represents the 15% downpayment amount that a loan of $120,700 requires (15% of $102,600 is $18,100). Now, since the cash providable by the borrowers ($35,000) is in excess of the required downpayment amount ($18,100), you compute your final price qualification under the form's Item B.1. of Section IV.

H. FINANCIALLY QUALIFYING YOURSELF IN AN FHA-BACKED LOAN SITUATION

As fully discussed in Chapter 5, the way the Federal Housing Administration (FHA), a federal government agency, helps home buyers to secure financing is by way of insuring the loans for lenders on the buyers' behalf. And because the government insures the loans, such loans are often obtained with smaller down payments (the minimum down payment for such loans is 3% on the first $25,000 of the loan and 5% on the remainder of the loan, on the average), and with lower interest rates than for conventional loans. Consequently, buyers who are unqualified for a conventional loan may be able to qualify for an FHA-backed loan. Currently the maximum loan amount set by the FHA for FHA-backed loans, is $124,815; however; higher limits are set for certain "high cost" areas of the country. [See Chapter 5 for more on the FHA Loan Program].

(a) Primary differences in Income Qualification Standards Between an FHA Loan and A Conventional Loan

In terms of the buyer's income figure used in the underwriting ratio, the FHA uses the NET monthly income, as opposed to the GROSS monthly income used in conventional loan qualification. Once the borrower's net income is determined, it is then compared against the total proposed housing expense. Under the FHA underwriting standards, the ratio of housing expense to net income may not be more than 38 percent.

(b) Procedures for financially Qualifying an FHA-backed Loan

1. First, calculate the borrower's monthly net income (primarily, deduct the amount of income tax paid each month from the monthly gross income).

2. Next, calculate the proposed housing expense by determining:
   - The proposed monthly mortgage payment
   - The principal, interest, taxes (property), hazard insurance (PITI), and homeowner's dues, if any.
   - The maintenance and repairs expenses
   - The utility expense (maintenance and utility costs are based on the square footage of the house and can be determined by using FHA formulated tables for the given area. Factors such as the age of the house, the structure, air conditioning, energy efficiency features, and the like, are considered by the FHA in making the cost determination).

3. Then, you are to calculate the buyer's other monthly expenses. They should include:
   - The social security (simply use 7.51% of the gross income) and retirement deductions.
   - Child support or alimony payments, if applicable
   - Childcare expenses
   - Insurance premiums
   - Union dues
   - Debts that will not be paid off in 6 months time. (Usually the FHA does not count a debt that will be paid off in 10 months or less. Credit card debts are also handled in the same manner unless they are excessive. However, because some mortgage companies would count any debt over 6 months, it is advised here that monthly payments of $100 or more be always included, even when the debt will be paid off in less than 6 months).[7]

---

[7] Note that, often, a debt can be below the minimum number of months to count as a debt and still be counted by the FHA or the VA or conventional lenders. The determining factor is often the relative size of the monthly payment amount. For example, 5 or 6 payments left on a car at $160 each, may not be counted, but if those payments are $300 or $350, they may be counted as part of the debt. Hence, it is very important that you know exactly what the mortgage company you are applying to will count as a debt against you. Here's what you must always do: simply ask the mortgage company's representative exactly what items are used in the calculations and, furthermore, whether the calculations are figured against the net income or gross income.

4. Finally, you apply this qualifying ratio: 38/53.[8] The first number in the ratio simply measures the percentage of income against the buyer's potential monthly housing cost, and says that your (the buyer's) net monthly income (income <u>after</u> taxes) must be high enough so that the proposed housing costs – comprised of the mortgage principal, interest cost, property taxes, insurance, maintenance, utility expense, homeowner's association dues and assessments – should add up to <u>no more than</u> 38 percent of your income.[9] The second number in the ratio (.53), represents the percentage of income against your total monthly obligations, including the potential housing costs. Simply put, this says that your payments on all your debts and obligations combined, <u>cannot exceed</u> 53 percent of your net income.

To find the "front end" ratio (i.e., the first number of the ratio), you simply multiply the first number, .38, by your net income. And to find the "back-end" ratio (i.e., the second number of the ratio), you multiply the second number, in this case .53, by your net income. You are deemed qualified for a loan if the calculated results for BOTH ratios are less than (below) the FHA qualifying ratios.

A simple Example:
Given a buyer's family monthly net income of $3,100, this net income figure is multiplied by the first number in the ratio, which is 38% (.38).

$$.38 \text{ x } \$3,100 = \$1,178.$$

This is the maximum total housing cost permissible; the total monthly housing costs (housing-related costs only) cannot exceed this amount.

Next, to get the second number in the ratio, which is 53% in this case, you multiply the monthly net income amount by the second number in the ratio (.53) as follows: $3,100 x .53 = $1,643.

The total monthly obligations including the mortgage costs, cannot exceed this amount. So, for this example, the ratio 38/53 is also equal to (the same thing as): <u>$1,178</u>
$1,643

This particular homebuyer's total monthly debts and financial obligations (all debts and obligations combined), cannot exceed this amount.

I. ALTERNATIVE METHOD: 'RESIDUAL INCOME' FORMULA FOR QUALIFYING AN FHA LOAN

FHA Loans
What if an FHA loan applicant does not qualify for a loan using the 38/53 percent ratios? There is an alternative method, called the ***residual income formula***, which the FHA rules say can be used to qualify an applying borrower under such a circumstance.

Basically, under this method, the monthly housing expenses and other expenses are subtracted from the net income to get the borrower's "residual income." This amount is then checked against the FHA's official residential income chart for the region of the country. If the borrower's residential income exceeds the amount

---

[8] As a rule, FHA ratios will normally be larger than ratios for conventional loans. The policy objective for this is to parallel conventional lenders and thereby increase the number of qualified buyers for Section 203(b) mortgage insurance.
[9] As a rule, gross or net income may be used in computing this ratio, depending on the institutional guideline used. However, because the FHA ratios are normally larger than in conventional-type loans, the FHA uses the net income instead of the gross monthly income used in conventional qualification. Conventional lenders generally use the gross income.

allowed on the FHA chart, he will qualify for the loan. The income chart takes into account the number of family members and may very from one area of the country to another. (See illustrated calculation using this formula, at the bottom part of Figure 15-2 on p.121).

Let's Work Out A Specific Buyer's FHA Loan Qualification Analysis

Most of the kinds of information and facts you'll need to have in order to financially qualify a borrower for an FHA-backed loan, are essentially the same as those required for a conventional type of loan. (See Section F above). Nevertheless, here, assume the following facts for the purposes of this loan qualification analysis exercise for an FHA loan:

- Mr. Jones, the principal buyer, a mechanical engineer, has an annual gross income of $34,000. Wife, a part-time clerk, earns gross income of $6,000. The couple's income is fairly stable (they have been at the job for 6 years), and goes up approximately 8 percent per year.

- Couple pays about $900 a month in income taxes.

- They pay $400 per month in total debt obligations on debts which still have more than 6 months to go on them.

- Taxes and hazard insurance costs payable on the kind of home located in the area the parties are looking at, amount to $150 per month.

- Utilizes and maintenance costs average $100 per month.

- Deductions made from salary for social security and retirement payments, approximately $250 per month.

- The mortgage is for 30 years at 10 percent interest rate.

- The price of the house being purchased by the couple is $79,000; they have a down payment of $4,000 (approximately 5 percent down), leaving a balance of $75,000 to finance.

Using the above information, an FHA qualification analysis under the 38/53 qualifying ratio, is worked out this way, as illustrated in Figure 15-2:

NOTE: There's an alternative method allowed by which to calculate the 38/53 ratio (see p. 121), which gives a borrower another way of looking at his financial position from a slightly different perspective. Assuming exactly the same set of facts and figures as in figure 15-2, the two relevant amounts for our purposes here are the borrower's Total (monthly) Proposed Housing Expense ($908), and the Total Obligations ($1,558). Given the fact that the FHA's allowable maximum housing expense is 38% of the borrower's net income, to get the minimum net income you'll need in order to qualify for making this level of housing expenses, you merely divide the proposed housing expense by the maximum allowable .38, as follows: $908.00 ÷ .38, to give you $2,389.47.

This is the minimum level of net income that will be necessary to afford a home having this level of housing expense under the FHA standards. Next, given that the maximum total obligations allowable by the FHA, is .53% of the borrower's net income, to get the minimum net income you'll need to have in order to qualify to bear this level of total obligations, you simply divide the proposed total obligations by the maximum allowable figure (.53), as follows: $\frac{\$1,558.00}{.53}$, to give you $2,939.62.

This is the minimum level of net income that will be necessary to afford a home of the size for which you'll bear the level of total obligations proposed.

FIGURE 15-2   Quantitative Buyer Qualification Worksheet (FHA Loan situation). An Illustration

Buyer's Name: _____

Step 1: Borrowers' net monthly income:

    $2,833   Borrower's income ($34,000 ÷ 12)
    $ 500   Co-borrower's income (6,000 ÷ 12)
    $3.333   Total gross income

   -$ 900   Minus federal taxes withheld
    $2,433   **Net income**

Step 2: Propose monthly payments:

    $ 658   Principal and interest (from amortization table, based on a 30-year loan of $75,000 @ 10%)
    $ 120   Taxes (property)
    $ 30   Hazard insurance
    $ 808   Total mortgage payment

    $ 100   Maintenance and utilities
    $ 908   **Total proposed housing expense for the new home**

Step 3: Add: Other monthly expenses (Fixed payments)

    $ 250   Social security and retirement payments (may vary based on borrower's employment situation. In this case the social security rate is used: .0751 x $3,333).
    $ 400   Monthly debt obligations (auto and personal loans, revolving credit card obligations, child support/alimony payment, etc.)
    $1,558   **Total Obligations**

Step 4: Apply ratios

Allowable housing expense ratio (front-end ratio) of .38:[10]
    $ 925   Allowable housing expense (net income $2,433 x .38).
           Since the proposed housing expense ($908) is below (less than) the allowable housing expense ($925), the Joneses would qualify for the loan.

Allowable total expense ratio (back-end ratio) of .53:
    $1,289   Amount of allowable total obligations (net income $2,433 x .53)
           Since the total obligation expense ($1,558) is <u>more than</u> the allowable total expense ($1,289), the Joneses would not qualify under this ratio.

Alternative Qualifying Method, Using the 'Residual Income' Formula

    $3.333   Gross income
    $ 900   Subtract federal taxes
    $ 908   Subtract housing expense
    $ 250   Subtract social security expense
    $ 400   Subtract debt expense
    $ 875   Residual income (the total income, minus the total expenses)

Using the sample Residual Income Chart below, we see that the minimum residual amount for a three-person family is $781. Since the Joneses residual income ($875) is in excess of that amount, they will qualify for the loan under this formula.

FHA provided Residual Income Chart Figures:[11]

    $ 409   One person
    $ 643   Two persons
    $ 781   Family of 3
    $ 868   Family of 4

---

[10] Note that while this couple will qualify under the first ratio (38%), they will not qualify under the second ratio (53%), since the net income required of them under this later ratio ($2,939.62) will be less than the actual net income they make, which is $2,433.

[11] These tables are subject to periodic changes and have different amounts for each geographic region of the country (there are four regions). Consult the FHA or a mortgage company for the most current figures.

$ 946   Family of 5
$1,026   Family of 6
$1,096   Family of 7

J. FINANCIALLY QUALIFYING YOURSELF IN A VA-BACKED LOAN SITUATION

The Veterans Administration (VA) loan guarantee program uses the cash flow qualifying method similar to the above-described FHA 'residual income' method (Section I above). Because the government guarantees this type of loan, they can be offered with little or no down payment and at a lower interest rate than conventional loans. The VA does not limit the amount of loan an eligible veteran may obtain. Nevertheless, lenders generally establish the maximum loan amount they will make based on the entitlement amount. The amount of a mortgage that the VA will guarantee depends on the size of the loan. Lenders will generally issue a VA mortgage for four times the sum of the guarantee and the down payment (if any) that you put down. Thus, if you qualify, you can get a VA mortgage of up to $184,000 without making any down payment. And you might get a $204,000 VA mortgage with as little as a $5,000 down payment.[12] [See Chapter 5 for more detailed discussion of VA loans].

(a) The Primary Differences Between the FHA and VA Income Qualification Standards

True, the VA uses the cash flow qualifying method similar to the FHA "residual income" method (Section I above). However, there are a few important differences. One major difference between qualifying the buyer for a VA loan and a FHA loan, is with respect to the income figure used in the qualifying ratio: unlike the FHA, which uses net monthly income, the VA uses gross monthly income. Also, generally speaking, the VA will count as a long-term monthly obligation any installment debt that has more than 6 monthly installments still remaining, whereas the FHA is not concerned with a debt unless there are more than 12 installments still to be paid. The expense-to-gross income ratio used by the VA is 41 percent; this compares to the allowable total expense-to-net-income ratio of 53 percent used for the FHA loans.

(b) Procedures For Financially Qualifying a VA Loan

The VA currently uses a two-point system for underwriting veteran loans. One method is a **Debt-to-income ratio** approach; the other method is called the **modified residual income** method. The VA states that both systems are to be used congruently (i.e., on an either-one-or-the-other basis), and that no veteran should be denied a loan based only on one approach.

Follow These Step-by-step Procedures in Qualifying for a VA Loan:

1. First, calculate the borrower's monthly gross income.

2. Next, calculate the total of all the monthly expenses of the borrower.

- These will include:
- Federal income taxes withheld.
- Social security and retirement deductions.
- Debts that will not be paid off before closing or in 6 months. (it's advisable to include all payment of $100 or more, even if the debt will be paid off in less than 6 months).
- Child support and alimony payments, if applicable.
- Childcare payments.
- Job-related expenses (minimum of $50 per working person), e.g. childcare, and the like.
- Proposed house payments and expenses (principal, interest, property taxes, hazard insurance, homeowners association dues, if any, etc.).
- Maintenance and repairs expenses.

---

[12] This works out this way. Four times the $51,000 ($204,000), which is the sum of the maximum $46,000 guarantee allowed by the VA, and your $5,000 down payment.

- Utility expense. (Maintenance and utility costs are based on the square footage of the house and can be determined by reference to the VA tables (see bottom part of p. 124 for a sample VA costs guidelines).

3. Next, apply the qualifying criteria. First, you use the **"Residual Income Formula"** to qualify the veteran. Under this method, the veteran's regular monthly expenses (all the housing and other expenses, as in item 2 above) are subtracted from the gross income. The amount left over, called the borrower's "residual income," is compared to the VA official residual income chart.[13] This amount must fall within a particular range allowable for qualifying. That is, this amount (the veteran's residual income figure) must be above the amount allowed on the VA chart for the borrower to qualify for the loan.

4. Next, you now use the SECOND method, the **"expense-to-income ratio"** formula, to qualify the veteran. To calculate the amounts using this ratio, you multiply the borrower's gross income by the VA qualifying ratio,[14] 41 percent. This resultant amount represents the VA's allowable total housing and other expenses – that is, the maximum amount that must not be exceeded by a veteran's total monthly housing and other expenses (exclusive of the federal taxes and social security expenses).[15]

> **NOTE:** It should be emphasized that the percentages (ratios) outlined herein, while being representative of the lending industry standards and falling within those commonly used by lenders, are only illustrative here. In practice, each lender has its own specific formula and percentages. Also, with most lenders, higher ratios which will, in effect, allow the borrower to borrow more and/or to do so on more lenient terms — may be justified by the presence of certain favorable factors, such as the following: large down payment by the borrower; borrower's demonstrated ability to allocate a greater proportion of his income to basic needs, such as housing expenses; higher energy efficiency of the house; having a private mortgage insurance or government loan guarantee (as in FHA or VA loans); borrower's demonstrated ability to sustain a good credit history and/or to maintain a low debt position; his accumulated savings; borrower's potential for increased earning as indicated, for example, by his education or job training; a degree of borrower's assets and net worth that's more than sufficient to evidence high probability he'll repay the loan, etc.

(c) Let's Work Out A Specific Buyer's VA Loan Qualification Analysis

For the sake of simplicity and consistency, let's just assume here for the purposes of this exercise, exactly the same buyer income and expense facts and information as in the proceeding case involving the FHA loan (See pp. 120). In addition, the VA buyers herein have no children; the home they are buying is a brick house, it has central air conditioning, and is 1,100 square feet.

VA qualification analysis using the *"residual income formula"* and the *"expense-to-income ratio"* methods [items 3 & 4 of Section J(b) above], is worked out as follows, as illustrated in Figure 15-3.

---

[13] Note that the chart varies in different areas of the country and are always changing from time to time. The most accurate information and updates on cost factors must be obtained from the VA or a mortgage broker or company. See Section ___ for more on this.

[14] Note that the 41% figure fluctuates around certain parameters, but is commonly viewed as a strong baseline, as any loan approvals beyond the 41% would generally require the approval of higher ranking officers further up the ladder, as well as an explanatory justification by the cooperating mortgage company involved.

[15] Some lenders (though not all of them) will be happy to tell you, as a courtesy to a potential borrower, their specific "threshold" percentages (ratios) and qualifying formulas. It will not hurt anything for you to ask your lender for such information, in any case.

FIGURE 15-3

Quantitative Buyer Qualification Worksheet (FHA Loan situation). An Illustration

Buyers: Mr. & Mrs Harrison(No Children)

Step 1: Borrowers' net monthly income:
$2,833   Borrower's income ($34,000 ÷ 12)
$ 500   Co-borrower's income ($6,000 ÷ 12)
$3,333   **Total Gross income**

Step 2: Subtract all monthly expenses:
$ 900   Subtract federal taxes withheld
$ 250   Subtract social security/retirement payment (may vary based on borrower's employment situation. In this case the social security rate is used: .0751 x $3,333).
$ 400   Subtract monthly debt obligations
$ 0   Subtract child support, alimony payments
$ 0   Subtract childcare payments
$ 100   Subtract job-related expenses
      $ 658   Principal and interest (from Amortization table, based on a 30-year loan of $75,000 @ 10%)
      $ 120   Taxes (property)
      $ 30   Hazard insurance
      $ 149   Maintenance & utilities (obtained from the VA chart, as below)
      $ 957
-$ 957   Subtract **total house expense payment**
$ 726   Amount remaining for family support (**"Residual Income"**)

Step 3: First, apply the VA qualification criteria
Residual income = $726. Because this amount ($726) is <u>more than</u> the allowable residual income for a veteran and spouse in the chart ($570), the Harrison would qualify under this criterion.
Next, using the **expense-to-income** ratio

$41%. Allowable total expense (excluding Federal and Social Security expenses), is $1,367 ($3,333 x .41)
Borrower's proposed total expenses is $1,457 ($400 + $100 + $957)
Since the proposed total expenses ($1,457) is more than (not below) the VA Allowable expense ($1,367), the Harrisons would <u>not</u> qualify under this ratio[16]

<u>VA Maintenance and Utilities chart</u>

	Frame	Frame w/AC	Brick	Brick w/AC
1,100 sq. ft. or less	10.5	15.0	9.0	13.5
1,101-1,700 sq. ft.	11.2	15.0	10.2	14.0
1,700 sq. ft. or more	9.5	12.7	8.0	11.2

VA - Provided Residual Income Chart
$ 400   One person
$ 570   Veteran and Spouse
$ 670   Family of 3
$ 760   Family of 4
$ 850   Family of 5
$ 940   Family of 6
$1,030   Family of 7
$1,120   Family of 8

---

[16] There is another way, an alternative method, of working out the expense-to-income qualifying ratio. Here, you simply divide the total housing and other expenses (all expenses, exclusive of the Federal tax and social security expenses) by the gross income. This results in a ratio. And if the resultant ratio is less than the 41% factor set by the VA, the veteran will qualify for the loan. For example, in the present example, this would be $\frac{\$1,457}{\$3,333}$, giving a ratio of 44% or .44. The calculated ratio is then compared to the .41 factor set by the VA. And since the proposed ratio in this instance (.44) is <u>in excess</u> of (and not below) the allowable VA ratio of .41, the borrower would not qualify under this alternative method.

K. ANOTHER ALTERNATIVE OR SUPPLEMENTARY QUALIFYING METHOD USED BY SOME LENDERS: THE "POINT SCORING SYSTEM"

Finally, one other method by which a lender may attempt to analyze a loan applicant and to get a sense of his or her financial standing and credit worthiness, is by use of the so-called ***"Point Scoring System."***

This system has been in use for credit card approvals for a number of years now. However, it is only just beginning to be adapted on a much more sophisticated level by a few major home loan investors. The idea here is simple: *"points"* are assigned to each section of a borrower's application and then tallied to arrive at a final lending decision. The scores may then be reviewed and graded by a computer point scoring system. The point scoring system and similar computer-oriented models are likely to be a major tool of the future for the evaluation of credit applications in the lending industry.

The following is a hypothetical example of such a system used by a credit card company or bank to grant credit.

Employment/current position held for:
Less than one year: -1 point
1 to 2 years: 2 points
More than 2 but less than 4 years: 2 points
More than 4 years: 3 points

Length of current residence:
Less than one year: 0 points
More than 1 year: 1 point
More than 2 years: 2 points
More than 3 years: 3 points

Gross monthly income:
Less than $1,000: -2 points
$1,001 to $1,999: 1 point
Over $2,000: 2 points

Over $3,000: 3 points
Over $4,500: 4 points

Savings account:
Yes: 1 point
No: 0 points

Checking accounts:
Yes: 1 point
No: -2 points

Current living arrangement:
Lives with parents: 0 points
Renting: 1 point
Homeowner: 2 points

Current lines of credit:
None: - 3 points
1-2: 1 point
3-5: 2 points
More than five: 3 points

Current/Previous loan or account at this bank:
No previous account history: 0 points
Previous account had more than one late payment: -3 points
Previous account has been paid in full with no lates: 3 points

Credit derogatories in the past two years:
None: 3 points
1-2: -2 points
3-4: -4 points
More than 4: -5 points

Scoring system:
16-20: Very good credit risk. Automatic approval.
12-15: Reasonable risk. Approval subject to supervisor's review and approval.
Less than 12: Automatic rejection.

Chapter 16
LET'S SEARCH FOR THE PROPER HOUSE, NEIGHBORHOOD, AND/OR BROKER FOR YOU

A. Consider What Kind of House and Neighborhood You Want

After you shall have secured your loan pre-qualification and pre-approval (the subject matter of Chapter 13), your next order of business would obviously be to go about searching for and locating a proper house with the right neighborhood characteristics to buy – within the limits imposed by the kind of price range you fall under (Chapters 9 and 13).

HERE ARE THE MAJOR FACTORS TO BE CONSIDERED:

• The Nature of the Community

• Taxes (remember that taxes are determined by <u>both</u> the tax rate and the property valuation practices of the given locality's assessors alone, and that these rates and practices widely differ from locality to locality.)

• The area's zoning laws and practices. [What type of houses—one-family or multiple-family, commercial or residential, or both, etc.—are permitted? Does the community permit easy variances in zoning laws? Are industrial and commercial buildings permitted near your house? Are conversions allowed? Etc.]

• The neighborhood—the location, the surroundings, the type of people who live there and their economic/ social level; accessibility of the location to schools, shopping centers, public transportation, etc. *[Experts assert that the 'neighborhood' factor is the single most important factor to consider in picking a home.]*

• Do you want a new or old house?   A single family house or one with rental units? Or a condominium?

[See Figure 3.1, "NEIGHBORHOOD INSPECTION CHECKLIST" on p. 20 below]

B. Now, Search for the Right House for You

Having determined the type of house you can afford (Chapter 9 at p.60) , and considered the kinds of housing and neighborhood characteristics you can live with within your budget range (Section A above), you are now finally ready to begin THE SEARCH FOR THE RIGHT HOUSE TO BUY.

1. The Three Basic Channels for Searching for a House

There are various ways by which you could shop for a house that is right for you and your family. Among such ways, are these three principal avenues by which houses are found or sold:

  i) through real estate advertisements contained in newspapers and magazines;
  ii) through real estate brokers; and
  iii) through direct purchase from the home owner.

128

In so far as a buyer (as opposed to a seller) is concerned, it really wouldn't matter from which source he makes his purchase or his find, providing the house at issue is the right one for him, and the price and terms of purchase are right. For one thing, it wouldn't matter whether he uses a broker as his source for finding the house to buy, since he wouldn't have to pay any fees or commission for the service, anyway, as the common rule is that it is only the property seller that pays the broker's commission. A wise approach would be to use all three sources as fully as possible in searching for a house—you are exposed to more opportunities and to a wider variety and options, this way!

2. The Advantages Of Using A Good Real Estate Broker In Finding Your Prospective House

If, eventually, you must make your purchase through a broker—and chances are that you probably would, since the overwhelming majority of home purchases (about 80%) are ultimately made through brokers—it is most essential that you be prepared to pick the right broker, and that you use the broker's services wisely. In deed, for a buyer—a wise buyer—*THE USE OF A GOOD BROKER FOR HELP IN FINDING A HOUSE COULD BE VERY USEFUL AND ADVANTAGEOUS:* the broker is often quite knowledgeable in the real property values of his area of operation and you can learn a lot from him about the general market conditions of the area's property, about what property is available and what they are really worth, about the general state and characteristics of the neighborhood, about what comparative property in the area has sold for in the recent past, and about what kinds of financing is available and where you stand in terms of being able to qualify for a purchase loan with the lenders, and much more.

Also, many of the larger brokers and brokerage chains provide an extensive, often computerized promotional and publicity networks, including newspaper and radio ads and, for those members which belong, the **Multiple Listing System (MLS).** Through such vast network systems (they include names like Match Maker, Electronic Realty Associates, Red Carpet, Better Homes & Gardens, Century 21, Partners, Re/Max, and Realty World), a prospective buyer in, say, New York, who wants to relocate to Houston, Texas, can learn of the listings in Houston without ever having left New York, thereby making for a wider, faster and easier matching of buyer and seller and on a national market.

Furthermore, since it is ultimately in the broker's interest that you make a purchase (he gets to collect his commission from the seller only if you make a purchase!), he frequently serves another important function which might prove just as relevant for you: that of helping you in the negotiating process with the seller, back and forth, on the terms and conditions of sale. Indeed, as we shall see in the chapters ahead [see, especially pp. 25-6], the role of a competent broker in being able to uncover and provide insight into the underlying "need to sell" situation of a home owner, the underlying needs that motivate him (or her) to put up his house for sale, is often crucial in enabling a buyer make intelligent negotiations with the home owner and to secure a property on a favorable and affordable financing or other terms.

don't hesitate, ask Questions!

Finally, aside from every other consideration by the home-buyer, for most people buying under today's market conditions, there has probably emerged one overriding consideration in making the selection of a broker: the broker's ability to aid you in your financing needs—how much expertise, experience, and ability the broker commands in locating sources of financing, and in packaging and arranging a feasible financing deal for you, the home buyer! One report* by the New York Times pointedly put it this way:

> "Because persistently high interest rates have put a crimp in the housing market, a home owner's choice of the right real estate agent can be crucial...Today, the best [real estate sales] agent may be someone who can skillfully maneuver buyers and sellers through the intricacies of 'creative financing'.*"

The report quoted a past president of the New Jersey Association of Realtors and Sales Manager of a Wayne, New Jersey real estate agency, Norman N. Kailo of the Soldoveri Agency: "There are at least 40 different ways of financing a sale [today], and if an agent can't name at least 10 right off the bat, you might want to find someone else."

In sum, in the final analysis, whether as a buyer or a seller, a good broker will save you both time and money in a host of ways. He will make one of the better efforts to discover your specific needs and could have the listings that will fit those needs. He will know about local financing sources and creative financial techniques, and will be able effectively to negotiate your needs with the seller or home owner, and to literally "sell" your offer to the home owner. He can help smooth the way in your dealings with appraisers, home inspectors, lawyers, town officials, escrow agents, home closing agents, and other parties that may be involved in a home sale arrangement.

3. General Pointers for Finding the Right House

Closely follow the following tips in looking for the proper house to buy or the proper broker to use, and you shall have likely selected the right house for yourself, in the end:

- In searching for property, peruse the advertisements in both the "classified ads" and the "real estate" sections of *two basic types* of newspapers: a large metropolitan newspaper covering the area (e.g., the N.Y. Times, the L.A. Times or the Washington Post), as well as a strictly local paper.

- The Federal Department of Commerce reports that 1 in 3 homes sell without the intervention of a broker. Hence, the point is that in searching for a house to buy (or to sell) you cannot afford not to take into account the great potential for business outside the traditional brokerage community. Look for the many sources of support and promotion of the for-sale-by-owner concept in your area for which there is a growing number in recent years. For example:
  —there are those mortgage lenders who offer free marketing videos and help with qualifying prospective home buyers and arranging the loan.
  —search through cable TV access channels for personally made videos, electronic billboards (like the one run by American Online and Prodigy) for sources of home-for-sale information.
  —there has been an exploding growth of regional give-away publications exclusively geared to advertising for-sale-by-owner properties. In the New York-New Jersey Metropolitan regions, for example, they include: For Sale By Owner, based in Coram, L.I., Hill's For Sale By Owner, based in Poughkeepsie, N.Y., FSBO Homes of New Jersey, based in Toms River, N.J., and For Sale By Owner Connection, based in Canton, Conn. [Nationally, there are now over 150 such publications. The publishers' National Trade Group, called By Owner Real Estate Association of America, can be reached as follows: Picket Fence Productions, Burlington, Vt., (802) 660-3167.]

- Let your friends and neighbors know that you are house hunting. Then take your time in shopping the market.

- Identify the area in which you want to buy – and are sure you can afford. Look around in that area and note any "for sale" signs. Narrow down your choice before you contact a real estate agent.

- Visit as many houses as possible and compare prices, housing features, and neighborhood conditions.

- Take a Sunday afternoon drive or a walk through the neighborhoods you desire. You may locate a few "House for Sale" signs and model homes on display.

"How to Choose a Real Estate Agent," The N.Y. Times, Sunday, Oct. 18, 1981.

- *Multiple Listing Service* companies and other independent companies in many areas publish booklets of information on homes for sale, and some even sponsor 30-minute television shows featuring listings. Having identified the area that fit your needs and price range, then contact these companies.

- Be thorough in your search, visit the house that appeals to you as many times as possible —two, three, four, or more times, and look it over and over.

- Inspect the house during the day, as well as at night (and also when it is raining, and/or snowing, if possible.)

- Check with all important sources of information—friends and relatives, real estate brokers, newspapers, people at work, neighborhood residents, supermarket bulletin boards, community organizations, City Hall (about taxes, schools, etc.), lenders in the area (for recent sales prices, etc.)

- *Ask questions, more questions, and still more questions* of the home owner, the seller or the broker, about the house—when it was built and bought, why the sale was being made, how long the house has been on the market, what major structural work have had to be done on the house and when and why, how much the owner had bought the property for, the major problems in the neighborhood, etc., etc?

4. General Pointers For Finding The Right Broker Who May Help You In Finding The Right House

- In looking for a good real estate broker, ask for recommendations by friends who have used the services of one, or call the mortgage officers of local banks and savings-and-loan associations. Notice which brokers run the most newspaper ads for the kind of houses you have in mind and in the desired neighborhood. (Of course, if all you are interested in is finding any real estate broker whatsoever, you can always find one in the local Yellow Pages under the heading "Broker" or "Real Estate"!)

- Remember, that, *as a buyer, the kind of sellers you are primarily interested in finding are sellers who are in a "need-to-sell" situation*—cases where the home owner/seller is under some degree of pressure to sell, such as a marriage, or business split-up, deteriorating physical health, job opportunities or relocation to another community, etc. Hence, your best prospect is to look for real estate brokers who are experienced in the specific geographical area you are interested in. Such a broker will usually have important exclusive listings and would be in a favorable position to hear about *need-to-sell* situations as they come on the market—in many cases even <u>before</u> they come on the market. But, be careful to make the proper distinction and selection. You've got to pick the big, successful, well-established brokerage firms. But, within the firms, themselves, you've also got to try to work with a broker or sales agent who has a depth of professional experience in both the area you're interested in and the type of housing situation you are looking for, rather than someone new to real estate or new to the community. (Pointer: simply ask the brokerage firm's manager for the name of the most successful real estate broker or salesperson in the organization, the top among the 20% of the sales force who usually make 80% of the sales. Such "crackerjack" salesperson is most likely to have the experience, know-how, or the drive, persistence, and negotiating skill to help you.)

   For the particular agent you pick to work with in the firm, insist on a specific answer to the question of whether the agent sells property full-time. You want someone who puts in 40 hours a week or more, whose sole means of livelihood is real estate selling.

- You can use the internal structure of a brokerage firm for a clue in gauging whether that's the kind of brokerage firm you should choose. The ideal one is a fairly large firm that has a large budget (this way it will be able to continue advertising in a slow market and not cut back); one that has lots of agents (the more agents, usually the more contacts and leads they will have, and the more homes and buyers and sellers they will have.) The firm should advertise a lot (a broker who advertises houses heavily week after week is sure to develop a list of prospective buyers than one who doesn't.)

   Visit any brokerage firm you're interested in. Is the office open at nights and on weekends? Are the agents actually working, or are they just reading newspapers or chatting around? Telephone the brokerage houses and inquire about the kind of house (describe it) you're interested in. Does the sales agent who comes to the phone try to sell you another house (as a good salesperson rightly should) if you say the house offered or advertised is too expensive or not to your liking?

- As stated above, as a buyer, your primary home buying need is to find a need-to-sell situation. In addition, you also want to be able to find an *affordable* house that will allow you some sort of creative financing. To be able to get this, you will be best served to work with many brokers—as many as you feel you can. By making your needs known to several brokers who have a depth of experience about the community you are interested in, as well as experience with creative financing and the art of negotiating, you directly multiply your chances of finding what you are looking for several times over.

- Check (ask the broker, if you have to), the type of listing arrangement a broker has on most houses he (she) has in his listing inventory—is it *"Exclusive Right To Sell"* arrangement, or *"Exclusive Listing,"* or *"Open Listing"?* ("Exclusive right to sell" listing means that the broker will have the exclusive right to sell the property, subject to the rate of the commission and conditions specified, and the broker will be entitled to a commission whether he sells the property or the home owner sells it; "exclusive" listing provides that the owner has the right to sell the property himself without having to pay a commission to the listing broker; and "open" listing is a listing that is as open to as many brokers as the home seller wishes).

  In the home sale business, houses for sale are a broker's stock-in-trade, and the listings are said to be "the very lifeblood" of a growing real estate office. Hence, if you find that a brokerage firm's listed inventory of homes consists mostly of Exclusive-Right-To-Sell listing, that's a good indication that the firm is probably a well-established broker since brokers who enter into such an arrangement are those with the financial security to plan a full-scale marketing program to sell the property. (The seasoned broker with exclusive listings on realistically priced property, will work hardest to sell property his own firm has listed (exclusive listing), since he doesn't have to share his commission with another firm. Furthermore, it's not just a matter of his trying to win the entire commission—it's a matter of pride.) If, on the other hand, a broker's listing consists mostly of the third type, the Open listings, or multiple listing or co-broker listings, or if the broker has next to nothing in the way of a listing inventory of homes for sale, that's not the kind of broker you should want to deal with— he (she) has been shut out of the all-important exclusive listings that invariably go to the established, respected local firms with a reputation for a solid sales performance, hence he probably is either too new or has some other problems preventing his firm from getting the all-important listing of the right type.

  Thirdly, if a brokerage firm doesn't belong to the local Multiple Listing Sevice, unless it can give you a good reason why it doesn't, you should pass it by. Such a firm won't have access to as many of the serious buyers in the area as will a firm that does belong to the multiple-listing service. A Multiple Listing Service is a system whereby agents from competing firms cooperate in selling all houses in the area in return for a sharing of the commission.

- Check the broker's listing in terms of its prices. Are the vast majority of his listings overpriced? If so, that's a good signal that that's the wrong broker for you. That's an indication either that there's a lack of knowledge on the broker's part about the current market values, or worse yet, that he might be one among the little crop of the overzealous but dishonest brokers, who, in their desire to get listings, will list a house well above current market prices in order to satisfy the sellers unrealistic desire to make a killing in the sale of his home.

- The agent or broker you need is not a high-pressure, promoter salesman type—one who is interested only in the "fast buck and the fast sale," and is interested in pushing the buyer (or even the seller) into something that fits his (the broker's) own needs, but not necessarily the buyer's needs. You need an agent who inspires confidence, but not necessarily by being a fast-talker.

  How do you make this differentiation? It's simple. If, for example, the buyer says "Hey, this house doesn't have a living room," the fast-talker type will say, "One less room for you to clean," explains one expert. The agent who inspires confidence will say, "That's true, and I know you'd prefer a house with a separate living room, rather than a combined living room/dining room, but that's why this house is so reasonably priced. You might pay $40,000 more for a house like this if it had a separate living room. That would make your monthly payments a lot higher, wouldn't it?' "

- Go to any "open house" in the areas of your interest. Talk to the real estate agents at each open house and tell them what you need.

- Real estate is not unlike any other area of business. It has its own share of people who lack personal ethics and integrity. And it will be your task to seek out those brokers who not only have the needed experience, but possess integrity. There are several ways you can size up a broker concerning this. Simply look to the way he deals with you. Does he come on or across as a fast-talking promoter? Does he make exaggerated claims? Does he make deceitful or misleading statements or indicate devious or unethical tactics? For example, if a broker engages in what is generally known as "puffing"—i.e., overselling—beware. That's a red flag, as when a broker tells you, for example, that the schools in the district are "the best in the country," or that the house he's showing you is "the most fantastic buy" he'd ever handled. Double-check him! Visit the schools and talk to the principal, for example, or ask the neighbors. If you can, while you are in the broker's office, listen to what and how he (or others who work with him) say to other brokers or customers on the telephone. Is the broker one who is always advertising unbelievable home sales and financial deals that always seem to vanish when you (or other customers) get to his office—the old "bait and switch" tactic, where the prospect is lured in with a sweet offer and then switched into "the better model for you"!? Be warned. That's a red flag.

- Does the broker generally take the time to ask you questions about your needs? Or, does his main thrust simply seem to be to persuade you to buy (or to sell, as the case may be) where he can make the bigger commission, rather than to fit your own needs?

- When it comes time for you to visit some houses listed under a particular broker or agent, deliberately and freely raise some objections with different aspects of the property and be attentive to see how he reacts or responds. Does he (she) fight you when you bring up an objection? Does he give you a put-down kind of response, a "you're-wrong-on-that-point," or "how-stupid-of-you-to-have-asked that-question" kind of answer? If so, that's a good sign that you're probably dealing with an inexperienced broker. The experienced real estate salesperson, on the other hand, will minimize the effect of a buyer's objection; even when he isn't agreeing with you, he'll still acknowledge your objection and convey the impression that he's taken it under consideration. Instead of fighting you or giving you the how-could-you-ask-such-a-question attitude, he'll let you feel that your questions are welcome, that he is giving you new information that more than compensates for your objection. He'll use such phrases as "that's an interesting point," or "I know what you mean, but..." or, "I agree with your thinking; however, don't loose sight of..."

- Independently check out the broker's claims or reputation—is he (or she) licensed to sell real estate (ask to see the license) ; is he a member of any reputable professional organization [e.g., a Graduate of the Realtors Institute, (G.R.I.)], or a holder of a Certified Residential Specialist (CRS) designation, or a member of the National Association of Realtors; how long has he been on the job; how many houses has he sold in the last 6 months, etc?

    If he is a member of the National Association of Realtors, for example, qualifying him to be called a "Realtor," you'll at least know that he will be required to take certain training courses and to obey a strict code of ethics, and that if you ever have a complaint against the broker, you will have someone to complain to. But don't rely exclusively on the certificates. They are no guarantee that the agent who has them will necessarily be a great agent, but they're a plus. As one expert, Edith Lank, author of The Homeseller's Kit, accurately warns, "They [the certificates], mean you've at least got someone who invested some time and effort and is experienced." A GRI designation requires about 90 hours of study, and about 90% of all relators hold a GRI. A CRS designation, on the other hand, which is the more impressive qualification, requires a minimum number of transactions, a GRI or ten years experience, and extra hours of study; only about 3% of all Relators hold a CRS.

- Before you eventually settle on some three or more major and experienced brokers, visit several brokers and find out what is available in the given areas within your price range. Ask to see each **broker's 'listing book,'** and make copies of the information for the houses you desire.

- Make sure the broker tells you about all, not just some, of the houses available in your price range.

- When visiting a house, **ASK QUESTIONS of the broker** about the house and the neighborhood. [Honest brokers will tell you about the faults of a house (or a neighborhood), as well as its good points. BUT TO GET IT, YOU'LL HAVE TO ASK—AND ASK THE RIGHT QUESTIONS! If a broker doesn't know or have answers to a particular question at the moment, make sure he gets the information for you. Don't let him brush it aside or forget it.

- Perhaps, the single most important consideration in ultimately settling on the right brokers to engage, is this question: does he (she) possess an expertise and experience in working out *"creative financing"* arrangements for the home buyer, and does he have a working relationship with banks, mortgage brokers, and financing sources? Ask him and ask other people he may have done this kind of service for, and satisfy yourself sufficiently on this.

A WORD OF CAUTION ON PICKING A BROKER: In all you do, it is important that you remember, nonetheless, NOT to rely solely or too heavily on the words or oral promises of the broker. Remember, the broker is not your partner; he is an independent third party. He is there, first and foremost, to NEGOTIATE for the highest possible price that you will pay and the lowest price the owner will accept; he is engaged by, and is therefore working principally for, the seller, and then for himself—not for you!

FIGURE *16-1*
Neighborhood Inspection Checklist

NEIGHBORHOOD QUALITY	YES	NO	NOT IMPORTANT
1. Are the homes well taken care of?	☐	☐	☐
2. Are there good public services (police, fire)?	☐	☐	☐
3. Are there paved roads?	☐	☐	☐
4. Are there sidewalks?	☐	☐	☐
5. Is there adequate street lighting?	☐	☐	☐
6. Is there a city sewer system?	☐	☐	☐
7. Is there a safe public water supply?	☐	☐	☐
8. Are the public schools good?	☐	☐	☐

NEIGHBORHOOD CONVENIENCE			
1. Will you be near your work?	☐	☐	☐
2. Are there schools nearby?	☐	☐	☐
3. Are there shopping centers nearby?	☐	☐	☐
4. Is there public transportation available?	☐	☐	☐
5. Will you be near child care services?	☐	☐	☐
6. Are hospitals, clinics, or doctors close by?	☐	☐	☐
7. Is there a park or playground nearby?	☐	☐	☐

NEIGHBORS			
1. Will you be near friends or relatives?	☐	☐	☐
2. Will you be near other children of your kids' *age*?	☐	☐	☐
3. Will you feel comfortable with the neighbors?	☐	☐	☐
4. Is there an active community group?	☐	☐	☐

DOES THE NEIGHBORHOOD HAVE ANY PROBLEMS, SUCH AS:			
1. Increasing Real Estate taxes?	☐	☐	☐
2. Decreasing sales prices of homes?	☐	☐	☐
3. Lots of families moving away?	☐	☐	☐
4. Heavy traffic or noise?	☐	☐	☐
5. Litter or pollution?	☐	☐	☐
6. Factories or heavy industry?	☐	☐	☐
7. Businesses closing down?	☐	☐	☐
8. Vacant houses or buildings?	☐	☐	☐
9. Increasing crime or vandalism?	☐	☐	☐

	GOOD	FAIR	POOR
WHAT IS YOUR OVERALL RATING OF THE NEIGHBORHOOD?	☐	☐	☐

APPENDIX A

APPENDIX A: (MORTGAGE) AMORTIZATION TABLES

How To Read The Tables In Appendix A

Appendix A tables show the monthly payments necessary to "amortize" (i.e., pay off) a loan at differing rates from 8 percent to 15 percent, and for amounts ranging from $50 to $100,000, and for terms of 5,10, 15, 20, 25 and 30 years.

However, note that, additionally, there are some few other simple, quick methods by which you may approximate, from the figures listed here, the monthly payments for other rates and amounts. For example, to estimate the payments for a loan at 9.125% interest, you may simply take the half-way point between 9 percent rate and 9.25 percent rate. For a mortgage of $81,000, you can multiply the $10,000 figure by 0.81. For $197,000 mortgage, you'll multiply the $100,000 figure by 1.97.

8.50%

Amount	5 Years	10 Years	15 Years	20 Years	25 Years	30 Years
50	1.03	.62	.50	.44	.41	.39
100	2.06	1.24	.99	.87	.81	.77
500	10.26	6.20	4.93	4.34	4.03	3.85
1000	20.52	12.40	9.85	8.68	8.06	7.69
2000	41.04	24.80	19.70	17.36	16.11	15.38
5000	102.59	62.00	49.24	43.40	40.27	38.45
10000	205.17	123.99	98.48	86.79	80.53	76.90
15000	307.75	185.98	147.72	130.18	120.79	115.34
20000	410.34	247.98	196.95	173.57	161.05	153.79
25000	512.92	309.97	246.19	216.96	201.31	192.23
30000	615.50	371.96	295.43	260.35	241.57	230.68
35000	718.08	433.95	344.66	303.74	281.83	269.12
40000	820.67	495.95	393.90	347.13	322.10	307.57
45000	923.25	557.94	443.14	390.53	362.36	346.02
50000	1025.83	619.93	492.37	433.92	402.62	384.46
55000	1128.41	681.93	541.61	477.31	442.88	422.91
60000	1231.00	743.92	590.85	520.70	483.14	461.35
65000	1333.58	805.91	640.09	564.09	523.40	499.80
70000	1436.17	867.90	689.32	607.48	563.66	538.24
75000	1538.74	929.90	738.56	650.87	603.93	576.69
80000	1641.33	991.89	787.80	694.26	644.19	615.14
85000	1743.50	1053.88	837.03	737.65	684.45	653.58
90000	1846.49	1115.88	886.27	781.05	724.71	692.03
95000	1949.08	1177.87	935.51	824.44	764.97	730.47
100000	2051.66	1239.86	984.74	867.83	805.23	768.92

8.75%

Amount	5 Years	10 Years	15 Years	20 Years	25 Years	30 Years
50	1.04	.63	.50	.45	.42	.40
100	2.07	1.26	1.00	.89	.83	.79
500	10.32	6.27	5.00	4.42	4.12	3.94
1000	20.64	12.54	10.00	8.84	8.23	7.87
2000	41.28	25.07	19.99	17.68	16.45	15.74
5000	103.19	62.67	49.98	44.19	41.11	39.34
10000	206.38	125.33	99.95	88.38	82.22	78.68
15000	309.56	188.00	149.92	132.56	123.33	118.01
20000	412.75	250.66	199.89	176.75	164.43	157.35
25000	515.94	313.32	249.87	220.93	205.54	196.68
30000	619.12	375.99	299.84	265.12	246.65	236.02
35000	722.31	438.65	349.81	309.30	287.76	275.35
40000	825.49	501.31	399.78	353.49	328.86	314.69
45000	928.68	563.98	449.76	397.67	369.97	354.02
50000	1031.87	626.64	499.73	441.86	411.08	393.36
55000	1135.05	689.30	549.70	486.05	452.18	432.69
60000	1238.24	751.97	599.67	530.23	493.29	472.03
65000	1341.43	814.63	649.65	574.42	534.40	511.36
70000	1444.61	877.29	699.62	618.60	575.51	550.70
75000	1547.80	939.96	749.59	662.79	616.61	590.03
80000	1650.98	1002.62	799.56	706.97	657.72	629.37
85000	1754.17	1065.28	849.54	751.16	698.83	668.70
90000	1857.36	1127.95	899.51	795.34	739.94	708.04
95000	1960.54	1190.61	949.48	839.53	781.04	747.37
100000	2063.73	1253.27	999.45	883.72	822.15	786.71

8.00%

Amount	5 Years	10 Years	15 Years	20 Years	25 Years	30 Years
50	1.02	.61	.48	.42	.39	.37
100	2.03	1.22	.96	.84	.78	.74
500	10.14	6.07	4.78	4.19	3.86	3.67
1000	20.28	12.14	9.56	8.37	7.72	7.34
2000	40.56	24.27	19.12	16.73	15.44	14.68
5000	101.39	60.67	47.79	41.83	38.60	36.69
10000	202.77	121.33	95.57	83.65	77.19	73.38
15000	304.15	182.00	143.35	125.47	115.78	110.07
20000	405.53	242.66	191.14	167.29	154.37	146.76
25000	506.91	303.32	238.92	209.12	192.96	183.45
30000	608.30	363.99	286.70	250.94	231.55	220.13
35000	709.68	424.65	334.48	292.76	270.14	256.82
40000	811.06	485.32	382.27	334.58	308.73	293.51
45000	912.44	545.98	430.05	376.40	347.32	330.20
50000	1013.82	606.64	477.83	418.23	385.91	366.89
55000	1115.21	667.31	525.61	460.05	424.50	403.58
60000	1216.59	727.97	573.40	501.87	463.09	440.26
65000	1317.97	788.63	621.18	543.69	501.69	476.95
70000	1419.35	849.30	668.96	585.51	540.28	513.64
75000	1520.73	909.96	716.74	627.34	578.87	550.33
80000	1622.12	970.63	764.53	669.16	617.46	587.02
85000	1723.50	1031.29	812.31	710.98	656.05	623.70
90000	1824.88	1091.95	860.09	752.80	694.64	660.39
95000	1926.26	1152.62	907.87	794.62	733.23	697.08
100000	2027.64	1213.28	955.66	836.45	771.82	733.77

8.25%

Amount	5 Years	10 Years	15 Years	20 Years	25 Years	30 Years
50	1.02	.62	.49	.43	.40	.38
100	2.04	1.23	.98	.86	.79	.76
500	10.20	6.14	4.86	4.27	3.95	3.76
1000	20.40	12.27	9.71	8.53	7.89	7.52
2000	40.80	24.54	19.41	17.05	15.77	15.03
5000	101.99	61.33	48.51	42.61	39.43	37.57
10000	203.97	122.66	97.02	85.21	78.85	75.13
15000	305.95	183.98	145.53	127.81	118.27	112.69
20000	407.93	245.31	194.03	170.42	157.70	150.26
25000	509.91	306.64	242.54	213.02	197.12	187.82
30000	611.89	367.96	291.05	255.62	236.54	225.38
35000	713.87	429.29	339.55	298.23	275.96	262.95
40000	815.86	490.62	388.06	340.83	315.39	300.51
45000	917.84	551.94	436.57	383.43	354.81	338.07
50000	1019.82	613.27	485.08	426.04	394.23	375.64
55000	1121.80	674.59	533.58	468.64	433.65	413.20
60000	1223.78	735.92	582.09	511.24	473.08	450.76
65000	1325.76	797.25	630.60	553.85	512.50	488.33
70000	1427.74	858.57	679.10	596.45	551.92	525.89
75000	1529.72	919.90	727.61	639.05	591.34	563.45
80000	1631.71	981.23	776.12	681.66	630.77	601.02
85000	1733.69	1042.55	824.62	724.26	670.19	638.58
90000	1835.67	1103.88	873.13	766.86	709.61	676.14
95000	1937.65	1165.20	921.64	809.47	749.03	713.71
100000	2039.63	1226.53	970.15	852.07	788.46	751.27

9.50%

Amount	5 Years	10 Years	15 Years	20 Years	25 Years	30 Years
50	1.06	.65	.53	.47	.44	.43
100	2.11	1.30	1.05	.94	.88	.85
500	10.51	6.47	5.23	4.67	4.37	4.21
1000	21.01	12.94	10.45	9.33	8.74	8.41
2000	42.01	25.88	20.89	18.65	17.48	16.82
5000	105.01	64.70	52.22	46.61	43.69	42.05
10000	210.02	129.40	104.43	93.22	87.37	84.09
15000	315.03	194.10	156.64	139.82	131.06	126.13
20000	420.04	258.80	208.85	186.43	174.74	168.18
25000	525.05	323.50	261.06	233.04	218.43	210.22
30000	630.06	388.20	313.27	279.64	262.11	252.26
35000	735.07	452.90	365.48	326.25	305.80	294.30
40000	840.08	517.60	417.69	372.86	349.48	336.35
45000	945.09	582.29	469.91	419.46	393.17	378.39
50000	1050.10	646.99	522.12	466.07	436.85	420.43
55000	1155.11	711.69	574.33	512.68	480.54	462.47
60000	1260.12	776.39	626.54	559.28	524.22	504.52
65000	1365.13	841.09	678.75	605.89	567.91	546.56
70000	1470.14	905.79	730.96	652.50	611.59	588.60
75000	1575.14	970.49	783.17	699.10	655.28	630.65
80000	1680.15	1035.19	835.38	745.71	698.96	672.69
85000	1785.16	1099.88	887.60	792.32	742.65	714.73
90000	1890.17	1164.58	939.81	838.92	786.33	756.77
95000	1995.18	1229.28	992.02	885.53	830.02	798.82
100000	2100.19	1293.98	1044.23	932.14	873.70	840.86

9.75%

Amount	5 Years	10 Years	15 Years	20 Years	25 Years	30 Years
50	1.06	.66	.53	.48	.45	.43
100	2.12	1.31	1.06	.95	.90	.86
500	10.57	6.54	5.30	4.75	4.46	4.30
1000	21.13	13.08	10.60	9.49	8.92	8.60
2000	42.25	26.16	21.19	18.98	17.83	17.19
5000	105.63	65.39	52.97	47.43	44.56	42.96
10000	211.25	130.78	105.94	94.86	89.12	85.92
15000	316.87	196.16	158.91	142.28	133.68	128.88
20000	422.49	261.55	211.88	189.71	178.23	171.84
25000	528.11	326.93	264.85	237.13	222.79	214.79
30000	633.73	392.32	317.81	284.56	267.35	257.75
35000	739.35	457.70	370.78	331.99	311.90	300.71
40000	844.97	523.09	423.75	379.41	356.46	343.67
45000	950.60	588.47	476.72	426.84	401.02	386.62
50000	1056.22	653.86	529.69	474.26	445.57	429.58
55000	1161.84	719.24	582.65	521.69	490.13	472.54
60000	1267.46	784.63	635.62	569.12	534.69	515.50
65000	1373.08	850.01	688.59	616.54	579.24	558.46
70000	1478.70	915.40	741.56	663.97	623.80	601.41
75000	1584.32	980.78	794.53	711.39	668.36	644.37
80000	1689.94	1046.17	847.50	758.82	712.91	687.33
85000	1795.57	1111.55	900.46	806.24	757.47	730.29
90000	1901.19	1176.94	953.43	853.67	802.03	773.24
95000	2006.81	1242.32	1006.40	901.10	846.59	816.20
100000	2112.43	1307.71	1059.37	948.52	891.14	859.16

9.00%

Amount	5 Years	10 Years	15 Years	20 Years	25 Years	30 Years
50	1.04	.64	.51	.45	.42	.41
100	2.08	1.27	1.02	.90	.84	.81
500	10.38	6.34	5.08	4.50	4.20	4.03
1000	20.76	12.67	10.15	9.00	8.40	8.05
2000	41.52	25.34	20.29	18.00	16.79	16.10
5000	103.80	63.34	50.72	44.99	41.96	40.24
10000	207.59	126.68	101.43	89.98	83.92	80.47
15000	311.38	190.02	152.14	134.96	125.88	120.70
20000	415.17	253.36	202.86	179.95	167.84	160.93
25000	518.96	316.69	253.57	224.94	209.80	201.16
30000	622.76	380.03	304.28	269.92	251.76	241.39
35000	726.55	443.37	355.00	314.91	293.72	281.62
40000	830.34	506.71	405.71	359.90	335.68	321.85
45000	934.13	570.05	456.42	404.88	377.64	362.09
50000	1037.92	633.38	507.14	449.87	419.60	402.32
55000	1141.71	696.72	557.85	494.85	461.56	442.55
60000	1245.51	760.06	608.56	539.84	503.52	482.78
65000	1349.30	823.40	659.28	584.83	545.48	523.01
70000	1453.09	886.74	709.99	629.81	587.44	563.24
75000	1556.88	950.07	760.70	674.80	629.40	603.47
80000	1660.67	1013.41	811.42	719.79	671.36	643.70
85000	1764.47	1076.75	862.13	764.77	713.32	683.93
90000	1868.26	1140.09	912.84	809.76	755.28	724.17
95000	1972.05	1203.42	963.56	854.74	797.24	764.40
100000	2075.84	1266.76	1014.27	899.73	839.20	804.63

9.25%

Amount	5 Years	10 Years	15 Years	20 Years	25 Years	30 Years
50	1.05	.65	.52	.46	.43	.42
100	2.09	1.29	1.03	.92	.86	.83
500	10.44	6.41	5.15	4.58	4.29	4.12
1000	20.88	12.81	10.30	9.16	8.57	8.23
2000	41.76	25.61	20.59	18.32	17.13	16.46
5000	104.40	64.02	51.46	45.80	42.82	41.14
10000	208.80	128.04	102.92	91.59	85.64	82.27
15000	313.20	192.05	154.38	137.39	128.46	123.41
20000	417.60	256.07	205.84	183.18	171.28	164.54
25000	522.00	320.09	257.30	228.97	214.10	205.67
30000	626.40	384.10	308.76	274.77	256.92	246.81
35000	730.80	448.12	360.22	320.56	299.74	287.94
40000	835.20	512.14	411.68	366.35	342.56	329.08
45000	939.60	576.15	463.14	412.15	385.38	370.21
50000	1044.00	640.17	514.60	457.94	428.20	411.34
55000	1148.40	704.18	566.06	503.73	471.02	452.48
60000	1252.80	768.20	617.52	549.53	513.83	493.61
65000	1357.20	832.22	668.98	595.32	556.65	534.74
70000	1461.60	896.23	720.44	641.11	599.47	575.88
75000	1566.00	960.25	771.90	686.91	642.29	617.01
80000	1670.40	1024.27	823.36	732.70	685.11	658.15
85000	1774.80	1088.28	874.82	778.49	727.93	699.28
90000	1879.20	1152.30	926.28	824.29	770.75	740.41
95000	1983.60	1216.32	977.74	870.08	813.57	781.55
100000	2087.99	1280.33	1029.20	915.87	856.39	822.68

10.50%

Amount	5 Years	10 Years	15 Years	20 Years	25 Years	30 Years
50	1.08	.68	.56	.50	.48	.46
100	2.15	1.35	1.11	1.00	.95	.92
500	10.75	6.75	5.53	5.00	4.73	4.58
1000	21.50	13.50	11.06	9.99	9.45	9.15
2000	42.99	26.99	22.11	19.97	18.89	18.30
5000	107.47	67.47	55.27	49.92	47.21	45.74
10000	214.94	134.94	110.54	99.84	94.42	91.48
15000	322.41	202.41	165.81	149.76	141.63	137.22
20000	429.88	269.87	221.08	199.68	188.84	182.95
25000	537.35	337.34	276.35	249.60	236.05	228.69
30000	644.82	404.81	331.62	299.52	283.26	274.43
35000	752.29	472.28	386.89	349.44	330.47	320.16
40000	859.76	539.74	442.16	399.36	377.68	365.90
45000	967.23	607.21	497.43	449.28	424.89	411.64
50000	1074.70	674.68	552.70	499.19	472.10	457.37
55000	1182.17	742.15	607.97	549.11	519.30	503.11
60000	1289.64	809.61	663.24	599.03	566.51	548.85
65000	1397.11	877.08	718.51	648.95	613.72	594.59
70000	1504.58	944.55	773.78	698.87	660.93	640.32
75000	1612.05	1012.02	829.05	748.79	708.14	686.06
80000	1719.52	1079.49	884.32	798.71	755.35	731.80
85000	1826.99	1146.95	939.59	848.63	802.56	777.53
90000	1934.46	1214.42	994.86	898.55	849.77	823.27
95000	2041.93	1281.89	1050.13	948.47	896.98	869.01
100000	2149.40	1349.36	1105.40	998.38	944.19	914.74

10.75%

Amount	5 Years	10 Years	15 Years	20 Years	25 Years	30 Years
50	1.09	.69	.57	.51	.49	.47
100	2.17	1.37	1.13	1.02	.97	.94
500	10.81	6.82	5.61	5.08	4.82	4.67
1000	21.62	13.64	11.21	10.16	9.63	9.34
2000	43.24	27.27	22.42	20.31	19.25	18.67
5000	108.09	68.17	56.05	50.77	48.11	46.68
10000	216.18	136.34	112.10	101.53	96.21	93.35
15000	324.27	204.51	168.15	152.29	144.32	140.03
20000	432.36	272.68	224.19	203.05	192.42	186.70
25000	540.45	340.85	280.24	253.81	240.53	233.38
30000	648.54	409.02	336.29	304.57	288.63	280.05
35000	756.63	477.19	392.34	355.34	336.74	326.72
40000	864.72	545.36	448.38	406.10	384.84	373.40
45000	972.81	613.53	504.43	456.86	432.95	420.07
50000	1080.90	681.70	560.48	507.62	481.05	466.75
55000	1188.99	749.87	616.53	558.38	529.16	513.42
60000	1297.08	818.04	672.57	609.14	577.26	560.09
65000	1405.17	886.21	728.62	659.90	625.37	606.77
70000	1513.26	954.38	784.67	710.67	673.47	653.44
75000	1621.35	1022.55	840.72	761.43	721.57	700.12
80000	1729.44	1090.71	896.76	812.19	769.68	746.79
85000	1837.53	1158.88	952.81	862.95	817.78	793.46
90000	1945.62	1227.05	1008.86	913.71	865.89	840.14
95000	2053.71	1295.22	1064.91	964.47	913.99	886.81
100000	2161.80	1363.39	1120.95	1015.23	962.10	933.49

10.00%

Amount	5 Years	10 Years	15 Years	20 Years	25 Years	30 Years
50	1.07	.67	.54	.49	.46	.44
100	2.13	1.33	1.08	.97	.91	.88
500	10.63	6.61	5.38	4.83	4.55	4.39
1000	21.25	13.22	10.75	9.66	9.09	8.78
2000	42.50	26.44	21.50	19.31	18.18	17.56
5000	106.24	66.08	53.74	48.26	45.44	43.88
10000	212.48	132.16	107.47	96.51	90.88	87.76
15000	318.71	198.23	161.20	144.76	136.31	131.64
20000	424.95	264.31	214.93	193.01	181.75	175.52
25000	531.18	330.38	268.66	241.26	227.18	219.40
30000	637.42	396.46	322.39	289.51	272.62	263.28
35000	743.65	462.53	376.12	337.76	318.05	307.16
40000	849.89	528.61	429.85	386.01	363.49	351.03
45000	956.12	594.68	483.58	434.26	408.92	394.91
50000	1062.36	660.76	537.31	482.52	454.36	438.79
55000	1168.59	726.83	591.04	530.77	499.79	482.67
60000	1274.83	792.91	644.77	579.02	545.23	526.55
65000	1381.06	858.98	698.50	627.27	590.66	570.43
70000	1487.30	925.06	752.23	675.52	636.10	614.31
75000	1593.53	991.14	805.96	723.77	681.53	658.18
80000	1699.77	1057.21	859.69	772.02	726.97	702.06
85000	1806.00	1123.29	913.42	820.27	772.40	745.94
90000	1912.24	1189.36	967.15	868.52	817.84	789.82
95000	2018.47	1255.44	1020.88	916.78	863.27	833.70
100000	2124.71	1321.51	1074.61	965.03	908.71	877.58

10.25%

Amount	5 Years	10 Years	15 Years	20 Years	25 Years	30 Years
50	1.07	.67	.55	.50	.47	.45
100	2.14	1.34	1.09	.99	.93	.90
500	10.69	6.68	5.45	4.91	4.64	4.49
1000	21.38	13.36	10.90	9.82	9.27	8.97
2000	42.75	26.71	21.80	19.64	18.53	17.93
5000	106.86	66.77	54.50	49.09	46.32	44.81
10000	213.71	133.54	109.00	98.17	92.64	89.62
15000	320.56	200.31	163.50	147.25	138.96	134.42
20000	427.41	267.08	218.00	196.33	185.28	179.23
25000	534.26	333.85	272.49	245.42	231.60	224.03
30000	641.11	400.62	326.99	294.50	277.92	268.84
35000	747.96	467.39	381.49	343.58	324.24	313.64
40000	854.82	534.16	435.99	392.66	370.56	358.45
45000	961.67	600.93	490.48	441.74	416.88	403.25
50000	1068.52	667.70	544.98	490.83	463.20	448.06
55000	1175.37	734.47	599.48	539.91	509.52	492.86
60000	1282.22	801.24	653.98	588.99	555.83	537.67
65000	1389.07	868.01	708.47	638.07	602.15	582.47
70000	1495.92	934.78	762.97	687.16	648.47	627.28
75000	1602.77	1001.55	817.47	736.24	694.79	672.08
80000	1709.63	1068.32	871.97	785.32	741.11	716.89
85000	1816.48	1135.09	926.46	834.40	787.43	761.69
90000	1923.33	1201.86	980.96	883.48	833.75	806.50
95000	2030.18	1268.63	1035.46	932.57	880.07	851.30
100000	2137.03	1335.40	1089.96	981.65	926.39	896.11

APPENDIX A: Amortization Tables

11.50%

Amount	5 Years	10 Years	15 Years	20 Years	25 Years	30 Years
50	1.10	.71	.59	.54	.51	.50
100	2.20	1.41	1.17	1.07	1.02	1.00
500	11.00	7.03	5.85	5.34	5.09	4.96
1000	22.00	14.06	11.69	10.67	10.17	9.91
2000	43.99	28.12	23.37	21.33	20.33	19.81
5000	109.97	70.30	58.41	53.33	50.83	49.52
10000	219.93	140.60	116.82	106.65	101.65	99.03
15000	329.89	210.90	175.23	159.97	152.48	148.55
20000	439.86	281.20	233.64	213.29	203.30	198.06
25000	549.82	351.49	292.05	266.61	254.12	247.58
30000	659.78	421.79	350.46	319.93	304.95	297.09
35000	769.75	492.09	408.87	373.26	355.77	346.61
40000	879.71	562.39	467.28	426.58	406.59	396.12
45000	989.67	632.68	525.69	479.90	457.42	445.64
50000	1099.64	702.98	584.10	533.22	508.24	495.15
55000	1209.60	773.28	642.51	586.54	559.06	544.67
60000	1319.56	843.58	700.92	639.86	609.89	594.18
65000	1429.52	913.88	759.33	693.18	660.71	643.69
70000	1539.49	984.17	817.74	746.51	711.53	693.21
75000	1649.45	1054.47	876.15	799.83	762.36	742.72
80000	1759.41	1124.77	934.56	853.15	813.18	792.24
85000	1869.38	1195.07	992.97	906.47	864.00	841.75
90000	1979.34	1265.36	1051.38	959.79	914.83	891.27
95000	2089.30	1335.66	1109.79	1013.11	965.65	940.78
100000	2199.27	1405.96	1168.19	1066.43	1016.47	990.30

11.75%

Amount	5 Years	10 Years	15 Years	20 Years	25 Years	30 Years
50	1.11	.72	.60	.55	.52	.51
100	2.22	1.43	1.19	1.09	1.04	1.01
500	11.06	7.11	5.93	5.42	5.18	5.05
1000	22.12	14.21	11.85	10.84	10.35	10.10
2000	44.24	28.41	23.69	21.68	20.70	20.19
5000	110.60	71.02	59.21	54.19	51.74	50.48
10000	221.19	142.03	118.42	108.38	103.48	100.95
15000	331.78	213.05	177.62	162.56	155.22	151.42
20000	442.37	284.06	236.83	216.75	206.96	201.89
25000	552.96	355.08	296.04	270.93	258.70	252.36
30000	663.55	426.09	355.24	325.12	310.44	302.83
35000	774.15	497.11	414.45	379.30	362.18	353.30
40000	884.74	568.12	473.66	433.49	413.92	403.77
45000	995.33	639.14	532.86	487.67	465.66	454.24
50000	1105.92	710.15	592.07	541.86	517.40	504.71
55000	1216.51	781.17	651.28	596.04	569.14	555.18
60000	1327.10	852.18	710.48	650.23	620.88	605.65
65000	1437.70	923.20	769.69	704.41	672.62	656.12
70000	1548.29	994.21	828.90	758.60	724.36	706.59
75000	1658.88	1065.23	888.10	812.79	776.10	757.06
80000	1769.47	1136.24	947.31	866.97	827.84	807.53
85000	1880.06	1207.26	1006.52	921.16	879.58	858.00
90000	1990.65	1278.27	1065.72	975.34	931.32	908.47
95000	2101.25	1349.28	1124.93	1029.53	983.06	958.94
100000	2211.84	1420.30	1184.14	1083.71	1034.80	1009.41

11.00%

Amount	5 Years	10 Years	15 Years	20 Years	25 Years	30 Years
50	1.10	.69	.57	.52	.50	.48
100	2.19	1.38	1.14	1.04	.99	.96
500	10.88	6.89	5.69	5.17	4.91	4.77
1000	21.75	13.78	11.37	10.33	9.81	9.53
2000	43.49	27.56	22.74	20.65	19.61	19.05
5000	108.72	68.88	56.83	51.61	49.01	47.62
10000	217.43	137.76	113.66	103.22	98.02	95.24
15000	326.14	206.63	170.49	154.83	147.02	142.85
20000	434.85	275.51	227.32	206.44	196.03	190.47
25000	543.57	344.38	284.15	258.05	245.03	238.09
30000	652.28	413.26	340.98	309.66	294.04	285.70
35000	760.99	482.13	397.81	361.27	343.04	333.32
40000	869.70	551.01	454.64	412.88	392.05	380.93
45000	978.41	619.88	511.47	464.49	441.06	428.55
50000	1087.13	688.76	568.30	516.10	490.06	476.17
55000	1195.84	757.63	625.13	567.71	539.07	523.78
60000	1304.55	826.51	681.96	619.32	588.07	571.40
65000	1413.26	895.38	738.79	670.93	637.08	619.02
70000	1521.97	964.26	795.62	722.54	686.08	666.63
75000	1630.69	1033.13	852.45	774.15	735.09	714.25
80000	1739.40	1102.01	909.28	825.76	784.10	761.86
85000	1848.11	1170.88	966.11	877.37	833.10	809.48
90000	1956.82	1239.76	1022.94	928.97	882.11	857.10
95000	2065.54	1308.63	1079.77	980.58	931.11	904.71
100000	2174.25	1377.51	1136.60	1032.19	980.12	952.33

11.25%

Amount	5 Years	10 Years	15 Years	20 Years	25 Years	30 Years
50	1.10	.70	.58	.53	.50	.49
100	2.19	1.40	1.16	1.05	1.00	.98
500	10.94	6.96	5.77	5.25	5.00	4.86
1000	21.87	13.92	11.53	10.50	9.99	9.72
2000	43.74	27.84	23.05	20.99	19.97	19.43
5000	109.34	69.59	57.62	52.47	49.92	48.57
10000	218.68	139.17	115.24	104.93	99.83	97.13
15000	328.01	208.76	172.86	157.39	149.74	145.69
20000	437.35	278.34	230.47	209.86	199.65	194.26
25000	546.69	347.93	288.09	262.32	249.56	242.82
30000	656.02	417.51	345.71	314.78	299.48	291.38
35000	765.36	487.10	403.33	367.24	349.39	339.95
40000	874.70	556.68	460.94	419.71	399.30	388.51
45000	984.03	626.27	518.56	472.17	449.21	437.07
50000	1093.37	695.85	576.18	524.63	499.12	485.64
55000	1202.71	765.43	633.79	577.10	549.04	534.20
60000	1312.04	835.02	691.41	629.56	598.95	582.76
65000	1421.38	904.60	749.03	682.02	648.86	631.32
70000	1530.72	974.19	806.65	734.48	698.77	679.89
75000	1640.05	1043.77	864.26	786.95	748.68	728.45
80000	1749.39	1113.36	921.88	839.41	798.60	777.01
85000	1858.73	1182.94	979.50	891.87	848.51	825.58
90000	1968.06	1252.53	1037.12	944.34	898.42	874.14
95000	2077.40	1322.11	1094.73	996.80	948.33	922.70
100000	2186.74	1391.69	1152.35	1049.26	998.24	971.27

12.50%

Amount	5 Years	10 Years	15 Years	20 Years	25 Years	30 Years
50	1.13	.74	.62	.57	.55	.54
100	2.25	1.47	1.24	1.14	1.10	1.07
500	11.25	7.32	6.17	5.69	5.46	5.34
1000	22.50	14.64	12.33	11.37	10.91	10.68
2000	45.00	29.28	24.66	22.73	21.81	21.35
5000	112.49	73.19	61.63	56.81	54.52	53.37
10000	224.98	146.38	123.26	113.62	109.04	106.73
15000	337.47	219.57	184.88	170.43	163.56	160.09
20000	449.96	292.76	246.51	227.23	218.08	213.46
25000	562.45	365.95	308.14	284.04	272.59	266.82
30000	674.94	439.13	369.76	340.85	327.11	320.18
35000	787.43	512.32	431.39	397.65	381.63	373.55
40000	899.92	585.51	493.01	454.46	436.15	426.91
45000	1012.41	658.70	554.64	511.27	490.66	480.27
50000	1124.90	731.89	616.27	568.08	545.18	533.63
55000	1237.39	805.07	677.89	624.88	599.70	587.00
60000	1349.88	878.26	739.52	681.69	654.22	640.36
65000	1462.37	951.45	801.14	738.50	708.74	693.72
70000	1574.86	1024.64	862.77	795.30	763.25	747.09
75000	1687.35	1097.83	924.40	852.11	817.77	800.45
80000	1799.84	1171.01	986.02	908.92	872.29	853.81
85000	1912.33	1244.20	1047.65	965.72	926.81	907.17
90000	2024.82	1317.39	1109.27	1022.53	981.32	960.54
95000	2137.31	1390.58	1170.90	1079.34	1035.84	1013.90
100000	2249.80	1463.77	1232.53	1136.15	1090.36	1067.26

12.75%

Amount	5 Years	10 Years	15 Years	20 Years	25 Years	30 Years
50	1.14	.74	.63	.58	.56	.55
100	2.27	1.48	1.25	1.16	1.11	1.09
500	11.32	7.40	6.25	5.77	5.55	5.44
1000	22.63	14.79	12.49	11.54	11.10	10.87
2000	45.26	29.57	24.98	23.08	22.19	21.74
5000	113.13	73.92	62.45	57.70	55.46	54.34
10000	226.26	147.84	124.89	115.39	110.91	108.67
15000	339.38	221.76	187.33	173.08	166.36	163.01
20000	452.51	295.68	249.77	230.77	221.82	217.34
25000	565.64	369.60	312.21	288.46	277.27	271.68
30000	678.76	443.52	374.66	346.15	332.72	326.01
35000	791.89	517.44	437.10	403.84	388.17	380.35
40000	905.02	591.36	499.54	461.53	443.63	434.68
45000	1018.14	665.28	561.98	519.22	499.08	489.02
50000	1131.27	739.20	624.42	576.91	554.53	543.35
55000	1244.40	813.12	686.87	634.60	609.98	597.69
60000	1357.52	887.04	749.31	692.29	665.44	652.02
65000	1470.65	960.96	811.75	749.98	720.89	706.36
70000	1583.78	1034.88	874.19	807.67	776.34	760.69
75000	1696.90	1108.80	936.63	865.36	831.79	815.02
80000	1810.03	1182.72	999.07	923.05	887.25	869.36
85000	1923.16	1256.64	1061.51	980.74	942.70	923.69
90000	2036.28	1330.56	1123.96	1038.44	998.15	978.03
95000	2149.41	1404.48	1186.40	1096.13	1053.60	1032.36
100000	2262.54	1478.40	1248.84	1153.82	1109.06	1086.70

12.00%

Amount	5 Years	10 Years	15 Years	20 Years	25 Years	30 Years
50	1.12	.72	.61	.56	.53	.52
100	2.23	1.44	1.21	1.11	1.06	1.03
500	11.13	7.18	6.01	5.51	5.27	5.15
1000	22.25	14.35	12.01	11.02	10.54	10.29
2000	44.49	28.70	24.01	22.03	21.07	20.58
5000	111.23	71.74	60.01	55.06	52.67	51.44
10000	222.45	143.48	120.02	110.11	105.33	102.87
15000	333.67	215.21	180.03	165.17	157.99	154.30
20000	444.89	286.95	240.04	220.22	210.65	205.73
25000	556.12	358.68	300.05	275.28	263.31	257.16
30000	667.34	430.42	360.06	330.33	315.97	308.59
35000	778.56	502.15	420.06	385.39	368.63	360.02
40000	889.78	573.89	480.07	440.44	421.29	411.45
45000	1001.01	645.62	540.08	495.49	473.96	462.88
50000	1112.23	717.36	600.09	550.55	526.62	514.31
55000	1223.45	789.10	660.10	605.60	579.28	565.74
60000	1334.67	860.83	720.11	660.66	631.94	617.17
65000	1445.89	932.57	780.11	715.71	684.60	668.60
70000	1557.12	1004.30	840.12	770.77	737.26	720.03
75000	1668.34	1076.04	900.13	825.82	789.92	771.46
80000	1779.56	1147.77	960.14	880.87	842.58	822.90
85000	1890.78	1219.51	1020.15	935.93	895.25	874.33
90000	2002.01	1291.24	1080.16	990.98	947.91	925.76
95000	2113.23	1362.98	1140.16	1046.04	1000.57	977.19
100000	2224.45	1434.71	1200.17	1101.09	1053.23	1028.62

12.25%

Amount	5 Years	10 Years	15 Years	20 Years	25 Years	30 Years
50	1.12	.73	.61	.56	.54	.53
100	2.24	1.45	1.22	1.12	1.08	1.05
500	11.19	7.25	6.09	5.60	5.36	5.24
1000	22.38	14.50	12.17	11.19	10.72	10.48
2000	44.75	28.99	24.33	22.38	21.44	20.96
5000	111.86	72.46	60.82	55.93	53.59	52.40
10000	223.71	144.92	121.63	111.86	107.18	104.79
15000	335.57	217.38	182.45	167.79	160.77	157.19
20000	447.42	289.84	243.26	223.72	214.35	209.58
25000	559.28	362.30	304.08	279.65	267.94	261.98
30000	671.13	434.76	364.89	335.57	321.53	314.37
35000	782.99	507.22	425.71	391.50	375.12	366.77
40000	894.84	579.68	486.52	447.43	428.70	419.16
45000	1006.70	652.14	547.34	503.36	482.29	471.56
50000	1118.55	724.60	608.15	559.29	535.88	523.95
55000	1230.41	797.06	668.97	615.22	589.46	576.35
60000	1342.26	869.52	729.78	671.14	643.05	628.74
65000	1454.12	941.98	790.60	727.07	696.64	681.14
70000	1565.97	1014.44	851.41	783.00	750.23	733.53
75000	1677.83	1086.90	912.23	838.93	803.81	785.93
80000	1789.68	1159.36	973.04	894.86	857.40	838.32
85000	1901.54	1231.82	1033.86	950.79	910.99	890.72
90000	2013.39	1304.28	1094.67	1006.71	964.57	943.11
95000	2125.25	1376.74	1155.49	1062.64	1018.16	995.51
100000	2237.10	1449.20	1216.30	1118.57	1071.75	1047.90

APPENDIX A: Amortization Tables

13.00%

Amount	5 Years	10 Years	15 Years	20 Years	25 Years	30 Years
50	1.14	.75	.64	.59	.57	.56
100	2.28	1.50	1.27	1.18	1.13	1.11
500	11.38	7.47	6.33	5.86	5.64	5.54
1000	22.76	14.94	12.66	11.72	11.28	11.07
2000	45.51	29.87	25.31	23.44	22.56	22.13
5000	113.77	74.66	63.27	58.58	56.40	55.31
10000	227.54	149.32	126.53	117.16	112.79	110.62
15000	341.30	223.97	189.79	175.74	169.18	165.93
20000	455.07	298.63	253.05	234.32	225.57	221.24
25000	568.83	373.28	316.32	292.90	281.96	276.55
30000	682.60	447.94	379.58	351.48	338.36	331.86
35000	796.36	522.59	442.84	410.06	394.75	387.17
40000	910.13	597.25	506.10	468.64	451.14	442.48
45000	1023.89	671.90	569.36	527.21	507.53	497.79
50000	1137.66	746.56	632.63	585.79	563.92	553.10
55000	1251.42	821.21	695.89	644.37	620.31	608.41
60000	1365.19	895.87	759.15	702.95	676.71	663.72
65000	1478.95	970.52	822.41	761.53	733.10	719.03
70000	1592.72	1045.18	885.67	820.11	789.49	774.34
75000	1706.49	1119.84	948.94	878.69	845.88	829.65
80000	1820.25	1194.49	1012.20	937.27	902.27	884.96
85000	1934.02	1269.15	1075.46	995.84	958.67	940.27
90000	2047.78	1343.80	1138.72	1054.42	1015.06	995.58
95000	2161.55	1418.46	1201.99	1113.00	1071.45	1050.89
100000	2275.31	1493.11	1265.25	1171.58	1127.84	1106.20

13.25%

Amount	5 Years	10 Years	15 Years	20 Years	25 Years	30 Years
50	1.15	.76	.65	.60	.58	.57
100	2.29	1.51	1.29	1.19	1.15	1.13
500	11.45	7.54	6.41	5.95	5.74	5.63
1000	22.89	15.08	12.82	11.90	11.47	11.26
2000	45.77	30.16	25.64	23.79	22.94	22.52
5000	114.41	75.40	64.09	59.48	57.34	56.29
10000	228.82	150.79	128.18	118.95	114.68	112.58
15000	343.22	226.19	192.27	178.42	172.01	168.87
20000	457.63	301.58	256.35	237.89	229.35	225.16
25000	572.04	376.98	320.44	297.36	286.68	281.45
30000	686.44	452.37	384.53	356.83	344.02	337.74
35000	800.85	527.77	448.61	416.31	401.35	394.03
40000	915.26	603.16	512.70	475.78	458.69	450.31
45000	1029.66	678.56	576.79	535.25	516.02	506.60
50000	1144.07	753.95	640.87	594.72	573.36	562.89
55000	1258.47	829.34	704.96	654.19	630.69	619.18
60000	1372.88	904.74	769.05	713.66	688.03	675.47
65000	1487.29	980.13	833.13	773.13	745.36	731.76
70000	1601.69	1055.53	897.22	832.61	802.70	788.05
75000	1716.10	1130.92	961.31	892.08	860.03	844.34
80000	1830.51	1206.32	1025.39	951.55	917.37	900.62
85000	1944.91	1281.71	1089.48	1011.02	974.70	956.91
90000	2059.32	1357.11	1153.57	1070.49	1032.04	1013.20
95000	2173.72	1432.50	1217.65	1129.96	1089.37	1069.49
100000	2288.12	1507.89	1281.74	1189.44	1146.71	1125.78

13.50%

Amount	5 Years	10 Years	15 Years	20 Years	25 Years	30 Years
50	1.16	.77	.65	.61	.59	.58
100	2.31	1.53	1.30	1.21	1.17	1.15
500	11.51	7.62	6.50	6.04	5.83	5.73
1000	23.01	15.23	12.99	12.08	11.66	11.46
2000	46.02	30.46	25.97	24.15	23.32	22.91
5000	115.05	76.14	64.92	60.37	58.29	57.28
10000	230.10	152.28	129.84	120.74	116.57	114.55
15000	345.15	228.42	194.75	181.11	174.85	171.82
20000	460.20	304.55	259.67	241.48	233.13	229.09
25000	575.25	380.69	324.58	301.85	291.42	286.36
30000	690.30	456.83	389.50	362.22	349.70	343.63
35000	805.35	532.97	454.42	422.59	407.98	400.90
40000	920.40	609.10	519.33	482.95	466.26	458.17
45000	1035.45	685.24	584.25	543.32	524.55	515.44
50000	1150.50	761.38	649.16	603.69	582.83	572.71
55000	1265.55	837.51	714.08	664.06	641.11	629.98
60000	1380.60	913.65	779.00	724.43	699.39	687.25
65000	1495.65	989.79	843.91	784.80	757.67	744.52
70000	1610.69	1065.93	908.83	845.17	815.96	801.79
75000	1725.74	1142.06	973.74	905.54	874.24	859.06
80000	1840.79	1218.20	1038.66	965.90	932.52	916.33
85000	1955.84	1294.34	1103.58	1026.27	990.80	973.61
90000	2070.89	1370.47	1168.49	1086.64	1049.09	1030.88
95000	2185.94	1446.61	1233.41	1147.01	1107.37	1088.15
100000	2300.99	1522.75	1298.32	1207.38	1165.65	1145.42

13.75%

Amount	5 Years	10 Years	15 Years	20 Years	25 Years	30 Years
50	1.16	.77	.66	.62	.60	.59
100	2.32	1.54	1.32	1.23	1.19	1.17
500	11.57	7.69	6.58	6.13	5.93	5.83
1000	23.14	15.38	13.15	12.26	11.85	11.66
2000	46.28	30.76	26.30	24.51	23.70	23.31
5000	115.70	76.89	65.75	61.28	59.24	58.26
10000	231.39	153.77	131.50	122.55	118.47	116.52
15000	347.09	230.66	197.25	183.82	177.70	174.77
20000	462.78	307.54	263.00	245.09	236.94	233.03
25000	578.48	384.42	328.75	306.36	296.17	291.28
30000	694.17	461.31	394.50	367.63	355.40	349.54
35000	809.86	538.19	460.25	428.90	414.64	407.79
40000	925.56	615.07	526.00	490.17	473.87	466.05
45000	1041.25	691.96	591.75	551.44	533.10	524.31
50000	1156.95	768.84	657.50	612.71	592.34	582.56
55000	1272.64	845.72	723.25	673.98	651.57	640.82
60000	1388.34	922.61	789.00	735.25	710.80	699.07
65000	1504.03	999.49	854.75	796.52	770.04	757.33
70000	1619.72	1076.37	920.50	857.79	829.27	815.58
75000	1735.42	1153.26	986.25	919.06	888.50	873.84
80000	1851.11	1230.14	1051.99	980.33	947.74	932.10
85000	1966.81	1307.02	1117.74	1041.60	1006.97	990.35
90000	2082.50	1383.91	1183.49	1102.87	1066.20	1048.61
95000	2198.20	1460.79	1249.24	1164.14	1125.44	1106.86
100000	2313.89	1537.67	1314.99	1225.41	1184.67	1165.12

14.50%

Amount	5 Years	10 Years	15 Years	20 Years	25 Years	30 Years
50	1.18	.80	.69	.64	.63	.62
100	2.36	1.59	1.37	1.28	1.25	1.23
500	11.77	7.92	6.83	6.40	6.22	6.13
1000	23.53	15.83	13.66	12.80	12.43	12.25
2000	47.06	31.66	27.32	25.60	24.85	24.50
5000	117.65	79.15	68.28	64.00	62.11	61.23
10000	235.29	158.29	136.56	128.00	124.22	122.46
15000	352.93	237.44	204.83	192.00	186.33	183.69
20000	470.57	316.58	273.11	256.00	248.44	244.92
25000	588.21	395.72	341.38	320.00	310.55	306.14
30000	705.85	474.87	409.66	384.00	372.65	367.37
35000	823.49	554.01	477.93	448.00	434.76	428.60
40000	941.14	633.15	546.21	512.00	496.87	489.83
45000	1058.78	712.30	614.48	576.00	558.98	551.06
50000	1176.42	791.44	682.76	640.00	621.09	612.28
55000	1294.06	870.58	751.03	704.00	683.19	673.51
60000	1411.70	949.73	819.31	768.00	745.30	734.74
65000	1529.34	1028.87	887.58	832.00	807.41	795.97
70000	1646.98	1108.01	955.86	896.00	869.52	857.19
75000	1764.63	1187.16	1024.13	960.00	931.63	918.42
80000	1882.27	1266.30	1092.41	1024.00	993.74	979.65
85000	1999.91	1345.44	1160.68	1088.00	1055.84	1040.88
90000	2117.55	1424.59	1228.96	1152.00	1117.95	1102.11
95000	2235.19	1503.73	1297.23	1216.00	1180.06	1163.33
100000	2352.83	1582.87	1365.51	1280.00	1242.17	1224.56

14.75%

Amount	5 Years	10 Years	15 Years	20 Years	25 Years	30 Years
50	1.19	.80	.70	.65	.64	.63
100	2.37	1.60	1.39	1.30	1.27	1.25
500	11.83	8.00	6.92	6.50	6.31	6.23
1000	23.66	15.99	13.83	12.99	12.62	12.45
2000	47.32	31.97	27.66	25.97	25.23	24.89
5000	118.30	79.91	69.13	64.92	63.08	62.23
10000	236.59	159.81	138.26	129.84	126.15	124.45
15000	354.89	239.72	207.38	194.76	189.22	186.68
20000	473.18	319.62	276.51	259.68	252.30	248.90
25000	591.48	399.52	345.63	324.59	315.37	311.12
30000	709.77	479.43	414.76	389.51	378.44	373.35
35000	828.07	559.33	483.88	454.43	441.52	435.57
40000	946.36	639.23	553.01	519.35	504.59	497.80
45000	1064.66	719.14	622.13	584.26	567.66	560.02
50000	1182.95	799.04	691.26	649.18	630.74	622.24
55000	1301.24	878.95	760.38	714.10	693.81	684.47
60000	1419.54	958.85	829.51	779.02	756.88	746.69
65000	1537.83	1038.75	898.63	843.94	819.96	808.91
70000	1656.13	1118.66	967.76	908.85	883.03	871.14
75000	1774.42	1198.56	1036.88	973.77	946.10	933.36
80000	1892.72	1278.46	1106.01	1038.69	1009.18	995.59
85000	2011.01	1358.37	1175.13	1103.61	1072.25	1057.81
90000	2129.31	1438.27	1244.26	1168.52	1135.32	1120.03
95000	2247.60	1518.18	1313.38	1233.44	1198.40	1182.26
100000	2365.90	1598.08	1382.51	1298.36	1261.47	1244.48

14.00%

Amount	5 Years	10 Years	15 Years	20 Years	25 Years	30 Years
50	1.17	.78	.67	.63	.61	.60
100	2.33	1.56	1.34	1.25	1.21	1.19
500	11.64	7.77	6.66	6.22	6.04	5.93
1000	23.27	15.53	13.32	12.44	12.04	11.85
2000	46.54	31.06	26.64	24.88	24.08	23.70
5000	116.35	77.64	66.59	62.18	60.19	59.25
10000	232.69	155.27	133.18	124.36	120.38	118.49
15000	349.03	232.90	199.77	186.53	180.57	177.74
20000	465.37	310.54	266.35	248.71	240.76	236.98
25000	581.71	388.17	332.94	310.89	300.95	296.22
30000	698.05	465.80	399.53	373.06	361.13	355.47
35000	814.39	543.44	466.11	435.24	421.32	414.71
40000	930.74	621.07	532.70	497.41	481.51	473.95
45000	1047.08	698.70	599.29	559.59	541.70	533.20
50000	1163.42	776.34	665.88	621.77	601.89	592.44
55000	1279.76	853.97	732.46	683.94	662.07	651.68
60000	1396.10	931.60	799.05	746.12	722.26	710.93
65000	1512.44	1009.24	865.64	808.29	782.45	770.17
70000	1628.78	1086.87	932.22	870.47	842.64	829.42
75000	1745.12	1164.50	998.81	932.65	902.83	888.66
80000	1861.47	1242.14	1065.40	994.82	963.01	947.90
85000	1977.81	1319.77	1131.99	1057.00	1023.20	1007.15
90000	2094.15	1397.40	1198.57	1119.17	1083.39	1066.39
95000	2210.49	1475.04	1265.16	1181.35	1143.58	1125.63
100000	2326.83	1552.67	1331.75	1243.53	1203.77	1184.88

14.25%

Amount	5 Years	10 Years	15 Years	20 Years	25 Years	30 Years
50	1.17	.79	.68	.64	.62	.61
100	2.34	1.57	1.35	1.27	1.23	1.21
500	11.70	7.84	6.75	6.31	6.12	6.03
1000	23.40	15.68	13.49	12.62	12.23	12.05
2000	46.80	31.36	26.98	25.24	24.46	24.10
5000	117.00	78.39	67.43	63.09	61.15	60.24
10000	233.99	156.78	134.86	126.18	122.30	120.47
15000	350.98	235.16	202.29	189.26	183.44	180.71
20000	467.97	313.55	269.72	252.35	244.59	240.94
25000	584.96	391.94	337.15	315.43	305.74	301.18
30000	701.95	470.32	404.58	378.52	366.88	361.41
35000	818.94	548.71	472.01	441.61	428.03	421.65
40000	935.93	627.10	539.44	504.69	489.18	481.88
45000	1052.92	705.48	606.87	567.78	550.32	542.11
50000	1169.91	783.87	674.29	630.86	611.47	602.35
55000	1286.90	862.26	741.72	693.95	672.62	662.58
60000	1403.89	940.64	809.15	757.04	733.76	722.82
65000	1520.88	1019.03	876.58	820.12	794.91	783.05
70000	1637.87	1097.42	944.01	883.21	856.05	843.29
75000	1754.86	1175.80	1011.44	946.29	917.20	903.52
80000	1871.85	1254.19	1078.87	1009.38	978.35	963.75
85000	1988.84	1332.58	1146.30	1072.47	1039.49	1023.99
90000	2105.83	1410.96	1213.73	1135.55	1100.64	1084.22
95000	2222.82	1489.35	1281.16	1198.64	1161.79	1144.46
100000	2339.81	1567.74	1348.58	1261.72	1222.93	1204.69

APPENDIX A: Amortization Tables

15.50%

Amount	5 Years	10 Years	15 Years	20 Years	25 Years	30 Years
50	1.21	.83	.72	.68	.66	.66
100	2.41	1.65	1.44	1.36	1.32	1.31
500	12.03	8.23	7.17	6.77	6.60	6.53
1000	24.06	16.45	14.34	13.54	13.20	13.05
2000	48.11	32.89	28.68	27.08	26.40	26.10
5000	120.27	82.21	71.70	67.70	65.99	65.23
10000	240.54	164.42	143.40	135.39	131.98	130.46
15000	360.80	246.62	215.10	203.09	197.97	195.68
20000	481.07	328.83	286.80	270.78	263.95	260.91
25000	601.33	411.03	358.50	338.48	329.94	326.13
30000	721.60	493.24	430.20	406.17	395.93	391.36
35000	841.87	575.44	501.90	473.86	461.92	456.59
40000	962.13	657.65	573.60	541.56	527.90	521.81
45000	1082.40	739.85	645.30	609.25	593.89	587.04
50000	1202.66	822.06	717.00	676.95	659.88	652.26
55000	1322.93	904.26	788.70	744.64	725.86	717.49
60000	1443.20	986.47	860.40	812.33	791.85	782.72
65000	1563.46	1068.67	932.10	880.03	857.84	847.94
70000	1683.73	1150.88	1003.80	947.72	923.83	913.17
75000	1803.99	1233.08	1075.50	1015.42	989.81	978.39
80000	1924.26	1315.29	1147.20	1083.11	1055.80	1043.62
85000	2044.53	1397.49	1218.90	1150.80	1121.79	1108.84
90000	2164.79	1479.70	1290.60	1218.50	1187.78	1174.07
95000	2285.06	1561.91	1362.30	1286.19	1253.76	1239.30
100000	2405.32	1644.11	1434.00	1353.89	1319.75	1304.52

15.00%

Amount	5 Years	10 Years	15 Years	20 Years	25 Years	30 Years
50	1.19	.81	.70	.66	.65	.64
100	2.38	1.62	1.40	1.32	1.29	1.27
500	11.90	8.07	7.00	6.59	6.41	6.33
1000	23.79	16.14	14.00	13.17	12.81	12.65
2000	47.58	32.27	28.00	26.34	25.62	25.29
5000	118.95	80.67	69.98	65.84	64.05	63.23
10000	237.90	161.34	139.96	131.68	128.09	126.45
15000	356.85	242.01	209.94	197.52	192.13	189.67
20000	475.80	322.67	279.92	263.36	256.17	252.89
25000	594.75	403.34	349.90	329.20	320.21	316.12
30000	713.70	484.01	419.88	395.04	384.25	379.34
35000	832.65	564.68	489.86	460.88	448.30	442.56
40000	951.60	645.34	559.84	526.72	512.34	505.78
45000	1070.55	726.01	629.82	592.56	576.38	569.00
50000	1189.50	806.68	699.80	658.40	640.42	632.23
55000	1308.45	887.35	769.78	724.24	704.46	695.45
60000	1427.40	968.01	839.76	790.08	768.50	758.67
65000	1546.35	1048.68	909.74	855.92	832.54	821.89
70000	1665.30	1129.35	979.72	921.76	896.59	885.12
75000	1784.25	1210.02	1049.70	987.60	960.63	948.34
80000	1903.20	1290.68	1119.67	1053.44	1024.67	1011.56
85000	2022.15	1371.35	1189.65	1119.28	1088.71	1074.78
90000	2141.10	1452.02	1259.63	1185.12	1152.75	1138.00
95000	2260.05	1532.69	1329.61	1250.96	1216.79	1201.23
100000	2379.00	1613.35	1399.59	1316.79	1280.84	1264.45

15.25%

Amount	5 Years	10 Years	15 Years	20 Years	25 Years	30 Years
50	1.20	.82	.71	.67	.66	.65
100	2.40	1.63	1.42	1.34	1.31	1.29
500	11.97	8.15	7.09	6.68	6.51	6.43
1000	23.93	16.29	14.17	13.36	13.01	12.85
2000	47.85	32.58	28.34	26.71	26.01	25.69
5000	119.61	81.44	70.84	66.77	65.02	64.23
10000	239.22	162.87	141.68	133.53	130.03	128.45
15000	358.83	244.31	212.52	200.30	195.04	192.67
20000	478.43	325.74	283.35	267.06	260.06	256.90
25000	598.04	407.18	354.19	333.83	325.07	321.12
30000	717.65	488.61	425.03	400.59	390.08	385.34
35000	837.25	570.05	495.87	467.36	455.10	449.57
40000	956.86	651.48	566.70	534.12	520.11	513.79
45000	1076.47	732.92	637.54	600.89	585.12	578.01
50000	1196.07	814.35	708.38	667.65	650.13	642.23
55000	1315.68	895.79	779.22	734.42	715.15	706.46
60000	1435.29	977.22	850.05	801.18	780.16	770.68
65000	1554.89	1058.66	920.89	867.95	845.17	834.90
70000	1674.50	1140.09	991.73	934.71	910.19	899.13
75000	1794.11	1221.53	1062.57	1001.48	975.20	963.35
80000	1913.71	1302.96	1133.40	1068.24	1040.21	1027.57
85000	2033.32	1384.39	1204.24	1135.01	1105.22	1091.79
90000	2152.93	1465.83	1275.08	1201.77	1170.24	1156.02
95000	2272.53	1547.26	1345.92	1268.54	1235.25	1220.24
100000	2392.14	1628.70	1416.75	1335.30	1300.26	1284.46

APPENDIX

APPENDIX B: TABLES OF OUTSTANDING BALANCES

How To Read The Tables In Appendix B

Appendix B tables show the amount of outstanding debt (unpaid balance) still remaining on your mortgage at particular points in time during your loan term—after 5, 10, 15, 20, 25, and 30 years of making payments.

To figure out the outstanding debt (balance) on your mortgage at a given point in time (at the 5, 10, 15, 20, 25, and 30-year points), here's what you do: (1) refer to the table having the applicable interest rate for your mortgage (2) select from the first column of the table (the "age of loan"), the line corresponding to the number of years that you've had the house or held the mortgage; (3) look at the number of years listed on top of each column. One of these numbers, the particular one that applies to you, represents the original term for your mortgage loan—the number of years for which you originally took out the loan; now, the percentage shown under the "years" column on the line corresponding to the age of you loan, is the proportion of the loan still remaining on your loan. For example, let's say the applicable age of your loan (the number of years you've held the mortgage) is 10 years; your loan was for $100,000, 30-year term at 10 percent interest. Reading from the "age of loan" column in the 10 percent table, the percentage shown for age 10 is 90.94. Therefore, on a $100,000 original mortgage, what you still owe today, after 10 years of paying on the loan, is about $90,940, as follows:

$$\$100,000 \text{ X } 90.94 = \$90,940$$

8.00%

Age of Loan	5 years	10 years	15 years	20 years	25 years	30 years
1	83.06	93.19	96.40	97.89	98.69	99.16
2	64.71	85.82	92.51	95.60	97.27	98.26
3	44.83	77.84	88.29	93.12	95.74	97.28
4	23.31	69.20	83.72	90.43	94.07	96.22
5	0	59.84	78.77	87.53	92.27	95.07
6		49.70	73.41	84.38	90.32	93.83
7		38.72	67.60	80.97	88.21	92.48
8		26.83	61.31	77.27	85.92	91.02
9		13.95	54.51	73.27	83.45	89.44
10		0	47.13	68.94	80.76	87.72
11			39.15	64.25	77.86	85.87
12			30.50	59.17	74.71	83.86
13			21.13	53.67	71.30	81.69
14			10.99	47.71	67.61	79.33
15			0	41.25	63.61	76.78
16				34.26	59.29	74.02
17				26.69	54.60	71.03
18				18.49	49.52	67.79
19				9.62	44.02	64.28
20				0	38.06	60.48
21					31.62	56.36
22					24.63	51.91
23					17.07	47.08
24					8.87	41.85
25					0	36.19
26						30.06
27						23.42
28						16.22
29						8.44
30						0

8.25%

Age of Loan	5 years	10 years	15 years	20 years	25 years	30 years
1	83.15	93.28	96.48	97.95	98.74	99.21
2	64.85	85.99	92.65	95.72	97.38	98.34
3	44.98	78.07	88.50	93.30	95.89	97.41
4	23.42	69.47	83.99	90.68	94.28	96.39
5	0	60.13	79.10	87.83	92.53	95.28
6		50.00	73.78	84.73	90.64	94.09
7		39.00	68.01	81.38	88.58	92.78
8		27.05	61.81	77.73	86.34	91.37
9		14.08	54.95	73.77	83.91	89.84
10		0	47.56	69.47	81.27	88.17
11			39.55	64.80	78.41	86.36
12			30.85	59.74	75.30	84.40
13			21.40	54.23	71.93	82.27
14			11.14	48.26	68.26	79.95
15			0	41.78	64.28	77.44
16				34.74	59.96	74.71
17				27.09	55.28	71.75
18				18.79	50.18	68.53
19				9.78	44.66	65.04
20				0	38.66	61.25
21					32.14	57.14
22					25.07	52.67
23					17.39	47.82
24					9.05	42.55
25					0	36.83
26						30.63
27						23.89
28						16.57
29						8.62
30						0

8.50%

Age of Loan	5 years	10 years	15 years	20 years	25 years	30 years
1	83.24	93.37	96.55	98.01	98.70	99.24
2	64.99	86.15	92.80	95.84	97.47	98.42
3	45.14	78.29	88.71	93.49	96.04	97.53
4	23.52	69.74	84.26	90.92	94.48	96.55
5	0.	60.43	79.42	88.13	92.79	95.49
6		50.30	74.16	85.09	90.94	94.34
7		39.28	68.42	81.78	88.93	93.08
8		27.28	62.18	78.18	86.74	91.71
9		14.22	55.39	74.26	84.36	90.22
10		0	48.00	69.99	81.77	88.60
11			39.95	65.35	78.95	86.84
12			31.19	60.30	75.88	84.92
13			21.66	54.80	72.54	82.83
14			11.29	48.81	68.90	80.56
15			0	42.30	64.95	78.08
16				35.21	60.64	75.39
17				27.49	55.95	72.46
18				19.09	50.85	69.27
19				9.95	45.29	65.80
20				0	39.25	62.02
21					32.67	57.90
22					25.51	53.43
23					17.71	48.55
24					9.23	43.25
25					0	37.48
26						31.20
27						24.36
28						16.92
29						8.82
30						0

8.75%

Age of Loan	5 years	10 years	15 years	20 years	25 years	30 years
1	83.33	93.45	96.62	98.07	98.84	99.28
2	65.14	86.31	92.94	95.96	97.57	98.50
3	45.29	78.51	88.92	93.66	96.19	97.64
4	23.63	70.01	84.53	91.16	94.68	96.71
5	0	60.73	79.75	88.42	93.03	95.69
6		50.60	74.53	85.43	91.24	94.58
7		39.56	68.83	82.18	89.28	93.36
8		27.50	62.61	78.62	87.14	92.04
9		14.35	55.83	74.74	84.81	90.60
10		0	48.43	70.51	82.26	89.02
11			40.35	65.90	79.48	87.30
12			31.54	60.86	76.45	85.43
13			21.93	55.36	73.14	83.38
14			11.44	49.36	69.54	81.15
15			0	42.82	65.60	78.71
16				35.68	61.30	76.06
17				27.89	56.62	73.16
18				19.39	51.50	69.99
19				10.12	45.93	66.54
20				0	39.84	62.77
21					33.20	58.66
22					25.95	54.18
23					18.04	49.28
24					9.41	43.95
25					0	38.12
26						31.76
27						24.83
28						17.26
29						9.01
30						0

APPENDIX B: Loan Progress Chart

9.00%

Age of Loan	5 years	10 years	15 years	20 years	25 years	30 years
1	83.42	93.54	96.69	98.13	98.88	99.32
2	65.28	86.47	93.08	96.08	97.66	98.57
3	45.44	78.73	89.12	93.84	96.33	97.75
4	23.74	70.28	84.80	91.39	94.87	96.86
5	0	61.02	80.07	88.71	93.27	95.88
6		50.90	74.89	85.77	91.53	94.81
7		39.84	69.23	82.57	89.62	93.64
8		27.73	63.04	79.06	87.53	92.36
9		14.49	56.27	75.22	85.24	90.96
10		0	48.86	71.03	82.74	89.43
11			40.76	66.44	80.00	87.75
12			31.90	61.41	77.01	85.92
13			22.20	55.92	73.74	83.92
14			11.60	49.91	70.16	81.73
15			0	43.34	66.25	79.33
16				36.16	61.97	76.71
17				28.29	57.28	73.84
18				19.59	52.16	70.70
19				10.29	46.56	67.27
20				0	40.43	63.52
21					33.72	59.41
22					26.39	54.92
23					18.37	50.01
24					9.60	44.64
25					0	38.76
26						32.33
27						25.30
28						17.61
29						9.20
30						0

9.25%

Age of Loan	5 years	10 years	15 years	20 years	25 years	30 years
1	83.51	93.62	96.76	98.18	98.93	99.35
2	65.42	86.62	93.22	96.19	97.75	98.64
3	45.59	78.95	89.33	94.01	96.47	97.86
4	23.84	70.54	85.06	91.61	95.05	97.00
5	0	61.32	80.39	88.99	93.51	96.06
6		51.21	75.26	86.11	91.81	95.04
7		40.12	69.63	82.95	89.94	93.91
8		27.96	63.47	79.49	87.90	92.67
9		14.62	56.71	75.70	85.66	91.31
10		0	49.29	71.53	83.21	89.82
11			41.16	66.97	80.52	88.19
12			32.25	61.97	77.57	86.40
13			22.47	56.48	74.33	84.44
14			11.75	50.46	70.78	82.29
15			0	43.86	66.89	79.93
16				36.63	62.62	77.35
17				28.70	57.94	74.51
18				20.00	52.81	71.40
19				10.46	47.18	67.99
20				0	41.01	64.26
21					34.25	60.16
22					26.83	55.66
23					18.70	50.73
24					9.78	45.33
25					0	39.40
26						32.90
27						25.78
28						17.96
29						9.39
30						0

9.50%

Age of Loan	5 years	10 years	15 years	20 years	25 years	30 years
1	83.60	93.70	96.83	98.24	98.97	99.38
2	65.56	86.78	93.35	96.30	97.84	98.71
3	45.74	79.17	89.53	94.18	96.60	97.96
4	23.95	70.81	85.32	91.84	95.23	97.14
5	0	61.61	80.70	89.27	93.73	96.24
6		51.51	75.62	86.44	92.08	95.25
7		40.40	70.03	83.33	90.27	94.16
8		28.18	63.89	79.92	88.27	92.97
9		14.76	57.14	76.16	86.08	91.65
10		0	49.72	72.04	83.67	90.21
11			41.56	67.50	81.02	88.62
12			32.60	62.51	78.11	86.87
13			22.74	57.03	74.91	84.95
14			11.91	51.01	71.39	82.84
15			0	44.38	67.52	80.52
16				37.10	63.27	77.97
17				29.10	58.59	75.17
18				20.30	53.46	72.09
19				10.63	47.81	68.70
20				0	41.60	64.98
21					34.78	60.89
22					27.27	56.39
23					19.03	51.45
24					9.96	46.01
25					0	40.04
26						33.47
27						26.25
28						18.31
29						9.59
30						0

9.75%

Age of Loan	5 years	10 years	15 years	20 years	25 years	30 years
1	83.68	93.78	96.90	98.29	99.01	99.41
2	65.71	86.94	93.49	96.41	97.93	98.77
3	45.89	79.39	89.72	94.34	96.73	98.06
4	24.06	71.07	85.58	92.05	95.41	97.27
5	0	61.91	81.01	89.54	93.95	96.41
6		51.81	75.97	86.76	92.35	95.46
7		40.68	70.43	83.71	90.58	94.41
8		28.41	64.31	80.34	88.63	93.26
9		14.89	57.57	76.62	86.49	91.98
10		0	50.15	72.53	84.12	90.58
11			41.97	68.02	81.51	89.03
12			32.95	63.06	78.64	87.33
13			23.01	57.58	75.48	85.45
14			12.07	51.55	71.99	83.38
15			0	44.90	68.15	81.10
16				37.58	63.91	78.59
17				29.50	59.24	75.82
18				20.61	54.10	72.77
19				10.80	48.43	69.41
20				0	42.19	65.70
21					35.30	61.62
22					27.72	57.12
23					19.36	52.16
24					10.15	46.69
25					0	40.67
26						34.04
27						26.72
28						18.67
29						9.79
30						0

10.50%

Age of Loan	5 years	10 years	15 years	20 years	25 years	30 years
1	83.95	94.03	97.10	98.45	99.13	99.50
2	66.13	87.39	93.88	96.72	98.16	98.94
3	46.35	80.03	90.30	94.81	97.09	98.33
4	24.38	71.85	86.33	92.68	95.90	97.64
5	0	62.78	81.92	90.32	94.57	96.88
6		52.70	77.03	87.70	93.10	96.04
7		41.52	71.59	84.79	91.47	95.10
8		29.10	65.56	81.56	89.66	94.06
9		15.31	58.86	77.97	87.65	92.90
10		0	51.43	73.99	85.42	91.62
11			43.17	69.57	82.94	90.20
12			34.01	64.66	80.19	88.62
13			23.84	59.21	77.13	86.86
14			12.54	53.16	73.74	84.91
15			0	46.45	69.97	82.75
16				38.99	65.79	80.35
17				30.72	61.15	77.68
18				21.53	56.00	74.73
19				11.33	50.28	71.44
20				0	43.93	67.79
21					36.88	63.74
22					29.05	59.24
23					20.36	54.25
24					10.71	48.71
25					0	42.56
26						35.73
27						28.14
28						19.72
29						10.38
30						0

10.75%

Age of Loan	5 years	10 years	15 years	20 years	25 years	30 years
1	84.04	94.10	97.16	98.49	99.16	99.53
2	66.27	87.54	94.00	96.82	98.23	99.00
3	46.50	80.24	90.49	94.88	97.20	98.41
4	24.49	72.11	86.57	92.88	96.05	97.75
5	0	63.07	82.22	90.57	94.77	97.03
6		53.00	77.37	88.00	93.34	96.22
7		41.80	71.98	85.14	91.75	95.31
8		29.33	65.97	81.95	89.98	94.31
9		15.45	59.29	78.41	88.02	93.19
10		0	51.85	74.46	85.83	91.95
11			43.58	70.07	83.39	90.56
12			34.36	65.19	80.68	89.02
13			24.11	59.75	77.66	87.31
14			12.70	53.70	74.30	85.40
15			0	46.96	70.57	83.28
16				39.47	66.41	80.91
17				31.12	61.78	78.28
18				21.84	56.62	75.35
19				11.50	50.89	72.09
20				0	44.50	68.47
21					37.40	64.43
22					29.49	59.94
23					20.69	54.94
24					10.90	49.37
25					0	43.18
26						36.29
27						28.62
28						20.08
29						10.58
30						0

10.00%

Age of Loan	5 years	10 years	15 years	20 years	25 years	30 years
1	83.77	93.87	96.97	98.35	99.05	99.44
2	65.85	87.09	93.62	96.52	98.01	98.83
3	46.04	79.60	89.92	94.50	96.85	98.15
4	24.17	71.33	85.83	92.27	95.57	97.40
5	0	62.20	81.32	89.80	94.16	96.57
6		52.10	76.33	87.08	92.61	95.66
7		40.96	70.82	84.07	90.88	94.65
8		28.64	64.73	80.75	88.98	93.53
9		15.03	58.01	77.08	86.88	92.30
10		0	50.58	73.02	84.56	90.94
11			42.37	68.54	82.00	89.43
12			33.30	63.60	79.17	87.77
13			23.29	58.13	76.04	85.93
14			12.22	52.09	72.58	83.91
15			0	45.42	68.76	81.66
16				38.05	64.54	79.19
17				29.91	59.88	76.45
18				20.91	54.74	73.43
19				10.98	49.05	70.09
20				0	42.77	66.41
21					35.83	62.33
22					28.16	57.83
23					19.69	52.86
24					10.34	47.37
25					0	41.30
26						34.60
27						27.20
28						19.02
29						9.98
30						0

10.25%

Age of Loan	5 years	10 years	15 years	20 years	25 years	30 years
1	83.86	93.95	97.03	98.40	99.09	99.47
2	65.99	87.24	93.75	96.62	98.09	98.89
3	46.20	79.82	90.11	94.65	96.97	98.24
4	24.28	71.59	86.08	92.48	95.74	97.52
5	0	62.49	81.62	90.06	94.37	96.73
6		52.40	76.68	87.39	92.86	95.85
7		41.24	71.21	84.43	91.18	94.88
8		28.87	65.15	81.16	89.33	93.80
9		15.17	58.44	77.53	87.27	92.61
10		0	51.00	73.51	84.99	91.29
11			42.77	69.06	82.47	89.82
12			33.66	64.13	79.68	88.20
13			23.56	58.67	76.59	86.41
14			12.38	52.63	73.16	84.42
15			0	45.94	69.37	82.21
16				38.52	65.17	79.78
17				30.31	60.52	77.08
18				21.22	55.37	74.08
19				11.15	49.67	70.77
20				0	43.35	67.10
21					36.35	63.04
22					28.61	58.54
23					20.03	53.56
24					10.52	48.04
25					0	41.93
26						35.16
27						27.67
28						19.37
29						10.18
30						0

APPENDIX B: Loan Progress Chart

11.50%

Age of Loan	5 years	10 years	15 years	20 years	25 years	30 years
1	84.30	94.34	97.34	98.63	99.26	99.60
2	66.69	87.99	94.37	97.10	98.44	99.14
3	46.95	80.86	91.03	95.38	97.51	98.63
4	24.82	72.88	87.29	93.45	96.48	98.06
5	0	63.93	83.09	91.29	95.32	97.42
6		53.89	78.38	88.87	94.01	96.71
7		42.64	73.11	86.15	92.55	95.90
8		30.02	67.19	83.10	90.91	95.00
9		15.87	60.56	79.68	89.07	93.99
10		0	53.12	75.85	87.01	92.86
11			44.78	71.55	84.70	91.59
12			35.43	66.74	82.11	90.17
13			24.94	61.34	79.21	88.57
14			13.18	55.28	75.95	86.78
15			0	48.49	72.30	84.77
16				40.88	68.20	82.52
17				32.34	63.61	80.00
18				22.77	58.46	77.17
19				12.03	52.69	73.99
20				0	46.22	70.44
21					38.96	66.45
22					30.82	61.97
23					21.70	56.96
24					11.47	51.33
25					0	45.03
26						37.96
27						30.03
28						21.14
29						11.18
30						0

11.75%

Age of Loan	5 years	10 years	15 years	20 years	25 years	30 years
1	84.38	94.41	97.40	98.68	99.30	99.62
2	66.83	88.13	94.49	97.19	98.50	99.19
3	47.10	81.07	91.20	95.51	97.61	98.70
4	24.93	73.13	87.52	93.63	96.61	98.16
5	0	64.21	83.37	91.52	95.49	97.55
6		54.19	78.71	89.14	94.22	96.86
7		42.92	73.48	86.47	92.80	96.09
8		30.25	67.59	83.47	91.20	95.22
9		16.01	60.97	80.09	89.41	94.24
10		0	53.54	76.30	87.39	93.14
11			45.18	72.04	85.12	91.91
12			35.78	67.25	82.57	90.52
13			25.22	61.86	79.70	88.97
14			13.35	55.80	76.48	87.21
15			0	49.00	72.86	85.24
16				41.35	68.79	83.03
17				32.75	64.21	80.54
18				23.08	59.07	77.75
19				12.21	53.28	74.60
20				0	46.78	71.07
21					39.48	67.10
22					31.27	62.63
23					22.04	57.62
24					11.66	51.98
25					0	45.64
26						38.51
27						30.50
28						21.50
29						11.38
30						0

11.00%

Age of Loan	5 years	10 years	15 years	20 years	25 years	30 years
1	84.12	94.18	97.22	98.54	99.20	99.55
2	66.41	87.69	94.13	96.91	98.31	99.05
3	46.65	80.45	90.67	95.10	97.31	98.49
4	24.60	72.37	86.81	93.07	96.20	97.86
5	0	63.36	82.51	90.81	94.95	97.16
6		53.30	77.71	88.29	93.57	96.39
7		42.08	72.36	85.48	92.03	95.52
8		29.56	66.38	82.34	90.30	94.55
9		15.59	59.71	78.84	88.38	93.47
10		0	52.28	74.93	86.23	92.26
11			43.98	70.57	83.84	90.92
12			34.72	65.71	81.17	89.42
13			24.39	60.28	78.19	87.74
14			12.86	54.23	74.86	85.87
15			0	47.47	71.15	83.79
16				39.94	67.01	81.46
17				31.53	62.39	78.87
18				22.15	57.24	75.97
19				11.68	51.49	72.74
20				0	45.08	69.13
21					37.92	65.11
22					29.94	60.63
23					21.03	55.62
24					11.09	50.03
25					0	43.80
26						36.85
27						29.09
28						20.43
29						10.78
30						0

11.25%

Age of Loan	5 years	10 years	15 years	20 years	25 years	30 years
1	84.21	94.26	97.28	98.59	99.23	99.57
2	66.55	87.84	94.25	97.01	98.37	99.10
3	46.80	80.66	90.85	95.24	97.41	98.56
4	24.71	72.63	87.05	93.26	96.34	97.97
5	0	63.64	82.80	91.05	95.14	97.30
6		53.59	78.05	88.58	93.79	96.55
7		42.36	72.73	85.82	92.29	95.72
8		29.79	66.79	82.72	90.61	94.78
9		15.73	60.14	79.26	88.73	93.74
10		0	52.70	75.39	86.63	92.57
11			44.38	71.07	84.27	91.26
12			35.07	66.23	81.64	89.80
13			24.66	60.81	78.70	88.16
14			13.02	54.76	75.41	86.33
15			0	47.98	71.73	84.29
16				40.41	67.61	82.00
17				31.93	63.01	79.44
18				22.46	57.85	76.57
19				11.86	52.09	73.37
20				0	45.65	69.79
21					38.44	65.78
22					30.38	61.10
23					21.36	56.29
24					11.28	50.69
25					0	44.42
26						37.40
27						29.56
28						20.79
29						10.97
30						0

148

12.50%

Age of Loan	5 years	10 years	15 years	20 years	25 years	30 years
1	84.64	94.63	97.57	98.80	99.38	99.67
2	67.25	88.68	94.83	97.44	98.68	99.31
3	47.56	81.68	91.72	95.90	97.89	98.89
4	25.26	73.89	88.19	94.16	96.99	98.42
5	0	65.06	84.20	92.18	95.97	97.88
6		55.07	79.68	89.94	94.82	97.28
7		43.75	74.57	87.41	93.51	96.59
8		30.94	68.77	84.54	92.03	95.81
9		16.43	62.21	81.30	90.36	94.93
10		0	54.78	77.62	88.47	93.94
11			46.37	73.45	86.32	92.81
12			36.84	68.74	83.89	91.53
13			26.05	63.40	81.14	90.08
14			13.84	57.35	78.02	88.45
15			0	50.50	74.49	86.59
16				42.74	70.49	84.49
17				33.96	65.97	82.11
18				24.02	60.84	79.42
19				12.75	55.04	76.37
20				0	48.46	72.91
21					41.02	69.00
22					32.59	64.57
23					23.05	59.55
24					12.24	53.87
25					0	47.44
26						40.15
27						31.90
28						22.56
29						11.98
30						0

12.75%

Age of Loan	5 years	10 years	15 years	20 years	25 years	30 years
1	84.73	94.71	97.63	98.84	99.41	99.69
2	67.39	88.70	94.94	97.52	98.73	99.34
3	47.71	81.88	91.88	96.02	97.97	98.95
4	25.36	74.13	88.41	94.32	97.10	98.50
5	0	65.34	84.47	92.39	96.12	97.98
6		55.36	80.00	90.20	95.00	97.40
7		44.03	74.93	87.71	93.74	96.74
8		31.17	69.16	84.89	92.30	96.00
9		16.57	62.62	81.68	90.66	95.15
10		0	55.20	78.04	88.81	94.18
11			46.77	73.91	86.70	93.09
12			37.20	69.22	84.31	91.85
13			26.33	63.90	81.60	90.44
14			14.00	57.86	78.51	88.83
15			0	51.00	75.02	87.02
16				43.21	71.05	84.95
17				34.37	66.54	82.61
18				24.33	61.42	79.95
19				12.94	55.61	76.93
20				0	49.02	73.50
21					41.53	69.61
22					33.03	65.20
23					23.39	60.18
24					12.43	54.49
25					0	48.03
26						40.69
27						32.37
28						22.91
29						12.18
30						0

12.00%

Age of Loan	5 years	10 years	15 years	20 years	25 years	30 years
1	84.47	94.49	97.46	98.72	99.32	99.64
2	66.97	88.27	94.60	97.27	98.56	99.23
3	47.25	81.27	91.38	95.65	97.71	98.77
4	25.04	73.39	87.75	93.81	96.74	98.25
5	0	64.50	83.65	91.74	95.65	97.66
6		54.48	79.04	89.42	94.43	97.00
7		43.20	73.84	86.79	93.05	96.26
8		30.48	67.99	83.83	91.49	95.42
9		16.15	61.39	80.50	89.73	94.48
10		0	53.95	76.75	87.76	93.42
11			45.58	72.52	85.53	92.22
12			36.13	67.75	83.02	90.87
13			25.50	62.37	80.19	89.35
14			13.51	56.32	77.00	87.64
15			0	49.50	73.41	85.71
16				41.81	69.36	83.53
17				33.15	64.80	81.08
18				23.39	59.66	78.32
19				12.39	53.87	75.20
20				0	47.35	71.69
21					40.00	67.74
22					31.71	63.29
23					22.37	58.27
24					11.85	52.61
25					0	46.24
26						39.06
27						30.97
28						21.85
29						11.58
30						0

12.25%

Age of Loan	5 years	10 years	15 years	20 years	25 years	30 years
1	84.56	94.56	97.52	98.76	99.35	99.66
2	67.11	88.42	94.71	97.36	98.62	99.27
3	47.41	81.48	91.55	95.78	97.80	98.83
4	25.15	73.64	87.97	93.99	96.87	98.33
5	0	64.78	83.93	91.96	95.81	97.77
6		54.78	79.36	89.68	94.63	97.14
7		43.48	74.21	87.10	93.28	96.43
8		30.71	68.38	84.19	91.76	95.62
9		16.29	61.80	80.90	90.05	94.71
10		0	54.37	77.19	88.12	93.68
11			45.97	72.99	85.93	92.52
12			36.49	68.24	83.46	91.21
13			25.77	62.89	80.67	89.72
14			13.67	56.84	77.52	88.05
15			0	50.00	73.95	86.15
16				42.28	69.93	84.02
17				33.56	65.39	81.60
18				23.70	60.26	78.87
19				12.57	54.46	75.79
20				0	47.91	72.31
21					40.51	68.38
22					32.15	63.93
23					22.71	58.91
24					12.05	53.25
25					0	46.84
26						39.61
27						31.44
28						22.21
29						11.78
30						0

APPENDIX B: Loan Progress Chart

13.00%

Age of Loan	5 years	10 years	15 years	20 years	25 years	30 years
1	84.81	94.78	97.68	98.88	99.43	99.71
2	67.53	88.84	95.04	97.60	98.79	99.38
3	47.86	82.08	92.04	96.14	98.05	99.00
4	25.47	74.38	88.63	94.48	97.22	98.57
5	0	65.62	84.74	92.60	96.27	98.08
6		55.66	80.31	90.45	95.18	97.53
7		44.31	75.28	88.01	93.95	96.89
8		31.64	69.55	85.23	92.55	96.17
9		16.86	63.03	82.07	90.96	95.35
10		0	55.61	78.47	89.14	94.42
11			47.16	74.37	87.07	93.36
12			37.55	69.71	84.72	92.15
13			26.61	64.40	82.05	90.78
14			14.17	58.36	79.00	89.21
15			0	51.49	75.54	87.43
16				43.67	71.59	85.40
17				34.77	67.10	83.10
18				24.64	62.00	80.47
19				13.12	56.18	77.49
20				0	49.57	74.09
21					42.04	70.22
22					33.47	65.82
23					23.72	60.81
24					12.63	55.11
25					0	48.62
26						41.23
27						32.83
28						23.27
29						12.39
30						0

13.25%

Age of Loan	5 years	10 years	15 years	20 years	25 years	30 years
1	84.90	94.85	97.73	98.91	99.46	99.72
2	67.67	88.97	95.15	97.67	98.84	99.41
3	48.01	82.27	92.20	96.26	98.13	99.05
4	25.58	74.62	88.84	94.64	97.33	98.64
5	0	65.90	85.00	92.80	96.41	98.18
6		55.95	80.62	90.70	95.36	97.64
7		44.59	75.63	88.30	94.16	97.03
8		31.64	69.93	85.56	92.80	96.34
9		16.86	63.43	82.44	91.24	95.55
10		0	56.02	78.88	89.46	94.65
11			47.56	74.82	87.44	93.62
12			37.90	70.18	85.13	92.44
13			26.89	64.90	82.49	91.10
14			14.33	58.86	79.48	89.58
15			0	51.98	76.05	87.83
16				44.13	72.13	85.84
17				35.18	67.66	83.57
18				24.96	62.56	80.98
19				13.30	56.75	78.03
20				0	50.12	74.66
21					42.55	70.81
22					33.91	66.43
23					24.06	61.42
24					12.82	55.71
25					0	49.20
26						41.77
27						33.29
28						23.62
29						12.59
30						0

13.50%

Age of Loan	5 years	10 years	15 years	20 years	25 years	30 years
1	84.98	94.92	97.79	98.95	99.48	99.74
2	67.81	89.11	95.26	97.74	98.89	99.44
3	48.16	82.47	92.36	96.37	98.21	99.10
4	25.69	74.87	89.05	94.80	97.43	98.71
5	0	66.18	85.26	93.00	96.54	98.26
6		56.24	80.93	90.94	95.53	97.75
7		44.87	75.98	88.58	94.37	97.17
8		31.87	70.31	85.89	93.04	96.50
9		17.00	63.83	82.81	91.52	95.74
10		0	56.42	79.29	89.78	94.87
11			47.95	75.26	87.79	93.87
12			38.26	70.66	85.52	92.73
13			27.17	65.19	82.92	91.42
14			14.50	59.36	79.95	89.93
15			0	52.47	76.55	88.22
16				44.59	72.66	86.27
17				35.58	68.21	84.04
18				25.27	63.13	81.48
19				13.48	57.31	78.56
20				0	50.66	75.22
21					43.05	71.40
22					34.35	67.03
23					24.40	62.03
24					13.02	56.32
25					0	49.78
26						42.30
27						33.75
28						23.97
29						12.79
30						0

13.75%

Age of Loan	5 years	10 years	15 years	20 years	25 years	30 years
1	85.07	94.99	97.84	98.98	99.50	99.75
2	67.94	89.25	95.36	97.82	98.93	99.47
3	48.31	82.66	92.51	96.48	98.28	99.15
4	25.80	75.11	89.26	94.95	97.53	98.78
5	0	66.45	85.52	93.19	96.68	98.35
6		56.53	81.23	91.17	95.69	97.86
7		45.15	76.32	88.86	94.56	97.30
8		32.11	70.69	86.21	93.27	96.66
9		17.15	64.23	83.17	91.79	95.92
10		0	56.83	79.69	90.09	95.08
11			48.34	75.70	88.14	94.11
12			38.61	71.12	85.91	93.00
13			27.46	65.87	83.35	91.73
14			14.66	59.86	80.41	90.27
15			0	52.96	77.04	88.60
16				45.05	73.18	86.69
17				35.98	68.76	84.49
18				25.59	63.68	81.97
19				13.67	57.87	79.08
20				0	51.20	75.77
21					43.55	71.98
22					34.79	67.62
23					24.73	62.63
24					11.21	56.91
25					0	50.35
26						42.83
27						34.21
28						24.33
29						12.99
30						0

14.00%

Age of Loan	5 years	10 years	15 years	20 years	25 years	30 years
1	85.15	95.06	97.89	99.02	99.53	99.77
2	68.08	89.38	95.46	97.89	98.98	99.50
3	48.46	82.85	92.67	96.59	98.35	99.19
4	25.91	75.35	89.46	95.09	97.63	98.84
5	0	66.73	85.77	93.38	96.80	98.43
6		56.82	81.53	91.40	95.85	97.96
7		45.43	76.66	89.13	94.76	97.43
8		32.34	71.06	86.53	93.50	96.81
9		17.29	64.63	83.53	92.05	96.10
10		0	57.23	80.09	90.39	95.28
11			48.73	76.13	88.48	94.35
12			38.97	71.58	86.28	93.27
13			27.74	66.36	83.76	92.03
14			14.83	60.35	80.86	90.61
15			0	53.44	77.53	88.97
16				45.51	73.70	87.09
17				36.38	69.30	84.93
18				25.90	64.23	82.45
19				13.85	58.42	79.59
20				0	51.73	76.31
21					44.05	72.54
22					35.22	68.21
23					25.07	63.23
24					13.41	57.50
25					0	50.92
26						43.36
27						34.67
28						24.68
29						13.20
30						0

14.25%

Age of Loan	5 years	10 years	15 years	20 years	25 years	30 years
1	85.23	95.13	97.94	99.05	99.55	99.78
2	68.22	89.51	95.56	97.95	99.02	99.53
3	48.61	83.04	92.82	96.69	98.42	99.23
4	26.03	75.59	89.66	95.24	97.73	98.90
5	0	67.00	86.02	93.56	96.93	98.51
6		57.11	81.83	91.63	96.00	98.06
7		45.71	77.00	89.40	94.94	97.55
8		32.57	71.44	86.84	93.72	96.95
9		17.44	65.02	83.88	92.31	96.27
10		0	57.64	80.48	90.68	95.48
11			49.12	76.56	88.81	94.57
12			39.32	72.04	86.65	93.53
13			28.02	66.83	84.17	92.32
14			15.00	60.84	81.31	90.93
15			0	53.92	78.01	89.33
16				45.96	74.21	87.49
17				36.79	69.83	85.36
18				26.21	64.78	82.91
19				14.03	58.97	80.09
20				0	52.27	76.84
21					44.55	73.10
22					35.65	68.78
23					25.41	63.81
24					13.60	58.09
25					0	51.49
26						43.88
27						35.12
28						25.03
29						13.40
30						0

14.50%

Age of Loan	5 years	10 years	15 years	20 years	25 years	30 years
1	85.32	95.19	97.98	99.08	99.57	99.79
2	68.35	89.64	95.65	98.02	99.06	99.55
3	48.76	83.23	92.96	96.96	98.49	99.27
4	26.14	75.83	89.86	95.37	97.82	98.95
5	0	67.28	86.27	93.74	97.04	98.58
6		57.40	82.12	91.85	96.15	98.15
7		45.99	77.33	89.66	95.12	97.66
8		32.81	71.80	87.14	93.93	97.09
9		17.58	65.42	84.23	92.56	96.43
10		0	58.04	80.87	90.97	95.67
11			49.51	76.98	89.13	94.79
12			39.67	72.49	87.01	93.77
13			28.30	67.31	84.57	92.60
14			15.17	61.32	81.74	91.24
15			0	54.40	78.48	89.68
16				46.41	74.70	87.87
17				37.19	70.35	85.78
18				26.53	65.32	83.37
19				14.22	59.51	80.58
20				0	52.79	77.36
21					45.04	73.65
22					36.09	69.35
23					25.74	64.39
24					13.80	58.66
25					0	52.05
26						44.40
27						35.58
28						25.38
29						13.60
30						0

14.75%

Age of Loan	5 years	10 years	15 years	20 years	25 years	30 years
1	85.40	95.26	98.03	99.11	99.59	99.80
2	68.49	89.77	95.75	98.08	99.10	99.58
3	48.91	83.42	93.11	96.89	98.55	99.31
4	26.25	76.06	90.05	95.51	97.90	99.01
5	0	67.55	86.51	93.91	97.16	98.65
6		57.68	82.41	92.06	96.30	98.24
7		46.26	77.66	89.92	95.30	97.77
8		33.04	72.17	87.44	94.14	97.22
9		17.73	65.80	84.57	92.80	96.59
10		0	58.43	81.24	91.24	95.85
11			49.90	77.39	89.45	95.00
12			40.02	72.94	87.37	94.01
13			28.58	67.78	84.96	92.87
14			15.34	61.80	82.17	91.55
15			0	54.88	78.94	90.02
16				46.86	75.20	88.24
17				37.59	70.86	86.19
18				26.84	65.85	83.81
19				14.40	60.04	81.06
20				0	53.32	77.87
21					45.53	74.18
22					36.52	69.91
23					26.08	64.96
24					13.99	59.23
25					0	52.60
26						44.92
27						36.03
28						25.73
29						13.81
30						0

APPENDIX B: Loan Progress Chart

15.50%

Age of Loan	5 years	10 years	15 years	20 years	25 years	30 years
1	85.64	95.46	98.17	99.20	99.64	99.83
2	68.90	90.16	96.03	98.26	99.22	99.64
3	49.37	83.98	93.53	97.17	98.72	99.42
4	26.58	76.76	90.62	95.90	98.15	99.15
5	0	68.35	87.22	94.41	97.48	98.85
6		58.54	83.26	92.68	96.70	98.49
7		47.09	78.64	90.66	95.79	98.07
8		33.74	73.24	88.30	94.72	97.58
9		18.17	66.95	85.55	93.48	97.02
10		0	59.62	82.35	92.03	96.35
11			51.06	78.61	90.34	95.58
12			41.08	74.24	88.38	94.68
13			29.43	69.15	86.08	93.63
14			15.85	63.21	83.40	92.40
15			0	56.29	80.27	90.97
16				48.21	76.62	89.30
17				38.78	72.37	87.36
18				27.79	67.41	85.08
19				14.96	61.62	82.44
20				0	54.87	79.35
21					46.99	75.74
22					37.80	71.54
23					27.09	66.63
24					14.58	60.91
25					0	54.23
26						46.45
27						37.37
28						26.77
29						14.42
30						0

15.00%

Age of Loan	5 years	10 years	15 years	20 years	25 years	30 years
1	85.48	95.33	98.08	99.14	99.60	99.81
2	68.63	89.90	95.84	98.14	99.14	99.60
3	49.06	83.61	93.25	96.99	98.61	99.35
4	26.36	76.30	90.24	95.64	97.99	99.06
5	0	67.82	86.75	94.08	97.27	98.72
6		57.97	82.70	92.27	96.43	98.33
7		46.54	77.99	90.17	95.46	97.87
8		33.27	72.53	87.73	94.34	97.35
9		17.87	66.19	84.90	93.03	96.74
10		0	58.83	81.62	91.51	96.02
11			50.29	77.80	89.75	95.20
12			40.37	73.38	87.71	94.24
13			28.87	68.24	85.34	93.13
14			15.51	62.27	82.59	91.84
15			0	55.35	79.39	90.34
16				47.31	75.68	88.61
17				37.99	71.37	86.59
18				27.16	66.38	84.25
19				14.59	60.57	81.53
20				0	53.84	78.37
21					46.02	74.71
22					36.95	70.46
23					26.42	65.53
24					14.19	59.80
25					0	53.15
26						45.43
27						36.48
28						26.08
29						14.01
30						0

15.25%

Age of Loan	5 years	10 years	15 years	20 years	25 years	30 years
1	85.56	95.39	98.12	99.17	99.62	99.82
2	68.76	90.03	95.94	98.20	99.18	99.62
3	49.22	83.79	93.39	97.08	98.67	99.38
4	26.47	76.53	90.43	95.77	98.07	99.11
5	0	68.09	86.99	94.25	97.38	98.78
6		58.26	82.98	92.48	96.57	98.41
7		46.82	78.32	90.42	95.63	97.98
8		33.51	72.89	88.02	94.53	97.47
9		18.02	66.57	85.23	93.26	96.88
10		0	59.23	81.99	91.78	96.19
11			50.67	78.21	90.05	95.39
12			40.73	73.81	88.05	94.47
13			29.15	68.70	85.71	93.38
14			15.68	62.75	83.00	92.13
15			0	55.82	79.83	90.66
16				47.76	76.16	88.96
17				38.38	71.88	86.98
18				27.47	66.90	84.67
19				14.77	61.10	81.99
20				0	54.36	78.86
21					46.51	75.23
22					37.38	71.00
23					26.75	66.08
24					14.39	60.36
25					0	53.70
26						45.94
27						36.92
28						26.43
29						14.21
30						0

Appendix C
GLOSSARY of Real Estate and Mortgage Terms

Abstract of Title   A short history of a piece of property, tracing its chain of ownership (title) through the years, plus a record of all liens, taxes, judgments or other encumbrances that may impair the title. Your title insurance company reviews the abstract to make sure the title comes to a buyer free of any defects (problems).

Acceleration clause   A clause in a mortgage or trust deed that calls all outstanding sums due in the event of certain specified occurrences, such as default, demolition, assignment or sale of the property, or any impairments to the mortgage security. To be enforceable, the clause and all its conditions must be stated in the original agreement. See also due-on-sale clause.

Accrued interest   The interest payable for the period of time that has elapsed since the previous fully paid period.

Adjustable mortgage loan (AML)   The recently authorized name for mortgage loans offered by federal savings and loan associations secured on one- to four-family dwellings on which the interest rate charged is periodically adjustable upwards or downwards. Rate fluctuations must follow the movement of a verifiable economic index not under the control of the lender; for example, six-month Treasury bills. Interest rate changes in AMLs are implemented by (1) changes in the periodic payment amount, (2) changes in the principal loan balance, (3) changes in the term of the loan, or (4) any combination of the three. Other AML variables include how often rate changes are made, whether payment caps are used, how much negative amortization is permitted, how much extension of the term is allowed and how much fluctuation is allowed in the interest rate.

Adjustable-rate mortgage (ARM)   The recently authorized name for residential mortgage loans having a periodically adjustable interest rate offered by nationally chartered banks. Similar to the adjustable mortgage loan (AML), with slight differences with regard to interest change caps, negative amortization and loan term. See also variable-rate mortgage and renegotiable rate mortgage.

Adjusted basis   The original basis of an asset, plus the costs of improvements, minus the expenses of depreciation, depletion, amortization or other loss. Adjusted basis is used for tax purposes and for deriving capital gains. The latter are obtained by subtracting the adjusted basis at the time of a sale from the net proceeds of the sale.

Ad Valorem   A latin phrase meaning "according to value."

Advance Commitment   A written offer by a lender to make a mortgage loan at a stated interest rate over a specific number of years.

Adverse Possession   The physical occupancy or possession of property in spite of, and in defiance of, someone else's legal title. If such possession continues for twenty years, legal title can be claimed by the one in possession.

Agreement for deed   See contract for deed.

Alienation clause   See acceleration clause, due-on-sale clause.

All-inclusive trust deed (AITD) (also called overriding or overlapping trust deed)   See wraparound.

Amortization   Repayment of a loan in periodic installments of principal and/or interest. At the end of the loan term both interest and principal will have been paid in full.

Annual percentage rate (APR)   Total finance charges—including fees, interest rate, points and other charges—expressed as a percentage of the total amount of the loan. Must be disclosed to borrower under federal Truth-in-Lending Law.

Annuity   A series of fixed-sum payments paid in a specified number of payment periods, usually monthly or annually.

Appraisal   An estimate of the market value of a home—that is, what it would sell for under normal conditions. 'Market value' is almost never the same as replacement cost, so an appraisal made by a lender is not adequate for insurance purposes.

Appraiser   A professional who charges to estimate the market or replacement value of a house.

Appreciation   An increase in the value of real or personal property above and beyond the value of improvements on such property.

Arbitrage   The spread, or difference, between a given set of interest rates, expressed in points. For example, in a wraparound loan, the arbitrage is the difference between the seller's loan to the senior mortgagee and the buyer's loan to the seller. If the seller's loan is 10 percent and the wraparound note is 12 percent, the seller enjoys an arbitrage of 2 points. Arbitrage can be positive income as in the above example, or it can be negative income (loss), as when the above situation is reversed.

Assessed value   The value of real property established for the purpose of assessing real property taxes.

Asset   An item having value. In accounting, assets have a specific, quantified value at any time and are summarized on a balance sheet along with the creditor's claims to the assets (liabilities) and the owner's claim against the remainder (net worth).

Assignment   The transfer of rights or interests in a property by an assignor to an assignee. Nonassignment clauses in contracts expressly limit the right of transfer of the contract.

Assumption   The financing technique wherein a buyer assumes the seller's existing mortgage loan and its obligations for payment. Usually involves a credit check and assumption fee by the lender. May require lender approval. See also due-on-sale clause.

Assumption clause   A clause in a mortgage note or deed that sets forth the lender's conditions and terms for the transfer of a mortgage to another mortgagor. The two concerns of the clause are: (1) the seller's continued liability and (2) possible renegotiation of the terms of the mortgage.

Balloon payment   The final payment of a loan, usually substantially larger than previous installments, which repays the debt in full.

Basis   A quantified value of an asset determined at the time the asset was acquired by its owner. In very simple cases, the basis of an asset is the cash paid for it, or its cost. Deriving the basis of assets, however, can be more complicated, as in the case of gifts, inheritances and real estate exchanges. Professional advice should be obtained when establishing an asset's basis.

Basis point   One-hundredth of one percent (.01 percent). Used to describe the change in value or market price of money assets, including mortgages. Also used to describe changes in yield. Do not confuse with a discount point (1 percent of face value of loan).

Biweekly mortgage   A loan that provides 26 payments a year with the size of the payments equal to one-half of the usual monthly payment. The borrower's equity builds rapidly with this type of loan.

Blanket mortgage   A mortgage loan secured by more than one property pledged as collateral. For example, a homeowner wishing to purchase two adjacent residences may obtain one mortgage by pledging both properties as collateral.

Blended-rate mortgage   See consolidated-rate mortgage.

Bridge loan (also called swing loan and interim financing)   A loan or loan offer, usually of short duration, that is taken out on a property and applied toward the purchase of another property prior to the sale of the first property. The bridge loan can be used to offset the sale of a residence by having the seller named as beneficiary or lienholder of the buyer's junior mortgage (the bridge loan) or trust deed. If the buyer's house is sold prior to or concurrent with the seller's house, the bridge loan can be cashed out before ever being executed (bridge loan option). The bridge loan and bridge loan option can alleviate the timing problem of the buyer's need to close on his or her home before buying another residence.

Builder contribution programs   Financial assistance programs wherein the builder contributes funds toward the homebuyer's debt obligation over a given time period. Can increase the homebuyer's mortgage eligibility and enable the builder to sell the home at less cost to himself or herself than would result from lowering the home's price to the point at which a buyer could qualify otherwise. See also buydown plans.

Buydown plans   Home financing arrangements that provide for mortgage payments to the lender by other parties as well as the buyer. The contributions made by other parties to the buyer's monthly payments reduce the interest amounts that the buyer pays on the mortgage balance. Hence the buyer, in effect, pays a lower interest rate on the loan; the loan's interest rate to the borrower is "bought down." Buydown programs have recently been accepted for purchase by FNMA if certain terms are met. See also builder contribution programs.

Call provision   See acceleration clause.

Capital gain (loss)   The positive or negative difference between the adjusted basis of an asset and the net proceeds resulting from its sale. Capital gains and losses are categorized as long-term (owned more than 12 months) and short-term (owned less than 12 months), and carry different tax consequences. One hundred percent of long-term gains and short-term gains are taxable as ordinary income. Long-term losses, on the other hand, are only 50 percent *deductible* from ordinary income (net of capital gains), at a rate not exceeding $3,000 per year. Short-term losses are fully deductible every year, with $3,000 again the maximum annual deduction.

Cash to loan   A method of acquiring property wherein a buyer assumes the seller's mortgage and pays the seller cash for the remaining balance.

Cloud (on title)   A claim or encumbrance against the title to a property that has the potential of impairing the property's marketability.

Collateral   Assets that are pledged to secure repayment of a loan.

Co-maker   A second party who signs a note with the borrower in order to increase the security of a loan. The co-maker then becomes jointly liable for repayment of the loan.

Compound interest   See interest.

Compounding   The arithmetic process of deriving the end-value of a payment or series of payments when compound interest is used.

Conditional sales contract   See contract for deed.

Consolidated-rate mortgage   A refinancing mortgage, typically offered by lending institutions, wherein a new loan is created carrying an interest rate that reflects the average rate between the old loan and that of a new loan, if it were to be issued at market interest rates. The WAMM (see weighted average money mortgage) also takes into account the outstanding balance and the amount of new money to be advanced. Thus, generally speaking, if an old $20,000 loan at ten percent were averaged with a new $10,000 loan at 15 percent, the resulting $\overline{\text{WAMM}}$ would be a $30,000 loan at 11.7 percent interest.

$$\frac{20,000 \times 10\% + 30,000 \times 15\%}{\$30,000}$$

Contract for deed (also called conditional sales contract, agreement for deed, installment sales contract, land contract, real estate contract) A method of transferring title to real property wherein the seller (vendor) is paid principal and interest, or interest only, by the buyer (vendee) for a specific period of time. At the end of the loan term the balance of principal and unpaid interest are paid to the seller, who then deeds the property to the buyer. Under the contract for deed, the seller holds legal title to the property and the buyer is granted equitable title and possession. Widely used when a minimum amount of cash is available.

Conventional loan A term describing the traditional fixed-rate, fixed-term, amortized mortgage loan that is not FHA-insured or VA-guaranteed. (Can be offered by private companies or investors.)

Conveyance The transfer of interest in real property by means of a deed.

Cross-defaulting clause A clause in a junior mortgage that specifies that a default on the senior mortgage triggers a default on the junior mortgage.

Debt service The amount of money needed to meet the periodic payments of a loan, including principal and interest.

Deed of trust (trust deed) A legal document that transfers title to property to a trustee as security for a debt obligation of the trustor (borrower) to the beneficiary (lender). Differs from mortgage insofar as a third party holds title and reconveys it to the trustor upon satisfaction of the obligation.

Default Failure to meet a contractual obligation when due.

Deficiency judgment A judgment levied against the borrower personally for the balance of a mortgage debt when a foreclosure sale fails to generate funds sufficient to satisfy the debt's outstanding balance.

Depreciation The gradual reduction in value of an asset. For tax and accounting purposes, depreciation refers to a deductible business expense on capital assets that is spread over the life of the assets. Ideally, this tax credit provides the incentive for the business to accumulate capital to replace the asset once it has lost its value. In practice, however, depreciation is a tax deduction that generates funds for any purpose. In addition, the "life" of the depreciable asset is somewhat arbitrary because an asset may in fact appreciate. To qualify for depreciation, the asset must be ruled depreciable. Land and nonincome-producing property are not depreciable.

Discounting The process of determining the present value of a deposit or series of deposits received at a certain time(s) in the future. A discount is the amount a mortgage has been reduced from its face value to its present cash value. Discounting a loan increases its effective yield to the holder/investor.

Discount points One percent of the face amount of a loan. Discount points are charged by lenders to raise the yield on below-market interest rate loans to a competitive level. Each face amount point deducted from a loan effectively raises its yield, or interest rate, 1/8 of 1 percent. For example, a $50,000 loan discounted 10 points bears a new face value of $45,000. If the same loan yielded 10 percent, the new yield would raise 10 points × 1/8 percent, or 1.25 percent, to 11.25 percent.

Disintermediation The act of consumers/depositors withdrawing their savings from banks, savings and loan associations and similar institutions in order to invest these funds directly in stocks, bonds, money market funds and other investments. Occurs when substantially higher yields than institutions can offer are available and easily accessible to consumers. Reduces institutional funds available for loans, for example, mortgage money when disintermediation occurs with savings and loan associations.

Due-on-sale clause A form of acceleration clause that specifically calls a mortgage loan due—at the lender's option—upon the sale or transfer of the property. The lender's primary concern with a due-on-sale clause is to renegotiate the interest rates if they have increased significantly since the loan's origination date. See also federal preemption.

Effective interest rate The actual rate or yield of a loan, regardless of the rate stated in the note. Applies particularly to the resulting yield from a mortgage that has been discounted. (See also nominal interest rate.)

Equity The market value of a property to the owner less all lien amounts outstanding against it. Equity is usually estimated by subtracting debts owed on the property from the property's estimated market value.

Equity participation agreement (EPA) A mortgage financing arrangement involving a third-party investor who joins with the borrower to finance a (residential) property. The investor/participant's involvement can have the impact of reducing the homebuyer's borrowing needs or of lowering the effective interest rate. The investor can also share in the monthly payment, if this is in the agreement. In return, the investor shares the equitable interest in the property and a percentage of the appreciation. Not to be confused with SAMs. See also shared appreciation mortgage.

Escalator clause Clause in a loan agreement that sets forth provisions for increases in payments or interest on the basis of some economic index (e.g., T-bill rates) or prescribed schedule. Usually escalator clauses supplant or eliminate the need for prepayment penalties.

Escrow A disinterested third-party agent who holds and releases money or documents in accordance with instructions given by the parties to the escrow. When the conditions of the escrow have been satisfied, the funds in escrow are delivered.

Fair Housing Law Title VII of the Civil Rights Act, prohibiting discrimination in residential housing on the basis of race, religion, color, sex, familial status, handicap or national origin. Does not apply to commercial or industrial properties.

Federal Home Loan Bank (FHLB) The federal regulatory agency that oversees all federal savings and loan associations. The FHLB's principal activity is managing association liquidity and providing reserve funds for members, particularly in local areas where there are temporary shortfalls of lendable funds.

Federal Home Loan Bank Board (FHLBB) The principal group of regulators within FHLB that issues rulings on regulations and policies.

Federal Home Loan Mortgage Corporation (FHLMC, Freddie Mac; renamed The Mortgage Corporation) A federal agency formed to purchase mortgages in the secondary market from insured banks and FHLB member savings and loan associations. The Mortgage Corporation also purchases VA and FHA loans. The purpose of the agency is to provide a means whereby lending institutions can sell their mortgages, maintain their liquidity from the proceeds and recycle available funds at market rates. FHLMC cycles its own portfolio by issuing mortgage-backed securities to the general public. Lenders wishing to sell loans to Freddie Mac must use approved forms and follow established procedures and processing guidelines.

Federal Housing Authority (FHA) A federal agency under the Department of Housing and Urban Development that was formed to standardize home financing and stabilize the mortgage market. FHA's principal activity is insuring approved lending institutions against mortgage loan defaults. Lenders must in turn follow FHA credit guidelines and restrictions. FHA neither buys nor originates loans.

Federal National Mortgage Association (FNMA, Fannie Mae) A private secondary mortgage market organization regulated by the federal government. FNMA specializes in the purchase of VA and FHA loans but also sometimes buys conventional loans. Its purpose, like that of other secondary mortgage market entities, is to buy qualified loans with bond-generated funds, thereby protecting lender liquidity and stimulating the recycling of mortgage funds. FNMA also stimulates lending by offering lenders commitments to buy as-yet unmade loans that will qualify under one of its commitment programs.

Federal preemption Regulatory or statutory actions taken by federal regulatory authorities, for instance the Office of the Comptroller of the Currency and the Federal Home Loan Bank Board, that expressly limit or overrule the provisions and/or enforceability of state law. For example, the OCC and FHLBB recently preempted state usury laws under certain conditions.

Federal Reserve Board (the banker's bank) A government institution that controls and regulates the operation of all nationally chartered banks.

Federal Savings and Loan Insurance Corporation (FSLIC) The parallel to FDIC, FSLIC insures deposits at member savings and loan associations.

Fiduciary Someone in a position of trust and confidence who acts accordingly as an agent for another.

Fifteen-year mortgage A variation of the fixed-rate mortgage. The interest rate and loan payments remain constant throughout the loan but the loan is paid off in only 15 years. It is usually available at an interest rate lower than a long-term loan rate.

Finance fee See origination fee.

Financial Institutions Deregulation Act A law enacted in March, 1980, authorizing the deregulation of several aspects of the banking and financing industry, in particular the deregulation of interest and earnings limits and the approval for savings and loans to have trust powers and make more consumer loans. One effect of the FIDA law is a lessening of the distinction between banks and savings and loan associations.

Financial intermediary A financial institution that acts as an investor for depositors and a lender for borrowers. Can be described as a loan "retailer" (lends small sums to borrowers) and an investment agent for depositors (pays yields on deposits).

First mortgage A legal document pledging collateral for a loan that was recorded as such before any other mortgages were recorded. Has priority over mortgages subsequently recorded.

Fixed-rate mortgage A mortgage in which the interest rate and monthly payments remain constant over the life of the loan.

Government National Mortgage Association (GNMA) A government agency that participates in the secondary mortgage market. It sponsors mortgage-backed securities programs backed by FHA and VA loans.

Graduated payment adjustable mortgage loan (GPAML) A new financing alternative that is essentially the adjustable mortgage loan's version of the GPM. Provides a graduated payment schedule for the principal and interest, with a variable interest factor built into the payment schedule and/or term and/or principal balance owed. See also graduated payment mortgage.

Graduated payment mortgage (GPM) Also known as the FHA 245 GPM, the financing method in which, under pre-established guidelines, the payments on a fixed-rate and -term, fully amortized mortgage are reduced in the beginning years of the mortgage. Unpaid interest is then added to the principal balance, and payments are increased annually to gradually retire the interest accrued. The graduated payment schedules eventually level off to a fixed payment for the remainder of the term. A standard loan for families with low but increasing incomes.

Grannie Mae A method for older homeowners to unlock the equity in their property. It involves the sale of the home to their children, who then give a lifetime lease to their parents with a monthly payment.

Gross income Income generated before any expenses have been subtracted. Often called "the top line."

Growing equity mortgage (GEM) A mortgage loan where the mortgagor makes extra principal payments every year in addition to the regular PI payments for the purpose of accelerating equity buildup.

Guaranteed loan A general term for a loan that is backed by payment guarantee from someone other than the borrower.

Home equity loan A loan based on the accumulated equity in the property. Can be either a lump sum or an equity line of credit, and is usually a junior mortgage.

Housing and Urban Development, Department of (HUD) The federal department that manages various housing programs throughout the nation; also the parent regulator of FHA and GNMA.

Hypothecation The pledging of a real property as mortgage security without surrendering possession of it.

Index The measure used by the lender to determine how much the interest rate on an ARM will change over time.

Individual reverse mortgage account (IRMA) A mortgage plan that includes characteristics of both a reverse annuity mortgage and a shared appreciation loan. Borrowers receive cash from the lender and when the borrower dies or the house is sold the lender receives the principal, accumulated interest and part of the property appreciation.

Installment sale A sale in which the seller spreads the receipt of the sale proceeds over two or more years. Installment sales—if certain provisions are met—qualify for deferred capital gains tax treatment.

Insured loan A mortgage or other loan that is insured against default in exchange for a premium paid by someone other than the borrower.

Interest Money paid, or charged, or accrued as rent for the use of money.
   Add-on interest. The method of computing interest wherein interest is charged on the entire sum of money over the term of the loan, regardless of any paydowns of principal during the loan term.
   Compound interest. Interest that is computed each period on the original principal as well as the accrued interest on the principal over the previous period.
   Simple interest. Interest that is charged only on the principal balance outstanding.

Interest rate Interest that is expressed as a percentage of the principal balance, usually the annual percentage.

Interim financing See bridge loan.

Involuntary lien See lien.

Judgment lien See lien.

Judicial sale A foreclosure sale of property by the court, effected to satisfy a mortgage debt.

Junior mortgage/lien A mortgage with a right or lien priority that is subordinate to another lien on the same property. The priority is determined by the chronological order in which the liens were recorded. The junior lien is less secure than the first lien or mortgage because upon default the first lien must be satisfied before the junior lien. Junior mortgages typically carry a higher interest rate because of the greater risk involved.

Land contract   See contract for deed.

Lease option (also called lease with option to buy)   A lease that allows a tenant the right to buy the leased property if and when certain conditions are met. Usually the rent payments are applied in part or in full to the purchase price if the tenant opts to buy.

Leverage   The use of borrowed money that, when coupled with one's cash or equity in an investment, increases the investor's return over and above the cost of funds and what the cash alone would have yielded. Reverse leverage in turn occurs when the cost of borrowed funds exceeds the net yield from the investment.

Lien   A legal claim upon the property of another as security for a debt obligation.
Involuntary lien. A lien imposed by law, usually for delinquent taxes.
Judgment lien. A lien placed upon a debtor as a result of a court decree.
Voluntary lien. A lien placed willingly on a property by the owner.

Liquidity   The cash position of an individual or business as it relates to the ability to pay obligations due. Synonymous with degree of cash available. A liquid asset or investment is one that can be converted readily into cash in an amount nearly equivalent to the investment's market value.

Loan constant   The percentage figure in loan constant tables that is used to tell an investor how much money is needed monthly or annually to amortize a loan—of any amount—given a fixed interest rate and period. To determine the cash needed to amortize a loan, the principal amount of the loan is multiplied by the monthly or annual loan constant.

Loan-to-value ratio (LTV)   The ratio between a mortgage loan and the market or appraised value, whichever is less. Used as a standard to measure the borrower's vested interest in the property and his or her consequent willingness to repay the loan. The higher the loan-to-value ratio, the riskier the loan because the borrower has less to lose upon default.

Lock-in clause/provision   A prepayment clause in a mortgage loan that expressly forbids prepayment of a loan in excess of the periodic payment. Practice common to lending policy of insurance companies.

Low-docs   A borrower making a higher down payment (20 percent to 30 percent) may have the loan approved without all or some of the usual credit checks, job and income verifications and tax statements.

Margin   The number of percentage points the lender adds to the index rate to calculate the ARM rate at each adjustment.

Market value   The highest price a buyer would pay for a property, assuming the property has a reasonable period of exposure to the market and that both buyer and seller are informed and not under duress.

Maturity   The date on which an obligation such as a real estate note comes due and payable.

Mortgage   A legal document that conditionally pledges a designated property as security for a loan. See also trust deed.

Mortgage banker   Represent funding sources such as life insurance companies and pension investors. Mortgage bankers locate borrowers, close the loans, and then service them for a fee.

Mortgage broker   An intermediary agent who, for a fee, brings together borrowers and lenders to effect loan transactions. Mortgage brokers also service loans and originate loans on behalf of lenders.

Mortgage constant   See loan constant.

Mortgagee The party in a mortgage transaction who holds the mortgage as security for a loan, usually the lender.

Mortgagor The party who gives the mortgage as security for debt; the owner of the debt collateral.

Negative amortization A loan balance that increases over time rather than decreasing. The result of monthly payments that are smaller than the interest accrued; the difference is subsequently added to the balance of the loan.

Negative spread The condition of a financial institution in which the aggregate loan portfolio's yield is less than the aggregate interest payable to depositors. Negative spread, usually expressed in percentage points, causes liquidity problems.

Net yield The portion of an investment's gross yield that remains after all costs have been deducted.

No-docs See low-docs.

Nominal interest rate The interest rate stated on the face of a contract, as opposed to the effective interest rate that results from discounting.

Note A debt instrument stating the loan amount, its interest rate, the term and method of repayment and the promise to repay.

Notice of default A written notice to a borrower of default on a loan. Frequently there is a clause in a contract for deed requiring the vendor (seller) to give notice of default and specifying a grace period for payment of the delinquent amount.

Office of the Comptroller of the Currency (OCC) The federal entity that regulates nationally chartered banks; the parallel organization to the Federal Home Loan Bank Board.

Origination fee Fee charged by the mortgagee for originating a mortgage loan. Covers credit inspection, appraisal fees, inspection of property, loan application processing and other administrative costs.

Payment cap A limit set on what an adjustable rate mortgage loan's periodic (usually monthly) payments can be. Payment caps may or may not be provided for in the mortgage. Exists as a device to maintain a loan's affordability despite increases in the adjustable interest rate. When payment caps are present, accrued interest is added to the principal, which may result in negative amortization.

PITI An abbreviation for principal, interest, taxes and insurance, commonly synonymous with the borrower's monthly payment on an amortized loan plus taxes and insurance paid monthly to an impound or escrow account.

Points See discount points.

Prepayment penalty/charge Similar to an early withdrawal charge; a levy against the borrower who repays a loan prior to its maturity. Commonly prescribed in an original loan agreement's prepayment clause, the penalty is designed to offset loan charges and loan servicing not recouped by the lender through interest earnings. Not permitted in adjustable rate mortgages after the first adjustment period.

Present value (PV) Stated in terms of one dollar, PV represents today's value of an amount of money that is not to be received until some time in the future. Can be understood as the current value of money less the compounded interest that would have been earned over the time period during which the money was not received.

Primary mortgage market The market in which loans are made by institutions or investors directly to borrowers.

Principal (1) The amount of a loan upon which interest is charged. (2) One of the main parties in a transaction, such as the seller of a home.

Private mortgage insurance (PMI) An insurance policy that protects the lender against losses up to the policy limits on a defaulted mortgage loan.

Promissory note See note.

Purchase-money mortgage The most common form of seller financing; a mortgage loan given to the buyer by the seller as part of the property's purchase price. Usually given in order to bridge the difference between a buyer's down payment and a new first mortgage.

Qualification In real estate finance, the process of obtaining a sufficient amount of information from a buyer and seller to determine the seller's financial objectives and the buyer's purchasing capacity.

Qualified monthly income (QMI) The amount of a borrower's monthly income necessary to qualify for a loan of a given amount at a given interest rate for a given term. Used as a lender's standard to determine how much a borrower can afford to borrow without creating undue risk or hardship. In most cases a QMI must be three to four times the monthly principal and interest payments on the loan.

Rapid payoff mortgage (RPM) An amortized mortgage loan where the loan term is significantly shorter than the customary 25- to 30-year term.

Real Estate Settlement Procedures Act (RESPA) A federal law requiring that all closing costs on a first mortgage be disclosed to the buyer and the seller of a one- to four-family residential property.

Recasting Rewriting a loan with new terms to accommodate a borrower threatened with default. A recast loan may lose priority over previously recorded junior liens.

Reconveyance Transferring title to a property from its present owner to the immediately preceding owner. A necessary practice in title theory states, where the trustor conveys title to the trustee as debt security. Upon satisfaction of the debt, the trustee reconveys the title to the trustor.

Refinancing-to-sell The practice whereby a seller refinances his or her home to maximize its loan-to-value ratio. Thus, when the property is offered for sale, the buyer may be able to assume the loan and purchase the home with a minimum amount of cash.

Regulation Z See Truth-in-Lending Law.

Renegotiable-rate mortgage (RRM) An adjustable-rate mortgage whose recent authorization has since been supplanted by the adjustable mortgage loan (AML) authorization. Because of this, the characteristics and limitations originally established for the RRM may or may not be allowed now. In general, the RRM is a first mortgage with an interest rate that is renegotiable every three to five years. Prior to the new AML regulations, the RRM had a nonextendable term, a maximum interest ceiling (5 percent) over the entire loan term, and an annual interest increase maximum equivalent to ½ percent. These restrictions no longer apply, although it is still possible that RRM-type loans can be made under AML regulations and restrictions. See also adjustable mortgage loan.

Return on investment (ROI) The net yield on an investment's equity, usually expressed as a percentage for a given time period.

Reverse annuity mortgage A mortgage arrangement established for elderly homeowners wherein the mortgagee makes equity advance payments to the mortgagors, then recoups the debt from the proceeds of the sale of the owners' property or estate.

Rollover note A short-term note that can be renewed upon maturity if certain conditions and terms are met. A debt instrument coming into use with adjustable-rate mortgages.

Second mortgage A mortgage that ranks immediately behind the first mortgage in priority.

Secondary mortgage market The market in which already existing mortgages are bought and sold. Dominated by major agencies and organizations, which buy discounted mortgages in order to (1) generate a yield for investors, (2) provide liquidity to mortgage sellers and (3) redistribute funds from cash-rich to cash-poor localities.

Security Something of value deposited or pledged to secure the repayment of a debt.

Seller carryback An idiom commonly used in real estate for whenever the seller, acting as a lender, holds or "carries back" a first or second mortgage note from the buyer. An example would be a purchase-money mortgage.

Shared appreciation mortgage (SAM) (also called appreciation participation mortgage and equity kicker) A first mortgage loan offered by a lender to a homebuyer at a lower-than-market interest rate in return for a percentage share in the property's appreciation. In practice, many forms of the SAM are possible—and as many serious legal questions can arise. The key variables in the SAM are: (1) the degree of mortgagee participation in increased value, (2) the degree of mortgagee liability should the property depreciate, (3) the borrower's right of alienation during the loan period, (4) when the appreciation is payable and (5) the quantitative relationship between the degree of participation and the degree to which the interest rate is reduced. The SAM as generally formulated does not confer a shared title interest, as in a joint tenancy, nor does it confer an interest in the original basis of the home at time of purchase. Do not confuse with equity participation mortgages, which involve a third-party investor.

"Subject to" mortgage A mortgage that confers equitable title on a purchaser without liability for payment of the mortgage note. Upon default, however, the mortgagor could lose his or her equity and the property in a foreclosure sale. The courts cannot order a deficiency judgment upon the mortgagor when there is a "subject to" mortgage. The "subject to" mortgage is similar to a contract for deed sale insofar as the mortgagor's liability is limited to his or her paid-in equity.

Swing loan See bridge loan.

Term loan/mortgage Nonamortized loan for a specified period of time in which interest only is paid per the agreement and the entire principal becomes due in full at maturity.

Trust deed See deed of trust.

Trustee The third-party holder of the trust for real property as security to the trustor's debt obligation.

Trustor The borrower whose property is held by the trustee until the debt obligation is satisfied.

Truth-in-Lending Law Enacted in 1969 under the Consumer Credit Protection Act; implemented by Regulation 7 of the Federal Reserve Board. Ensures disclosure of credit costs by lenders, including disclosure of all fees and charges associated with a loan but separate from its quoted interest rate.

Underwriting The financial analysis of a borrower made to determine the borrower's ability to repay a loan. Also used to describe the act of purchasing securities for the purpose of reselling or distributing them to investors.

Usury Charging more interest on a loan than the legal limit. Usury laws vary widely from state to state and in certain instances have been preempted by federal regulations and rulings.

VA-insured loan   A loan made by a VA-approved lender at rates and under conditions established by the Veterans Administration. If the conditions are followed and the borrower has obtained his or her certificate of eligibility, the Veterans Administration will guarantee the lender the first $27,500 of the loan in the event of default.

Variable-rate mortgage (VRM) (also called variable interest rate loan [VIR])   The VRM, like the renegotiable-rate mortgage, is one of the new experiments with adjustable interest rates that have been supplanted by AML and ARM authorizations. See also adjustable mortgage loan and renegotiable-rate mortgage.

Vendee   The purchaser or borrower involved in a contract-for-deed transaction. More simply, a buyer.

Vendor   The seller or lender in a contract-for-deed transaction.

Veterans Administration (VA)/VA mortgage   A federal agency that provides services for veterans of U.S. Armed Forces. In real estate finance, the VA insures lenders against defaults on loans made to qualified veterans. Also assists veterans by guaranteeing higher-risk loans and loans with lower-than-market interest rates.

Voluntary lien   See lien.

Weighted average money mortgage   See consolidated-rate mortgage.

Wraparound (also called all-inclusive trust deed, overriding loan/trust deed and overlapping loan/trust deed)   A junior lien, usually given by the seller to the buyer, for the difference between the selling price and the buyer's down payment. In a wraparound arrangement, the seller continues his or her payments on and liability for senior liens of record, and the buyer's payments flow directly to the seller.

Yield   The rate of return on an investment, e.g., the effective interest rate on a mortgage loan.

Zoning   The legal power of a local municipal government (city or town) to regulate the use of property within the municipality.

Appendix D
SOME RELEVANT BIBLIOGRAPHY

Shaun Aghili, *The No-Nonsense Credit Manual* (I.L.S. Publishing, Irvine CA: 1998)

William R. Allen, *New York Real Esate Practices* (National Real Estate Institute, Redmond, Washington)

American Homeowners Foundation, *How To Sell Your Home Fast* (Arlington, VA)

Harley Bjelland, *How To Sell Your House Without A Broker* (Cornerstone Library, N.Y. 1979)

James E. Bridges, *Mortgage Loans. What's Right For You?* (Betterway Books, 4th ed., Cincinnati, OH:1997).

Stephen R. Mettling and Gerald R. Cortesi, *Modern Residential Financing Methods: Tools of the Trade*, 2nd ed. (Real Estate Education Company, A Div. of Longman Financial Services Institute Chicago, IL.: 1990).

David Crank, *Godly Finances:The Bible Way To Pay off Your Home* (David Publications, St. Louis Mo., 1996)

John R. Dorfman, ed., *The Mortgage Book* (Consumer Reports Books, Yonkers, N.Y. 1992)

The Editors of Rodale Press, *Cut Your Spending In Half Without Settling For Less* (Rodale Press, Emmaus, PA: 1994)

Vijay Fadia, *How To Cut Your Mortgage In Half* (Penguin Books, New York: 1990)

Federal Trade Commission, *The Mortgage Money Guide* (Washington, D.C.)

Richard F. Gabriel, *How To Buy Your Own House When You Don't Have Enough Money!* (Signet, New America Library, N.Y. 1982)

Earl C. Gottschalk Jr., "Picking the Wrong Mortgage Broker Can Become A Homeowner's Nightmare." *The Wall Street Journal,* 26 March 1992: C1, C18.

HALT, *Real Estate* (Washington, D.C.)

HSH Associates, *How To Shop For Your Mortgage* (Butler, N.J. 1989)

Robert Irwin, *The For Sale By Owner Kit* (Dearborn Financial Publishing, Chicago, IL)

Danielle Kennedy, *Double Your Income in Real Estate Sales* (John Wiley & Sons, N.J.)

Kiplinger's Personal Finance Magazine, "Selling Your Home Do It Yourself?" (Feb. 1995), p. 86-9.

James E. A. Lumley, *How To Get A Mortgage in 24 Hours* (John Wiley & Son: 1990).

Andrew J. McLean, *Investing in Real Estate* (John Wiley & Sons, N.J.)

Peter G. Miller, *How To Save Money When You Hire A Real Estate Broker,* (The Springhill Press, Silver Springs, MD)

Robert G. Natelson, *How To Buy and Sell A Condominium* (Simon & Schuster: 1981)

N.Y. Times, "Picking The Best Broker," Sunday Section 10, June 12, 1994; "Your Home: Haggling Do's and Dont's," Sun. Sec. 10, Aug. 7, 1994; "An Appellate Ruling Rekindles Disclosure Debate," Sun., April 24, 1994, Sec. D., p. 9.

Frank R. Pajares, *For Sale By Owner* (New Trend Publication, Tampa, FL)

Pete, Marwick, Mitchell & Co., *RESPA: The 1979-80 Evaluation, Vol. I: Executive Summary* (October 1980)

Alex Rachun, *How To Inspect The Older House* (N.Y. State College of Human Ecology, Cornell University, N.Y.)

Robert Schwartz, *The Home Owner's Legal Guide* (Collier, Macmillan Publishers, N.Y. 1965)

Martin M. Shenkman and Warren Boronson, *How To Sell Your House In A Buyer's Market* (John Wiley & Sons N.Y. 1990)

C. F. Sirmans, *Real Estate Finance*, 2nd ed. (McGraw-Hill Book Company, New York: 1989).

Paulette Thomas, "Federal Data Detail Pervasive Racist Gap in Mortgage Lending," The Wall Street Journal, 31 March 1992: A1,A12.

Michael C. Thomsett, *Save $ On Your Mortgage: The Mortgage Acceleration Techniques* (John Wiley & Sons: 1989)

Michael C. Thomsett, *Your Home Mortgage* (John Wiley & Sons: 1992)

U.S. Department of HUD, *House Buyer's Information Package: A Guide For Buying and Owning a House* (Washington, D.C.)

Appendix E

LIST OF OTHER PUBLICATIONS FROM
DO-IT-YOURSELF LEGAL PUBLISHERS

Please DO NOT tear out this page. Consider others!

The following is a list of books obtainable from the Do-It-Yourself Publishers/Selfhelper Law Press of America.

(Customers: For your convenience, just make a photocopy of this page and send it along with your order. All prices quoted here are subject to change without notice.)

1. How To Draw Up Your Own Friendly Separation/Property Settlement Agreement With Your Spouse
2. Tenant Smart: How To Win Your Tenants' Legal Rights Without A Lawyer (New York Edition)
3. How To Probate & Settle An Estate Yourself Without The Lawyers' Fees ($35)
4. How To Adopt A Child Without A Lawyer
5. How To Form Your Own Profit/Non-Profit Corporation Without A Lawyer
6. How To Plan Your 'Total' Estate With A Will & Living Will, Without a Lawyer
7. How To Declare Your Personal Bankruptcy Without A Lawyer ($29)
8. How To Buy Or Sell Your Own Home Without A Lawyer or Broker ($29)
9. How To File For Chapter 11 Business Bankruptcy Without A Lawyer ($29)
10. How To Legally Beat The Traffic Ticket Without A Lawyer (forthcoming)
11. How To Settle Your Own Auto Accident Claims Without A Lawyer ($29)
12. How To Obtain Your U.S. Immigration Visa Without A Lawyer ($25)
13. How To Do Your Own Divorce Without A Lawyer [10 Regional State-Specific Volumes] ($35)
14. How To Legally Change Your Name Without A Lawyer
15. How To Properly Plan Your 'Total' Estate With A Living Trust, Without The Lawyers' Fees ($35)
16. Legally Protect Yourself In A Gay/Lesbian Or Non-Marital Relationship With A Cohabitation Agreement
17. Before You Say 'I do' In Marriage Or Co-Habitation, Here's How To First Protect Yourself Legally
18. The National Home Mortgage reduction Kit (forthcoming) ($26.95)
19. The National Home Mortgage **Qualification** Kit ($28.95)

Prices: Each book, except for those specifically priced otherwise, costs $26, plus $4.00 per book for postage and handling. New Jersey residents please add 6% sales tax. **ALL PRICES ARE SUBJECT TO CHANGE WITHOUT NOTICE**

CUSTOMERS: Please make and send a zerox copy of this page with your orders)

ORDER FORM

TO: **Do-it-Yourself Legal Publishers**
 60 Park Place # Suite **1013,** Newark, NJ 07102

Please send me the following:
1._____copies of _____
2._____copies of _____
3._____copies of _____
4._____copies of _____

Enclosed is the sum of $_____ to cover the order. *Mail my order to:*
Mr./Mrs.//Ms/Dr. _____
Address (include Zip Code please): _____
_____
Phone No. **and area code:** ( )_____ Job: ( )_____
*New Jersey residents enclose 6% sales tax.

IMPORTANT: Please do NOT rip out the page. Consider others! Just make a photocopy and send it.

INDEX

A

Ability to pay, evaluating your, 72, 74
Adjustable-rate mortgages, 21, 31
  advantages of, 31
  affordability of, 32
  availability of, 32
  disadvantage of, 33
  contrast between adjustable and fixed rate mortgages, 28
Affordability factor, 11, 32
Affordability of a house for a buyer, rule-of-thumb guideline for guaging, 65; see also qualified
Affordability workshop, 66
Aghili, Shaun .1, The No-nonsense Credit manual, 94
Alienation clause, 37
Amortization table, 7, 8
Annual Percentage Rate
  assumption under, 52
  definition of, 51
  contents and make up of, 51
  daily interest compounding factor in, 52
  use of to comparison-shop, 92
Application,
  don't file when you still have large credit card balances, 94
  ideal conditions for making an, 93
  what to do if denied a loan, 106
Application fee, 68
Apples and oranges, 73
Applying for mortgage loan, typical procedures for, 71
Appraisal fee, 69
Appraised price of a home, 72
APR, see Annual Percentage Rate
Assessment
  of your present financial condition, 55
  of your character, ability and willingness to pay by loan officer, 72, 74
Assets, your, 57
Association of Community Organizations for Reform (ACORN), 1991 study on discrimination by, 107

Assumability, 33, 37; of VA loans, 39
Assumable mortgage, 24
Attorney's fees, 68
Attraction, the, of the fixed-rate type of mortgages, 28
Average Joe, 7

B

Back-end ratio, 119
Background material chapters, 3
Bad quality loan, 75
Bait and Switch tactics by brokers, 132
Balloon mortgage, 22
Balloon payment, 13
Bankruptcy, history of by borrower, 97, 102
Basic principles of Mortgage finance and calculations, 2; see also mortgage finance
Better Homes and Garden, 128
Big Five, The, of mortgage types, 20
Big Three factor, using, in planning the term of the mortgage to get, 9
Brokerage commission, 70
Buy-down, 25; consumer buy downs, 26
By Owner Real Estate Association of America, 129

C

Caps, 21, 31, aggregate cap, 21; rate cap, 21; periodic cap, 21; placed on permissible frequency of rate increases, 31; placed on the degree of interest rate increases permissible annually, 31
Carter, Will and Tammy, 72
Cash adjusted, 115
Cash-on-hand qualification, 113
Cash reserve, 56, 57
Census report, average stay of Americans in a home, 92
Centerpiece, 3
Central quandary, 48
Century 21, 128
Certified Residential Specialist (CRS), 132
Chicago Sun-Times, 86
Chicago Fair Housing Alliance, 1998 study on discrimination by, 107
Closing costs

average closing costs for a home purchase, 67
closing costs on VA loans, 43
definition of, 67
how and why you can still negotiate and amend, 67, 70
points as the biggest closing costs, 70; points vs. loan origination fee in, 67
sample closing costs, 70
summary of the main closing costs, 67
Closing the loan, 15
Collaterals, 5
Commercial banks, 14
Comparison-shopping for a mortgage, as the single most vital cost-effective element in mortgage decisions, 87
  potential savings from, 87
  ten-year analysis in, 92
  using phone poll for, 88
  why you must do some before you settle on a final pick, 87
Compounded interest, 10
Computerized Mortgage Search Organization, 85, 86
Congress, U.S., 35, 73
Consumer buy-downs, 26
Consumer Protection Act of 1969, 51
Contracted costs of a house, 5
Controller of the Currency, 107
Conventional loan, 35
Council of Better Business Bureaus, 108
Cousins of the Savings and Loans Banks, 14
Counter-offer, on loan commitment, 76
Cover letter, 97, 98
Creative financing
  highlighting the essentials of, 27
  methods of, 19
  reasons for proliferation of, 19
  some major methods of today, 20
Credit bureaus, see credit reporting agencies
Credit card debts,
  close down most of before you apply for a loan, 94
  pay down before you apply for a loan, 94
Credit check, charge for, 68;

methods of, 74
Credit report, correct and clean out your, 94
Credit reporting agencies, 94; list of, 95
Credit Unions, 16
Creditworthy customers, 21

D

Daily interest compounding, 52
Deadening, of debt, 7
Dead wrong, 1
Debt-to-income ratio, 64; 109; using the Pre-qualifier worksheet to figure out the, 65; using the 28/36 ratio rule to figure out your, 64
Deed of Trust, 4
Deed to secure Debt, 4
Default, 4
Demand deposits, 14
Department of Commerce, Federal, report by, 129
Department of Housing and Urban Development (HUD), 35
Direct endorsers of the FHA, 36
Disclosure statement, 51, 78
Discount, 47
Discount points, 67
Discrimination, what to do if you're a victim of, 106
Document preparation fee, 70
Don't of a loan application, 93
Dorfman, John R.
citing some studies on housing discrimination, 107
on the laws of economics, 43
on the limitations of the APR as a loan shopping tool, 52
on variations in cost of escrow charges, 67, 70
on potential savings from comparison-shopping for loans, 87, 88
Down payment verification, 74
Due-on-sale clause, 24, 25, 37

E

Electronic Realty associates, 128
Eligibility for VA loans, 41
Equal Credit Opportunity Act (ECOA), 106
Equifax, 95
Equity conversion, 26
Escrow account, 68; escrow account

method in FHA and VA loans, 69
Escrow fee, 68
Experian (TRW), 95

F

Family and job stability, 94
Federal Department of Commerce, report by, 129
Federal Deposit Insurance Corporation, 107
Federal Home Loan Bank Board interest rate, 21, 31
Federal Housing Administration, see FHA
Federal National Mortgage Association (Fannie Mae), 64; guidelines set by, 112-112
Federal Reserve Bank data, 107
Federal Reserve Bank rate, 31
Federal Reserve System, 107
Federal Reserve System APR Tables, 52
Federal Truth-in-Lending Act of 1969, 73
Federal Truth-in-Lending Law, 4
FHA and VA mortgages account for 20% of all U.S. mortgages, 35
FHA financing, 22
advantages of, 38
closing costs on, 36
contrasts with VA mortgages, 35
different types of programs in, 39
distinction between conventional loans and, 37
escrow account method in, 69
insuring of loan under, 35
impounds, 37
loan and discount points on, 38
MIP, 36, 37, 38
mortgage assumability issues in, 37
mortgage insurance premium on, see MIP
prepaid items, 37
procedures of the loan programs under, 36
regional offices of, 44
secondary financing, 37
section 203b, the standard FHA loan program, 39
surcharge on, 36
FHA mortgage, 22
Financial indices, 21
Financial ratios, analysis of, 75, 109; typical ratios used in conventional loans, 75; PITI debt ratio, 75
Financial profile, 99
Financial qualification methods, 109

Financially qualifying yourself
conventional loan situation, 114
FHA-backed loan situation, 118
FHA-backed vs. conventional loan income qualification standards, 118
FHA-backed vs. VA-backed loan income qualification standards, 122
financial ratios in conventional loans, 111-112
financial ratios in FHA loans, 119
financial ratios in VA loans, 112
residual income formula in FHA and VA loans, 119-122
Finder's fees, 87
First mortgage, 46
Fixed-rate mortgage (FRMs), 20, 28, 31
attraction of, 28, 90
fixed-rate vs. adjustable-rate mortgages, 28
privilege of having a, 29
advantages of having a, 29, 31
disadvantages of having a, 29, 33
affordability of, 32
availability of, 32
Flexible-rate mortgage, 31
Foreclose, 4
Formulas, two quick, 49; to prequalify yourself, 62
For Sale By Owner, 129
Front-end ratio, 119
FSBO Homes of New Jersey, 129
Full disclosure, the best policy for loan applicant, 97, 103
Fundamental flaw in the typical way of buying a home, 1
Fundamental premise of the book, 1
Fundamental reason why prospective homebuyers fail to obtain the lender's mortgage approval, 1
Funding fee, 43

G

Gabriel, Richard F., on potential savings from comparison shopping for loan, 88
GI Bill of Rights, 35
Guarantee, VA-bank loans provides, 35
Glue, 3
Good Faith Estimate of settlement charges, 57, 73, 83, 97
Graduated Payment Mortgage, 23

Graduate of the Realtors Institute (GRI), 132
Growing Equity Mortgage, 23
Guidelines to seek out the best possible mortgage sources, 84

H

Highlighting the essentials of creative financing, 27
High quality loan, 75
Holding the Title during the mortgage period, 4
Home for Sale Listing, 1
Home inspection fee, 70
Home price range you can afford first determine the, 60
rule-of-thumb methods of determining, 62
Home Sellers, The, 13
Houston Post, 86
How long a loan to get, 10
HSH Associates, a mortgage search service, 86; report by, 88
HUD, a survey by, 17

I

Ideal conditions for a loan application, 93
Impound account, 69
Income, per capita, 23
Income qualification, 109
Insurance companies and pension funds, 16
Installment sale or land contract method, 46
Insured loan, 35
Interest, compounded, 10
Interest factor, 6
Interest factor table, 6
Interest, introductory rates in mortgages, 85
Interest, payment of in mortgage amortization, 8
Interest rates, comparing points to, 48

K

Kailo, Norman, N., 129
Korean and Vietnam wars, veterans of, 35

L

Land contract, 25
Lank, Edith., author of the Homeseller's Kit, 132
Lender's profit, interest as, 7
Liabilities, figuring out your, 57
Lien on real property, 4, 5
Lifetime cap, 31
Living from paycheck to paycheck, 93

Loan amortization, how it works, 7
Loans and discount points, 38
Loan application, the reverse order of what the proper sequence should be, 9
Loan committee, 72
Loan commitment letter or contract, 76, 101
Peeke LoanFax Inc, 86
Loan organization fee, 67
Loan proposal, 97
Lock-in fee, 69; lock-in on loan commitment, 76
Long-term cost factors of a house, 5
LT Debt ratio, definition of, 109-110; what it measures, 110; when it's commonly used by loan officers, 110

M

Ronnie Mae, 87
Magic or easy gimmicks, 2
Match maker, 128
Gary S. Meyers & Associates, a mortgage search service, 86
Modified residual income, 122; see also residual income formula
Mortgage as a contract, 4; as a promise to pay, 4
Mortgage 'Big Three,' 5, 9
Mortgage Brokers, 15, 84
Mortgage deed, 4
Mortgage finance, analytical or computational dimensions of basic, 2, 3; basic principles of, 2, 3
Mortgage fundamentals, 1
Mortgage Information Form, use of to collect basic loan information from lenders, 91, 103, 104
Mortgage insurance, the two types of, 69; mortgage life insurance, 69; mortgage default insurance, 69
Mortgage Journal, The, 85
Mortgage loan, 5; the three major attributes of a, 5
Mortgage loan making
assessment of your character and ability/willingness to pay, 72, 74; credit check, employment verification, and down payment verification in, 74
good faith estimate of settlement charges in, 72
ideal conditions for filing an application in, 93
methods of borrower analysis, evaluation, and scoring system in, 71
primary documentations for loan

applicant in, 71
property survey, appraisal and inspection methods in, 72
size of your income as most important criterion in assessing your qualification for, 75
standard loan application forms used in, 77-78
truth-in-lending disclosure statement, 73, 81
Mortgage registration tax, 69
Mortgage sources, guideline to seek out the best, 13, 84; computerized sources, 85, 86
Mortgages, the five basic types of, 20; contrasting the fixed-rate and the adjustable-rate types, 28
Mountain of extra costs in interest, 10
Multiple Listing System among brokers, 128, 130, 131; Listing book of, 132
Mutual Savings Banks, 14

N

National Association of Realtors, 87, 132
National banks, what is a, 107
National Credit Union Administration, 107
National Housing Act, 35
National Mortgage Weekly newspaper, 85
Need-to-sell, sellers with, 128, 130
Negotiate, always, 93
Neighborhood, 1
Net worth, definition of, 57; figuring out your, 57; worksheet for figuring out your, 58, 59
New York Times, 107, 129
Non-assumability, 30
Notary fees, 70

O

Office of Thrift Supervision, 107
Owner-financed mortgage, 24
Owner financing, 45

P

Paper, see second mortgage
Partners, 128
Per capita income, 23
Periodic cap, 21
Phone poll, use of for comparison shopping, 88
PITI debt ratio, 110-111
Plain vanilla American mortgage, fixed-rate mortgage as, 28
Pledged account buy-down mortgages,

22
Points
  as discount or loan fees, 47
  definition of, 47
  interest rates versus points, 48
  two quick formulas for comparing
  interest-rates relative to points, 49
Points equivalency table, 49
Point scoring system, 75, 100, 125
Pre-approval and approval phases of a
  loan application, 61, 96, 97; see also
  pre-qualified
Prepaid items, 37
Prepayment penalty, 41
Prequalification, see prequalified
Prequalified
  advantages of getting yourself
  prequalified first, 61
  first, get yourself, 61
  rule-of-thumb methods to prequalify
  yourself, 62
Prime rate, 21
Principal, 4, 5; payment of in
  mortgage amortization, 8
Private Mortgage Insurance (PMI), 36,
  37, 38, see also mortgage insurance
Privilege of having a fixed-rate, 29
Profile, 72
Programmatic System, 3
Promissory note, 46
Property taxes, 68, 69
Puffing, by a broker, 132
Purchase money mortgage, 46

Q

Qualitative Buyer Qualification
  Workshop, conventional loan
  situation, 116
Qualitative Buyer Qualification
  Worksheet, FHA loan
  situation, 121
Qualitative Buyer Qualification
  situation, VA loan situation,
  124
Quality of loan, underwriter's
  determination of, 75

R

Rennie Mae, 87
RAM, 26
Rapid payoff mortgages, 23
Rate cap, 21
Rate commitment on loan, 101
Ratio analysis, 107
  for conventional loans, 100
  debt-to-income ratios, 109
  LT debt ratio, 109

PITI debt ratio, 110
LTV (loan-to-value) ratios,
  113
Real estate brokers
  advantages of using to find a
  house, 128
  exclusive listing, 131
  exclusive right to sell, 131
  multiple listing system among,
  128, 120, 130, 131
  open listing, 131
  pointers for finding, 130
  selection of broker with ability
  to locate sources of financing
  is paramount, 129, 133
Real estate brokers and agents,
  17
Real estate industry secrets, 2
Real Estate Settlement Procedures
  Act, 97
Recording fee, 70
Red carpet, 128
Red flag, 93, 95
Redlining, 106
Re/max, Realty World, 128
Rent with option to buy, 21
Reserve account, 69
Residual income, 119
Reverse annuity mortgage, 26
Reverse order of what the
  proper sequence of loan
  application should be, 1
Review of income and job
  history, 100
Risk, default type of, 74
Risk Factors, 96
Rollover mortgages, 21
Rule-of-thumb formulas to prequalify
  yourself, 62

S

Savings and Loan Associations,
  13
Secondary mortgage market,
  37, 72
Second trust, 24
Second mortgage, 24, 45;
  purchase money mortgage
  under, 46
Section 203b FHA loan
  program, 39
Security for the borrowed
  money, 4
State assistance, in locating
  sources of funds, 17
Seller-assisted loan, 13, 45; see
  also Owner Financed

Mortgage
Seller take-back mortgage, 24,
  45
Sellers with Need-to-Sell, 128,
  130
Selling yourself to the lender,
  97
Seldin Organization, a mortgage
  search service, 86
Settlement Costs Guide, 74
Shared Appreciation Mortgage,
  23
Shared Equity Mortgage plan,
  24
Short list of lending rules and
  criteria, 1, 2, 3, 89
Sirmans, C.F., author of Real
  Estate Finance, 72
Sources for mortgage money,
  13
Standard loan application
  forms, 12
Step-by-step procedures to get a
  mortgage approval almost
  everytime you apply, 90
Structure of mortgage
  amortization, 7
Sure-fire formula to get a
  mortgage in 24 hours, 89
Survey fee, 68

T

Taking back a mortgage, 45
Tax returns, copies of your, 99
Ten-year Analysis Table, The,
  53
Ten-year Analysis, The, 52; use
  of to comparison-shop for
  loans, 92
Terms of the approved
  mortgage, 102
Thomsett, Michael C., on
  potential savings from
  comparison-shopping for loan,
  87
Tips, on selecting the best
  mortgage sources, 17
Title insurance, fee for, 68
Title search costs, 68
Transfer tax, 69
Transunion, 95
Trouble in paradise, do not start
  an application if there is, 93
Trust deed, 4
Truth-in-Lending Disclosure
  Statement, 57, 73, 81, 97
Truth-in-Lending Law, 51

Twenty-eight/Thirty-six (28/36)
  ratio rule, 64

U

Underwriter, of loan, 71, 72
U.S. Census report, 30
U.S. Commerce Department
  index, 23
U.S. Congress, 35
U.S. Treasury bill rate, 21, 31

V

Variable interest mortgage, 21
Verification, of deposit, 97; of
  employment, 97
Veterans Administration (VA)
  financing, 22, 35
  procedures of the loan programs
  under, 40
  assumability of, 39 40
  closing costs on, 43
  eligibility for, 41
  escrow account method in, 69

W

Wall Street Journal, 107
World War II Veterans, 35
Wraparound, 25

Z

Zero Rate and Low Rate
  Mortgage, 26